THAT'S WHAT
SHE SAID

THAT'S WHAT SHE SAID

Contemporary Poetry and Fiction by Native American Women

EDITED BY

RAYNA GREEN

INDIANA UNIVERSITY PRESS
BLOOMINGTON

Library of Congress Cataloging in Publication Data
Main entry under title:
That's what she said.
Bibliography: p.
1. American literature—Indian authors. 2. American
literature—Women authors. 3. American literature—20th
century. 4. Indians of North America—Women—Literary
collections. I. Green, Rayna.
PS508.I5T46   1984   810'.8'009287   83-49002
ISBN 0-253-35855-8
7 8

CONTENTS

Paula Gunn Allen

Diane Burns

Contents

Gladys Cardiff

Nora Dauenhauer

Charlotte de Clue

Contents

Louise Erdrich

Rayna Green

Joy Harjo

Linda Hogan

Wendy Rose

Carol Lee Sanchez

Mary TallMountain

Judith Mountain Leaf Volborth

Annette Areketa West

Roberta Hill Whiteman

Shirley Hill Witt

PREFACE

This collection of fiction and poetry by Native women writers came to be for many reasons. It is, in many respects, the classic labor of love. The material, I thought, deserved the widest and most appreciative audience it could find, and since no one had yet given the work this expansive a forum, I took the task to heart. Because the material can, I feel, stand on its own merits, I decided to offer an "uninterpreted" work. Although I have looked for high artistic quality, I have not examined the works in a literary-critical sense. To guide readers through the work, I have provided a historical and contextual introduction and a glossary of terms and concepts used throughout the poems and stories.

Ritual but sincere apologies must be made for any shortcomings of the work. Several fine writers do not appear in these pages for a variety of reasons, chiefly because of the technicalities of permissions. I have tried to include their published works in the bibliography, in which I have aimed for tribal, regional, stylistic, and artistic diversity. The bibliography includes references to videotapes and to presses that regularly publish Native women's writing. I can only urge readers to seek out and enjoy more of the writers included, as well as those missing from these pages.

This anthology has its antecedents in other works and other writers' efforts. It is true that Native women have been included in anthologies of "Third World" writers and in collections of materials by American Indian writers, so that this book builds on the efforts of those who understood and appreciated good writing and who gave it new exposure. Yet, as with all women's work, this body of writings still needs special attention, and not just to remedy the not so selective neglect of the distant past. With the exception of Leslie Silko, whose extraordinary work receives some of the good critical attention it deserves, most writers in this volume are unfamiliar to the general reading public and even to readers of the most esoteric poetry and fiction. In spite of inclusion of their works in anthologies, prizes, awards, fellowships, and readings throughout the country, the writers find appreciation primarily among a specialized audience—Indian, feminist, politically attuned. Since, with a few exceptions, most writers herein publish with small or "obscure" presses, their work is hard to obtain; it is rarely found on the shelves of mainstream bookstores. So, the limited accessibility of these voices did somewhat determine my interest in producing a single volume from a major press. But need, in that market-attuned sense, could not suffice to create this book. I felt, quite simply, that these women have something important to say and that they say it elegantly, profoundly, and beautifully. Sharing one another's literary company here would, I thought, augment the artistic, social, and political strength of their individual voices.

Besides those who preceded me in recognizing the power in these women's art, there are many to thank. The network of personal relationships among these artists precipitated the book as much as the obvious need for it. This work comes from talking and sharing ideas with many people, most of them the writers themselves—men and women from the Native community in this country. Long visits and good friendship with Joy Harjo and Linda Hogan over the last several years and expanding acquaintance with other Indian writers in this country—Wendy Rose, Maurice Kenney, Joe Bruchac, Hanay Geiogamah, Simon Ortiz, Diane Burns, Paula Gunn Allen, Geary Hobson—culminated in 1981 at the American Writers' Congress. One fine night of reading and joking at the American Indian Community House Gallery in New York brought us all the kind of spirit that makes books and more seem possible. Unquestionably, my relationships with the women writers and my feeling for their work made the book imperative for me. The very title, and not coincidentally, the spirit which impelled it, comes from Joy Harjo's fine work *What Moon Drove Me to This?* I gratefully acknowledge her permission to use "That's What She Said" in description of these women's art.

Still others deserve praise and thanks for their assistance. The editors of past anthologies and those associated with small presses that published previous works—Maurice Kenney, Geary Hobson, Joe and Carol Bruchac, and Dexter Fisher—tracked down people I couldn't find on my own and provided encouragement along the way. Michael Green and Andy Wiget, my colleagues in Native American Studies at Dartmouth, took personal and professional interest in the work, inviting some of the authors to read at Dartmouth and serving as gracious and interested toilers-in-the-same-vineyard.

The authors included here just laughed when I said I'd reveal everything I knew about them. They dutifully and graciously responded to my many inquiries and harassments and took time from their personal and professional lives to work with me on the book's many details. Significantly, in the best of Indian tradition, where honor goes to those who give what they have to others, these writers have waived any interest in fees or royalties in order to establish a fund for support of Indian women writers and the presses who publish them. In addition, the Muskiwinni Foundation, long interested in the work and careers of Native women, provided funds to me in 1981–82 for the completion of this work and of my previous volume from Indiana, *Native American Women: A Contextual Bibliography*. To all of them, I am happily indebted.

This book is dedicated to those early American Indian women writers who labored alone and largely in obscurity, and to Leslie Silko, who cleared the way. The women's dance, the women's circle moves on. They sing, and the song is ours.

RAYNA GREEN

The Ronan Robe Series

Spring 1979 Moon of the Buttercups

Part I: In the Beginning

The glaciers pushed
and the People moved
The glaciers pushed
And the People moved
Onward and downward
Onward and downward
And the Mother gave birth
To a new nation
To a new nation

Part II: The People

There has been established
An incontestable record
Showing that the mountain and plateau region
Was occupied by Homo Sapiens
At least eleven thousand years ago.
The *Scheligu* did not make pottery
But were expert weavers
And fashioned numerous utensils
Of stone, wood, and horns.
They made leggings and clothing
Of fur and skins.
Later they possessed quantities
Of buffalo robes
Which were highly prized
And valuable items of trade.

Part III: The Woman

The Woman's father was a trader.
A horse trader. The oldest profession.
Contrary to belief, prostitution is not the
    oldest.
Barter must take place before the act of sex.

The Woman's grandmother
Was Lodge Grass People
Coming from the south
With a Great Basin dialect.

Part IV: The Chant

Watch me move my hands
They are moving
They are moving

Watch me move my soul
It is moving
It is moving

Watch me make my art
All is moving
All is moving

Part V: The Image

She creates them from her dreams
Half awake and half asleep
During the twilight time
Images race and flicker
Need to be caught
What is captured
Remains in the daylight world
As evidence
Of the dream world
Which is where all creativity originates.

Part VI: The Work

Then shape appears to the Woman
And she cuts the canvas
Sometimes in the shape of an elk
Sometimes in the shape of a bison
Sometimes in the shape of new things
Heads to the left
Tails to the right
Stripes going round

Then a color appears to the woman
And she dyes the canvas

Sometimes in the color of leather
Sometimes in the color of grass
Sometimes in the color of new things
Heads to the left
Tails to the right
Stripes going round

And then a design appears to the Woman
And she paints the canvas
Sometimes in the manner of mapping
Sometimes in the geometry of line
Sometimes in the way of new things
Heads to the left
Tails to the right
Stripes going round

Then fire appears to the Woman
And she smokes the canvas
Sometimes passing it north south
Sometimes passing it east west
Sometimes passing it up down
Heads to the left
Tails to the right
Stripes going round

Part VII: The Bridge

Then daylight evidence of the twilight dream
Appears to the Woman
And she senses the past and present sealed in
    the wax
Heads to the left
Tails to the right
Stripes going round.

JAUNE QUICK-TO-SEE-SMITH

THAT'S WHAT
SHE SAID

Introduction
Rayna Green

She never lives at home anymore. But she thinks about it. Call it the Rez.
Call it Second Mesa. That Indian bar in Pierre. Maybe it's the road between here and there. A horse's back or truck cab. I first met her at the
Indian Center in L.A. But she thinks of it all like Grandma's house, in the
winter when she first heard all the stories, out in the hills in the full cold
moon. Call the place Home. That's where you might find her tonight
when you go looking, or at least where she's thinking she'd like to be. But
tomorrow when you try to find her, she'll be there, laughing with some
other women—teasing her cousin maybe or making fun of some coyote
who thinks he can teach her something she doesn't already know. She
could be mad and asking for trouble, asking for trouble with him or her
or her with him. Too much trouble. Too much beer. Maybe not enough
yet to stop the thoughts about what ought to be or where she could be.
She'll do something she'll be sorry for unless she goes down to the Indian
Center to make fry bread with the others. There's bingo tonight, and
with flour on her hands for a while, maybe she'll make it through—even
with that cough and him not working. She worries a lot about him—the
things he does when he's got too much time on his hands. And then he
worries about his mom, back home. She's like that South Dakota girl sitting in the Bronx bar with the Mohawk steelworkers who started to
wonder how she came this far. But her sister works in the IHS emergency
ward on the Rez and her cousin is wearing a hard hat, watching Mr. Pea-
body's coal shovel dig up the Black Hills. Things are changing, but sometimes, it's hard to see. So she might have a story tonight when you find
her. I guess she'll always have a story to tell. Some of what she has to say
is just gossip. What her auntie told her mom about those Navajo wolves
over near Gallup or what Winona said yesterday about why Bob Two
Bears can't come home anymore. How she got those boots she's wearing
or the ribbon shirt she gave you or the car she might drive to Anadarko
Fair next week.

Someone else might have to tell that story for her . . . maybe make it just
a little bit crazier than even she would have. Sometimes she might give
you the story, just because she likes knowing you'll tell it everywhere you
can. It's the only way everyone will know what happened. I know she's
sold the stories to people, when she ran out of food or had to pay the
doctor something that year the kid was so sick. Once, she just figured

she'd told it enough, then gave it to her sister because she wanted to argue with her over which version was the right one. Some of the best fights she's had have been over who was telling the story right. Whatever her reasons, she always wants the story told, and besides, if you don't tell it yourself, someone else is always going to make trouble for you by telling it all wrong. Most of the things she tells just show how crazy Indians really are. But it's important to remember, at least for Indians—just to say the names over and over—to think all over again what home looks like when you think you'll never get there again. Even when it's not pretty, what she says—except for the moon and horses, except for the red rock and canyons, except for the way Grandmother Woman looks when she fools Coyote again, except for the way she tells it—well, you know it's worth telling. But I won't tell you the worst, like about the time she put dried coyote prick in the tribal chairman's beer and what he did afterward—or when she dared that dog soldier to a race and ran off with the horse instead—or how she won the Eskimo Olympics. But we can finish a six pack of red pop and Colorado Kool-Aid while I tell you the rest. I'm just telling you what she told me, eyy?

The clay shapers, fiber twisters, picture makers, and storytellers—the ones who said what was and what will be—they've always been important in Indian Country. Whether it comes directly from the storyteller's mouth and she writes it down or someone writes it for her, the story has to be told. Sometimes she hears or dreams something and makes a story out of it. That's the way it often happens. Before European writing, there were voices to sing and speak, dances to make real the stories that the People told or to honor the retelling anew. There were hands that talked and drew and shaped. Some tales could be told with one or two small marks—because the artist knew how to put them together so that those who saw would be reminded of where they came from just from seeing the marks. Others would take eight nights to sing the words so that someone could be healed and the others could remember. And others might get the story as they watched the women weave it into the rug. They'd have to remember what their duties were toward the People because the rug told them every time they looked at it. Whichever way it was, the story got told, and it gets told now. The old ways of speaking aren't gone. They've changed, of course. There has always been change; there are always new ways to remember. The same people still give shape to mass, color to substance, music to ideas, and words to feelings. Not everyone knows how to do these things, but everyone sees or hears and touches, and some have the special gift to say the right words. They kept them even when no one asked to hear them—even when the whiteeyes came and asked only the men what they knew.

Thus the women have always kept the stories, in clay or reeds, in wool or cotton, in grass or paint or words to songs. Somewhere they began to keep them in ink and paper (and eventually in electronic impulses transferred to paper from magnetic tape). Sequoyah taught some to write; the priests taught others. Some learned in the Cherokee Female Seminaries and a very few were sent to Mount Holyoke and Quaker schools in the East. Others went to Carlisle, then Haskell—Indian schools. Now they take M.F.A's at Iowa or Ph.D.'s at the University of New Mexico. Some still go to Indian schools, and some don't go at all or drop out. But they write and they've been writing for quite a while.

Some of the earliest writers—Humishuma (1888–1936), Ella Deloria (1888–1971), Pauline Johnson (1861–1913)—wrote and retold old tribal stories, because they wanted to preserve tribal culture and because previous Anglo writers had gotten the stories so wrong that they wanted to set the record straight. Eventually, they wrote their own work too—short stories or poems, a novel, autobiographies. Bonnin, for example, was best known for her political activities on behalf of Indian people, but as a classically trained violinist, she wrote a musical play that was successfully produced and well received around the country. Humishuma (or Chrystal Quintasket) started writing because she wanted to preserve the stories of the Okanogan people but ended up writing a novel, *Co-go-wea, The Half-Blood*, for which she is now best known. Ella Deloria began as an assistant to anthropologists and ended as a scholar in her own right, contributing a massive body of work to the scholarship on the linguistics and folklore of the Dakota Sioux. And Pauline Johnson, a Canadian Mohawk actress, wrote volumes of popular poetry known throughout Canada to both Native and non-Indian people. There were others, of course, not so well known. Sarah Callahan, for example, a well-born Creek, may have written the first novel by a Native woman (and not Humishuma, as previously assumed).

While some tribes, like the Cherokees, had their own presses, publications, and traditions of publication, most did not, and the world of white publication was alien to all but a few. Still, Indians wrote prolifically and they wrote well in the contexts of their own age. The works of Johnson and Humishuma stemmed, naturally, from their own environments and times. Their stylistic heritage was, in many respects, a Victorian one. Johnson's poetry resembled Victorian ladies' literature, with its pious tone and inspirational messages, while Humishima's writing—because of the interference of her male amanuensis—was replete with high-flown political rhetoric and polite phraseology, interspersed with the Western and vernacular language that makes the book more interesting.

Many of these women, like their male counterparts, had Anglo support-
ers who encouraged them and assisted them in putting their stories down
in writing or seeing them to publication. Some women did not even begin
their careers as writers. Activists like Bonnin (1876–1938) and the La
Flesche sisters (1854–1903 and 1865–1915) were taken up as darlings
of the various reform movements—the early female-suffrage movement
or the assorted political reforms of the early twentieth century—and
their speeches and writings were widely reproduced. Humishuma's Anglo collaborator nearly took over her work as his own, imposing his opin-
ions and style on her writing, to its detriment, yet his intervention was
essential for the publication of a fine novel by an interesting and compel-
ling artist. Most of these women, fearful that cultural dissolution and European education would wipe out their languages and artistic heritages,
sought out whites who had the same fears—though they shared them for
different reasons—and acted as best they could to preserve what they
saw. But except for Deloria, whose passion for preservation made her devote her life to it, the concerned women became creators rather than preservers, and in doing so established a new form of expression for Native
people.

Combined with the autobiographies, journal articles, and tale collections, these plays, poems, stories, and a few novels constitute a scant but
powerful literary heritage for contemporary Native women. Unfortunately, that heritage was virtually unknown to contemporary women until a few years ago, when scholars and writers began to turn their attention to reprinting and discussing those materials so important to the
literary history of Native people—of Native women. The works show a
thematic continuity, but there is also change, primarily in style, as anyone
might guess. And life has changed for Native people. Life has certainly
changed for Native women since the period when Johnson and Bonnin
wrote. But the interest in Indian politics, in national politics as they affect
Native people, in the lives and tragedies of Native people, in the languages, in the old stories, has changed not at all. The hell-raising tradition flourishes alongside the storytelling tradition. In these poems and
stories, we are treated to reiterations of themes and characters that Indian women have always written about, and the bulk of Native women's
writing since the mid-nineteenth century has been "preservative." In it
all, political or not, the jokes and the people, the scenes and the language,
the names and the places belong to Indian Country. You can see it through
their eyes. Rarely on the contemporary scene, however, does anyone re-
tell stories in their entirety; only in the works of Leslie Silko—not represented here—do complete tales become the center of the story or poem-
tale. In the writings here, the references to traditional myth figures and

stories set the stage or make the point or take the reader from one point to another. The psychic and symbolic landscape of Indian Country—complete with animals, spirits, parts of the natural landscape—combines with specifically tribal or pan-Indian social references—foods, dances, ceremonies, joking—to produce the "Indian" parts of these works. Wendy Rose has said that any writer comes from a community, speaks to, about, and for that community; thus Indians attuned to their community will inevitably write and speak about it. Rather than re-creating the consciously Indian world, retelling the stories in toto, the modern writer may hark back to the traditional world but moves on to the referential framework of contemporary life. But the spiritual and symbolic "baggage" remains, either to be dealt with or to be shunted aside. The bottom line here, however, is the harsh knowledge that race and gender superimpose on experience.

Sometimes she thinks it's funny the way the stories change when she tells them. She doesn't know Indian Country the way Grandma knew it, and no matter how much she might wish she looked like the old ladies out in the plaza sometimes, she knows she never will. It's bluejeans and sunglasses for her after all—save the fringed shawl for powwow. One of her cousins called her a Disco Indian last week. But still, she's not as hip as she looks sometimes. It's not that she could ever get away from the old stories, even if she wanted to. She can't tell them the way Grandma did, but she's hardly ever in situations like the ones Grandma thrived on. Still some of the stories took root so deeply in her that she tells them without thinking, in new forms, especially the ones that have to do with being a woman or being someone with a name. Spending so much time with women from other tribes—in Indian school and now in the city—gives her even more stories and names—so many she doesn't remember what tribe they came from anymore. She thinks the names belong to her now, and she's right. Clan Mother, White Buffalo Calf Woman, Beloved Woman, Early Morning Woman, Night Wind Woman, Earthwoman, Corn Mother, Iyetiko, Persimmon Woman, Rainwater Woman, Grandmother Turtle, White Shell Woman, Ohlone Woman, Brave-Hearted Woman, Message-Bringer Woman, Spider Woman, the Woman Hanging from the 13th-Floor Window, Suicid/ing (ed) Indian Women, the Pueblo Woman Who Got Down in Brooklyn. She knows her names now, just the way she knows the places and languages she wasn't born to. But every time she starts to tell a story, she remembers more, as though she'd always known. The way she'd always known the laughter and the trouble. Sometimes, she chants them over to herself, the way she'd sing a song. Just for the comfort of it, especially when things get bad or when she feels really out touch with what Grandma calls "Indian-ness."

When things do get bad, she sews. Last week, when I was there with her, she was making ribbon shirts—for the family and to sell at the next pow-wow. She tried to learn quillwork from that Chippewa woman last year but decided she ought to put the earrings she made out of their misery. We joked that we both had so few traditional skills that we would have been put out to die or left behind in the old days. But she's an impressive artist, and I've been trying to convince her to go to the Institute of American Indian Art and study. Her paintings—of those Appaloosas and of the Indian women at the rodeo—are incredibly good—neo-realist art, I guess it could be called. She says now she's doing paintings of what she dreams, and I said I had nightmares better than that, eyy? She knows I love her work though, so she showed me some things she's started to write. After she read that book by Silko last year, she got all excited about reading about real worlds she knows. So she asked if the institute taught writing too. Maybe she would apply, she said. The dreams take color and shape, but they're beginning to have words.

The physical and psychological environments contemporary women occupy are as diverse as their tribal identities. Some—like Carol Lee Sanchez, Paula Gunn Allen (Sanchez's sister), Wendy Rose, Mary Tall-Mountain, Nora Dauenhauer, and Diane Burns—live utterly urban lives. And yet, they all go—metaphorically and literally—back to the Rez, where they recount the tales, textures, and meanings of rural New Mexico, Minnesota, Arizona, Alaska, and Oklahoma. Bar coyotes, rodeo cowboys and wino trash, the Saturday-night flirts and sometime lovers, Grandma and Grandpa, Uncle and Auntie, the Black-robes and nuns populate the bars and houses, the roads and rodeos, the fairs and schools, the Indian centers, hospitals, and government offices that contemporary Indian people inhabit. Others, like Gladys Cardiff, Judith Mountain Leaf Volborth, Charlotte de Clue, Shirley Hill Witt, and Annie Arkeketa West go back in their work, to historic themes, older times, historical characters that have tribal and personal relevance. Still others—Roberta Hill Whiteman, Harjo, Burns, and Sanchez—take their themes and characters from their own lives and those of their contemporaries—from the experiences of a farming community in rural Oklahoma or the tough urban life of Albuquerque or New York. A few—Erdrich, Witt, Hogan, Green, and Allen—interweave the experiences of people who are not Indian (or metaphorically Indian) into their writings. One of Hogan's voices belongs to Amanda McFadden, part of the Oneida Community of the nineteenth century. For Witt, the personae of Malinche, Mexican Indian consort of Cortez, and of the Woman of Courage—both Hispanic—are the vehicles through which she talks about the female experience. Erdrich's world is peopled with whites and breeds who interact and reproduce and carry on in a marginal, sleazy, funny, lower-class soap opera. And Allen's world, when it's not Laguna, comes close to California— white lawyers, Japanese lovers, Bay Area poets, stoned left-over hipsters, and political activists of a very modern stripe.

The Place is really more often the Road, for there is no home to many of these wanderers. Harjo is always on the road, whether she's driving the Turner Turnpike in Oklahoma, trying to find herself in Creek country again, or out with Noni Daylight, loose and drunk and crazy in the New Mexico moonlight. Erdrich's women wander the North Dakota hills in a pink Mustang, live briefly in rented rooms, or stay home while their men do the wandering, in and out of prison, on another road. The twentieth century brought government relocation—a new Trail of Tears—and urban migration to Indian people, and so it brings it to their writings. Men did not walk alone on the Trail of Tears or the Long Walk. The women walked and died, and they do it now in spirit the way they did it in the nineteenth century. But the reasons are different. They go to the towns for jobs or to follow their husbands and families. They go to school someplace and they never go home again permanently, or the city becomes home. Sometimes they get to go back to the Rez. Maybe it's someplace they never were before, and that new experience becomes part of the searching. They can be looking for something Indians call "Indianness"—what sociologists call "identity" and Bicentennial patriots called "heritage." Because most of them—with few exceptions—are "breeds," "mixed-bloods," not reserve-raised, they aren't "traditional," whatever that might mean now. Some might say that writing is just their role. That's what breeds do. They stand in the middle and interpret for everyone else, and maybe that's so. That's what they are. But "identity" is never simply a matter of genetic make-up or natural birthright. Perhaps once, long ago, it was both. But not now. For people out on the edge, out on the road, identity is a matter of will, a matter of choice, a face to be shaped in a ceremonial act.

In such women's lives, the taking of new names and the reshaping of old names is the essential process for becoming, for becoming through writing. In the stories and poems of these contemporary writers, there are characters invented to serve the authors' purposes, who have names like Noni Daylight (Harjo), or there are women who stand for specific types and have real-life names like Delilah (Allen) or Monahsetah (deClue). But some personae, like Iyetiko, Grandmother Turtle, and White Buffalo Calf Woman, are spirits and mythological forebears of Native people—governing symbolic women who gave the people life or taught them how to behave. Others take their names from social or political titles, like the

Iroquoian Clan Mother or the Beloved Woman, which is what the Cherokees called the highest Clan Mother of the Tribe. Some are sisters, grandmothers, or aunts—real kin or fictive kin made blood in the intensity of symbolic relationship. Some—like Harjo's Woman Hanging from the 13th-Floor Window or Allen's Suicid/ing(ed) Indian Women—become all women, waiting with them to climb back and live or die. Their names are called so that we all remember our names, and that we remember the names that empower us. "Oh, woman," Harjo tells us, "remember who you are. It is the whole earth." Receiving names, realizing you own names you never knew, taking new names, giving names—all are part of the deepest religious process for Native people. In conferring names or in simply calling them—sometimes for the first time in a non-public ceremonial, these writers create ceremony, invoking the powers of the often forgotten female spirits, giving women—and themselves—power to speak and create and know—power to remember, the most powerful of tools, and power to endure for those named. The names can evoke place, time, continuity, difference, and contradiction. They map the women's place.

Her first chapbook came out last week—illustrated with her own drawings—and she was so excited she almost forgot to take a copy home when she left for the summer. But when she got there, all the excitement died in her. Her uncle told her the words would lose power if she wrote them down, and her high-school teacher said writers never made any money anyway. Why didn't she stick to painting, they all asked? She could make some money at that, and besides, that was better for women to do. So, she said over the phone, she just went down to that bar over the reservation line and got ripped with her cousins. Did they all go through this garbage, she asked, and she didn't want to hear the answer when I said, yes, yes, they all did. And worse, I didn't tell her.

But then, of course, back on the Rez, she saw so much more material for her work, she got to writing again. She can't stop it now, it just comes and it has to. Her auntie told her not to listen to Uncle, and now she's teaching her some words in what she calls "In'din." Those get into the poems now, and she's beginning to experiment with old songs from the women's house. The old ladies decided to tell her some things they hadn't told anybody about before or had lied about once when asked. Maybe, if she would write it down and show them how she'd written it, they said, they would help her even more. Maybe it was time, they thought, for one of their own to tell the truth. So many wrong things said before. Now she would get it right. So, she's decided to stay home and learn what they have to teach.

The notion of vocation for contemporary Indian women is as blurred as it was for earlier writers. Most women writers enjoy some form of extended education. Some, like their older counterparts, play many roles besides that of writer. Harjo makes films. Rose trained as an anthropologist. Allen is a literary critic. Erdrich was a working journalist. Dauenhauer is a linguist. Some of these writers teach, full or part time. Allen, Rose, Sanchez, and Whiteman teach in Native American Studies programs. All of them do ritual service for arts councils through the Poets in the Schools programs, occasionally teaching in Indian schools, but rarely. Few are able to devote themselves to writing full time and survive. Their major exposure to the public comes from the usual round of city and university promotion tours for new books, readings, lectures, and classroom discussions. For those with children to support, the way of life is even more demanding than for those alone. For all of them, the time to work, to write, is torn from the time spent working for income.

Most Native writers, male and female, are poets. Few novelists and playwrights have yet emerged. But most attempt to write in new genres. Several poets have produced works primarily for children—TallMountain and Whiteman, for example. Hogan wrote a play, produced once but as yet unpublished, entitled *A Piece of Moon*. Harjo is moving toward film and theater as a medium, as is Green. Allen's novel, *The Woman Who Owned the Shadows*, is in press, and Erdrich has one novel completed and another in progress. Several authors, of whom Erdrich is currently the most visible, write both short fiction and poetry. And a number of these women are artists as well. Jaune Quick-to-See-Smith, primarily a visual artist, writes poetry with a strongly visual dimension, which she often incorporates into her artistic work. Rose, Harjo, Sanchez, and Burns are accomplished artists, who frequently illustrate their own poetry. Some, like Dauenhauer, think of themselves not primarily as writers in the creative sense, but rather as cultural preservers and illuminators. The bulk of Dauenhauer's work rests in community cultural development, in linguistic translation and preservation. The variants are many, showing both the impossibility of surviving on an income generated solely from writing and the enormous and diverse talent of these women. Thus, for these women, the expression of life as a "writer" can take many different forms, moving between genres and even into other media that extrapolate vision from writing.

Readers will want to know about the politics of these writers, partly because they will be certain that any "Third World" writer will be political in very specific ways and partly because most of what they know of modern Indian peoples involves the political. Certainly, some of the writers

treat political issues in their poems—whether specifically Indian concerns, such as lands, water, and treaties, or broader concerns such as
racist abuse or human rights. Some of these writers are old enough to
have been part of the Indian activist movements of the early sixties, such
as the American Indian Movement, which staged actions centering on
fishing rights and treaty rights; others are younger but have participated
in latter-day efforts like the Black Hills Survival Gathering of 1981 or are
involved with groups like the Women of All Red Nations. Others remain
unaffiliated with movements or organizations; some identify with mainstream groups; still others with a wide range of activities, left and center,
but rarely right. Of late, some specific concerns—the imminence of nu-
clear war, for example—have been addressed in the works of Allen,
Hogan, and Rose. But in most of the writings, the politics are subtle—as
in Wendy Rose's continuing critique of academe and scholarship, especially the discipline of anthropology, in which she is trained, or Paula
Allen's and Joy Harjo's feminist critique of the desperate lives of Indian
women, worn by poverty, the abuse of men, the silence and blindness of
whites. As I have written elsewhere, Native women from many tribes
show a natural appreciation of feminist concerns since they either come
from tribes that were matriarchal and matrifocal in nature—and there-
fore find themselves dispossessed by the encroachment of European pa-
triarchal forms—or come from tribes where female spheres of power
remain denigrated in favor of male power. Obviously, throughout the
writing here and elsewhere, a pained recognition of the condition of
many Indian women causes writers to express concern, but the root of
their problem appears attributable to the callousness and sexism of Indian men and white society equally. In their evocations of female gods
and spirits and in their descriptions of traditional societies, the writers
often reveal a poignant desire to return to older social and ceremonial
forms, which intertwine men and women in mutual, complementary
roles as religious leaders, healers, political figures, and educators. Tightly
wound indeed is the double bind of race and gender.

The political dimension, these women might say (and I believe), is an inherent part of their writing because it is an inherent part of their lives.
In Erdrich's comic story "Scales," one of the Indian characters, Gerry
Nanabush, continually escapes from prison to be with his lover, Dot, and
the law continually captures him, thus extending his sentence. Erdrich
expresses no overt rage, makes no political statement regarding Gerry's
plight. He is presented neither as an unjustly abused person nor as a bad
guy. He is simply lower class, Indian, and in trouble, predictably, inevitably, finally—the perpetual condition of all the characters. But other
works rage openly at injustice, laying bare the battered lives of Native

women and men. And so it goes with Indian writers. Suicide, alcoholism, wasted lives, battered women are part of the Indian turf, and the presentation of those lives constitutes integral political comment. The writers, as all writers will say, simply tell what they see, and what they see in the Indian world demands comment.

Lest readers think, however, that the Indian world women writers see is completely grim, completely hopeless, let them look again more closely. This Indian world fills the empty spaces with laughter, with humor. Laughing is one way Indians, like all people, get around the tragedy, the trouble, the one-way street they stumble into. Burns's and Harjo's poems, Erdrich's short fiction are filled with laughter, some mockery, some fun, and teasing. "Which part do you want?" Harjo asks the part-Indian guy she's just told she's part Creek and part white. Burns re-creates a modern Indian ritual, the '49 dance, for us, with Modene, the Roller Derby Queen, and other "nontraditional" characters. And Erdrich's Chippewa bar world includes comic-opera police chases, escapes, jealous rivalries, and absurd happenings in the not so black-humored craziness that constitutes the marginal life in the Dakota hills. "Hey, honey," they all sing, like in the '49, "I don't care if you're married, I'll love you anyway." The women's barbed humor almost always concerns relationships, misunderstandings, sex, and the sharp edges of racial conflict between whites and Indians. The joking is like gossip in some ways, telling all the stories that people share about other people who've gotten themselves into ridiculous situations. For some, it's just telling stories on themselves. Call it what you will. The women just call it remembering.

She called me again last night, really depressed, and said they'd turned her down again for the writing fellowship, the one to write the tribal women's history. She wasn't "qualified," the panelists said. She didn't have a Ph.D. With the second chapbook out now, she thought this time she'd get it, even though she knew they regarded her as a young and "minor" writer. She's having trouble making it financially, so she was hoping. The little teaching she's able to get just doesn't cover expenses, not for her and the kids too. And she can't write if she works full time. I ought to just forget it, she said, and I've heard that before. I don't blame her either. Just hang on for a little while, though, I said. You're doing everything right, I told her. I didn't tell her about sitting on the panel and hearing the white boys talk about the "esoteric and irrelevant" small presses and "ethnic" writers. I just gave her my usual speech about hanging tough and quoted her own lines, from "Spider Women," the way I always do.

> Wrapped in the weaver's dreams
> you'll know that spinning is everything,
> more than dreaming.
> women's hands are never empty
> women's mouths are never empty
> women's arms are never empty
> standing heart-bare, stripped,
> they fill hands, arms, bellies.
> This woman's spindle turns
> and the loom fills with the dance of women,
> their arms spilling over with tomorrow's rich design.

It was a cheap trick, using her own words on her, and she knew it. So I told her about the verse I made up last week at the '49.

> If you leave me, sweetheart
> I'll love you anyway
> But I'll look for your body somewhere, heya!

And when she started to laugh, I knew I had her back again—thinking about the difference she makes. Don't tell me what kind of trash you made up yesterday, she said. That's worse than telling me who you snagged at the dance. No, it's worse than *not* telling you, I said. You'll never let me wallow in self-pity, will you, she said? Not unless you wallow in print and make it good, I told her. Let's write an Indian soap opera. That'll get you the money to survive. You mean the story of my life, she laughed. No, the story of *my* life—more sex, more action, more . . . It won't matter whose story it is, you know, she interrupted, serious again, it'd all come out the same no matter which of us we chose. Let's call her Winona. She could live in Dallas. Apache maybe, or Navajo. Jesus, not *that*, I said, but yes, that sounds like her. Jeans, sunglasses, and a worn purple shawl. Right, I said, but we've got to have a story line—you know, a beginning, a middle, an ending. No, she said, just a beginning.

That's what she said.

Paula Gunn Allen

Grandmother

Out of her own body she pushed
silver thread, light, air
and carried it carefully on the dark, flying
where nothing moved.

Out of her body she extruded
shining wire, life, and wove the light
on the void.

From beyond time,
beyond oak trees and bright clear water flow,
she was given the work of weaving the strands
of her body, her pain, her vision
into creation, and the gift of having created,
to disappear.

After her,
the women and the men weave blankets into tales of life,
memories of light and ladders,
infinity-eyes, and rain.
After her I sit on my laddered rain-bearing rug
and mend the tear with string.

Snowgoose

North of here where
water marries ice,
meaning is other than what
I understand.

I have seen in pictures how
white the bulge of the glacier
overshadows the sea,
frozen pentecostal presence,
brilliant in the sun—
way I have never been.

I heard the snowgoose cry today
long-wheeled wings overhead,

sky calling untroubled blue
song to her and morning.
(North wind blowing.)

Coyote's Daylight Trip

Poled to its environment, shored,
an imagined thing made by hand does not connect—
senses of accuracy in the machine are light
etched on paper,
means:

   Bringing Home the Fact.

Men each day go out, return, though mourning the sight:
questions posed in photographs, whether of the mind or not.
And loony poor Bud deranges life; all literature a spindly bough
that cannot hold true, Sapling grown in spring is gone in snow—
disactualized.

   History Happens.

How it comes chemical, charged, is no matter
of fact but Photograph and
Type. Did they make pictures of Calley's, Ellsberg's
damaged psyche? I
am inconsequential as the wind. No
picture can be made of formulations called myself: mere
corpses show on the plate, true as fact, grow
monstrous in every quiet place, an
institution.

   I See Myself As Death.

Vapors play poorly in the light, leave tracings that once swam
onto the page and fixed themselves through careful eye: I
cannot care for this—ancestors' shades fixed on the wall.
I bury my dead. I mourn
for four full days.

The Trick Is Consciousness

I must have been mistaken.
Taken for a ride, an eternity of them,
masked strangers driving me hundreds of miles in
unidentifiable cars down nameless highways,
dark sideroads of a thousand tales and thoughts—I
must have misunderstood the terms of the agreement
between time and place, identity and surmise, those roads
led somewhere, I thought, and those someones would take me
swiftly there. I must have been wrong.
It has, I suppose, to do with temporality—
sensation, duration, whatever we know of time:
with how waves swell and break, how sand blows from one
county to the next, how light blooms pale and deep
one year from another, yet still remains the light.
I think about long ago
as they say or said *humma ho* when the tale began,
and wonder how the earth has changed, not I but
it in twenty years, wonder at the completeness of it,
getting, forgetting, sudden realization, no
excuses, no surprise,
there it is.

I remember the corral behind the house,
the wooden stairs up to it, chicken house, stall, rabbit pen,
pigeon pen, the high rocks shading.
It was full during the war. My father
didn't want us to want—there were chickens, rabbits, a cow
that gave enough for the whole village, sheep, pigeons,
a huge pig.
They made *chicharrones* when they slaughtered it.
I was maybe four.
Later the corral was empty.

Used to wander around in it, wondering.
I still do, at night, at dream.
And I remember grandma's mulch bed—
and crazy lily pond she ran us out of,
the tamarack tree behind the coal shed, deep
shadows there, spider webs, trumpet vine, I
dream about them now, sound, smell, shade and light
so complete—I have changed nothing.

The key is in remembering, in what is chosen for the dream.
In the silence of recovery we hold
the rituals of the dawn,
now as then.

Star Child Suite

written the week John Lennon died

For Lo, I bring you tidings of great
joy which shall be unto all people; for
on this day unto you is born a savior
who is Christ the Lord.

I

Crepe paper christmas
green and red, turns
and twists symmetrically
around the walledup room—"open space" filled with sound
voices, mechanical and electronic noises everywhere
untouched books, glossy and neat with disuse sit mute
waiting—above the groan and clatter a highmigraine screech
pulses, unidentified, predictable, sets teeth on edge.
My brainends turn, twist, try to tune themselves to
unpredictability, to something textured, recognizable.
Still, I inhabit this universe too, am scheduled,
punitive, traumatic: I hold the chalk.

electronic mornings creep over the horizon
fill the days with danger, hang ominous over the river—
chase the mesas north. On the highway early, I
saw sunrise, gold and dayglopink billow on the smoke
of an unnamed installation near Bernalillo north of Albuquerque. So
much beauty in certain destruction, filling the December
crystal air—winter settling on the land. The
soft, frozen grass pointed northward, the way I was going.
Last night they announced his death. He died climbing
the stairs. Remembering when I was on the other side of the desk,
I wept. We had moved together for so long: how had we come to this?

II

The best of the world slumps before me—minds
that eighteen years ago first turned earthward, blinking.
oh yeah.
Wasted.
Turned off.
Tuned in to video narcosis,
stereophonic flight, transfixed.
naked angels burning their hopes, mine, on dust and beer.
They talk of Ever Clear, laughing—though they don't know
what that might otherwise mean. They have grown into
electronic commodities, and haven't the will left to fight back:
stoned, martyrs of the old faith, they go on down their days
not understanding how they've been crucified, or by who:
they make do with plastic reveries sunk in unspoken desperation—
synthetic clutter dusts their days, makes electrochemical
tissue of their breath. What world is this:
cut off, torn away, shattered, they dream of when it will get
better, of when they will be free.

III

180 Proof.
Neither womb nor honest texture provides
rough comfort nor sure throbbing grasp,
quivering, the desperados hide under sneer and sham,
behind closed eyes, disheveled hair
what do they become, these and my own—
children I watch staggering, see despair rise
brown and stinking like the desert air
to billow, golden and dayglopink around their heads,
shivering: piles of helpless memories pollute
what used to pass for dreams: they do not plan.
There is no future they can bear.
I would cradle them, murmuring, keep them from knowing
what I hear. I will not let them see me weep: I'll
fight with them instead, sneer and rage. Tell them
to sit down.

IV

No munchkin voices. An English sharptop
point breaks with a smug tap. Muffled sounds rise

in my ears, the sweet bite of lemon fills the air.
They pass pieces of it around, sweet juice sticking
to their hands. I am surrounded by eyes
that measure me, canny, dull—from faces
no more than nineteen years old. Artificially-induced
boredom barely masks rage at dust and plastic rivers
barely differentiated into carpet, cinderblock, dividers,
chalkboards, cheap plastic desks: they understand
the nature of their punishment. They do not comprehend
their sin. They sit behind faces barely differentiated
into closed and sick.

V

Touch skin:
one's own
dewy with petrochemicals
soft for now.
Remember wood
gleaming and warm
accepting you—
smells and oils,
polishing.
Handle plastic
that refuses to recognize
whatever it is you are
huddled into petrochemical cloth
acrylic
cold
no energy in it
know the exact dimension
of a dying soul.

VI

Tired.
Day nearly done
mind
a tree
dead bark peeling
litters the ground
waiting
for the last molecule

to be released
this rubble of ash
held together by despair
blocks glazed and battered
roughshod voices ride
the lockerlined corridors
murmuring on the brink
of suicide
the principal stalks the halls
and tiny snackbar beyond the door
collaring those who loiter
in these sacred halls,
haranguing, ordering,
brown face merely tired
body familiar, mexican: he knows what he sees.
The students allow his harsh ministrations,
return to their loitering, necking, playing
pinball when he's gone. Two o'clock.
Ten more minutes I'll be free.
I teach the students lost
to plastic rugs and chairs,
watch silted minds,
grainy to the fingers' touch
ooze onto the bright acrylic floor:
warm and smooth, one face reflected
in hand-held glass gleams.

VII

Wood steel overemotional motivation sullen
firetaste smoke harsh hash herbs gross grass
bitter lemonpeel coffee grounds awful seeds
like wood burning nutcrust walnutskin goats
milk the aftertaste liquidy resin kumquats
sour cherries sharp attar burning tongues
streams chillful harpoon spiraling too tight
grapefruit spaced-out daydream waking from
green apricots sour blackberries air groggy
kind of asleep stomach pain sad chest light
tingly upgoing muscles energized pulse speed
adrenalin rush going up taking off flying
rising meadows of pleasure sour cream rancid
cheese fresh milk rain taste of blood coats

warm throat what do we do with the hole he's
left staggering bleeding on the steps ripe
ripped apart on the powered air stale burning
rising sweet incense nicotine sweet fingers
nauseating air content powdered sugar hills
fish ride lakes no longer clear calm defined
space strawberry brick walls plastic fields
time grows long soft fiber molded lemon air

VIII

Around me
the faces are forests
retreating into snow they
whisper about taking her down
giggle defiant
prepared for punishment
because they know.
My words fall on history-reddened ears
she   /   he
"you know *he's* talking to *her*
because the voice is male and he says
let me take you down" they tell me.
They do not mention the tone of grief.
Winter here, we wish for spring
for ease maybe somewhere
for running across fields
forever alive for free
(that freeze-dried recurrent daydream)
but red with ridicule and self-abuse
in front of me their postures are
vaguely tied to the true red of rage
that right to the quick bites deep
touches in me that secret place
where no one dares to go, not even me,
that inward lifelong sentence, a
single thought that holds a life together
now bruised, bleeds sweet juice
on the forever frozen grass.

IX

The noise and clutter of each separate day
fuses into sound: learned

in grit, in multi-decible shriek
learned to say what there is to say
under bricks, under rubble of dead elephant dreams
heaps of ivory hedge against inflation
learned that daddy won't come home
because he was never there anyway
to take it step by step like one child stepped
upward climbing in death—
trying to get home—
scrambling among words groping for comprehension
cut off in the frozen air
sufficient for that time—
a life and a not necessary death
still, quiet.
Later that day it rained.

The Beautiful Woman Who Sings

a beautiful woman at Laguna
isn't much like a beautiful woman
in L.A. except for some parts
of it, of her. who carried
beauty in her eyes. the strength
of her hands. not gentle, though,
of course gentle, but power.
those women were large. big.
round. smiling. serious.
selfcontained. private.
kept right on. with what they
were. doing. beautiful.
not for its own sake. not
devoid of meaning. ovoid. not
void. full. not empty. but
not noisy either. maybe that
was the beauty of them.
not full of noise. laughing,
to be sure . . . and sure. the
beautiful women. beautiful
corn woman. woman like corn:
ripe and full. sweet. self

generating. tasseled.
blowing in the wind. meeting.
juicy. feeding. coming back
every time. coming home.
filling the fields with green.
making the people dance.
gathering.
making the children laugh.
making butterflies sing.

Suicid/ing(ed) Indian Women

I. Kyukuh

broken, a
tremble like
windowpane in gusted
wind I envision you
Kyukuh
on the southern shore writing
stepping slowly in the circle
as traditional in your view
as Wolverine in any metropolis
but your shaken
voice, is it a small wind
we carry in our genes?
A fear of disappearance?
An utterance that hovers
at the edges of the lips,
forever to-be-said?
The stories around Laguna say
that She, Iyetiko, left the people
longtimeago. There was a drought.
She gave them some toys for gambling,
you know, but the men gambled everything,
no matter how their wives pleaded, or
even their aunts, and hid in the kivas so the women
couldn't nag, and they wouldn't even do the necessary
dancing. So Iyetiko got angry and went away. That's
what the story says, and maybe it's so.

Maybe She knew that we could do without her presence
in the flesh, and She left the perfect ear of corn
behind to remind them that she was near, to honor
women, the woman in the earth, and in themselves,
but they call themselves her name, they call themselves
Mother, so maybe they sent her away and made up the rest.

II. Laguna

small woman huddled on the couch
soft light and shadows try to comfort you
Laguna would-be-suicide
why do you cling
to the vanished lakebed?
Even the water has left
the village.
You hardly speak
except to say confusion fills your mind
how can you escape the ties of brutaldrunken father
gossipy sisters/aunts scolding uncles/brothers
who want you to buy and cook their food
you eat little yourself you say
why must you in your beauty and strength
huddle helpless on the edge of the couch
laugh mocking your own helpless pain
why are things so terrible at Laguna that you
can't see another world around you like the lamps
soft and comforting around this room?

III. Navajo

earthwoman
as authentic as any whiteman
could wish you
marry out and
unhappy you beautiful/strong/brown
and your flowing black hair
Navajo maiden you can't
understand why your squawman sits in a chair
orders you and your young sisters about
you knew the reservation was no place to be
you giggle about the agonies of your past
the men your mother married

it will not be like that for you,
and you know
it must unless you get away
but how divide yourself
from your flesh? Division
does not come easy to a woman,
it is against the tribe
laws which only women honor
nor do you understand that
so you perch uneasily
on the edge of the reservation
and make joking fantasies
do for real

IV. Shipapu

Beautiful corn woman
lost all those centuries ago
stolen as your children
for generations have been
and it is not right
that this should be
but the law is such.
They abandoned you,
defied the women,
gambled and lost.
And you left them.
They don't tell how they
put women out of the center
except your emblem,
but death and destruction
have followed them,
the people lost the beautiful
first home, KUSHKUTRET
to the raging gods of war
and wander homeless now
beside the dead lake.
They have taken your name.

Poem for Pat

I wanted you to hear that song, she told me
so I listened and listened
trying to understand why
even admitting it was lovely
heart provoking
I still wondered
it took me clear through winter
and past full-bodied trees
into another snow.
Well I'll be damned, here comes your ghost again—

it happened to be on the day
we found each other again, she said,
and we were shivering at what we contemplated
locked together on the sandstone mesas at star rock
we were looking everywhere
Dine country spread at our feet, we could
hear the coydogs howling far off
and watched the chindis, dust devils whirling
on the floor below—
watched for rain.
Our breath comes out white clouds, mingles and hangs in the air
There were cedars twisted near where we sat.
It was spring.

Today the sun flows softly through my window
and I'm listening to the song,
thinking of her again on that mesa,
wondering what magic materialized out of that wind,
and if it rained.

Donna

Persimmon woman
flooding afternoon with your light
cactus garden far from here your home
spines
mingled green

essence of almost sweet
that orange
light welling filling garden
sky
exotic plant watching
growing
unconscious
broods and blossoms
full fat fruit, spiny pears, bitter seeds.
your thoughts are sharp/as day
enters night
as song.

Robin

Rainwater woman
your voice rises from your thoughts
like water from the meadows of earth
rainwater woman. voice breaking on the shores of sound
somewhere a tin roof waits
hot for your meaning.
Do you hear the tears in your voice,
the grey drops on a slant,
the barely begun wind just behind
driving the water sidewise in its fall?
There is angularity in rain
how it slices the space
between spirit and ground
cloud, rock
curving its return/that rise.
Somewhere a hot roof waits
spine thrust into the sky
for your sound.

Womanwork

some make potteries
some weave and spin
remember
the Woman/celebrate
webs and making
out of own flesh
earth
bowl and urn
to hold water
and ground corn
balanced on heads
and springs lifted
and rivers in our eyes
brown hands shaping
earth into earth
food for bodies
water for fields
they use
old pots
broken
fragments
castaway
bits
to make new
mixed with clay
it makes strong
bowls, jars
new
she
brought
light
we remember this
as we make
the water bowl
broken
marks the grandmother's grave
so she will shape water
for bowls
for food growing

for bodies
eating
at drink
thank her

Madonna of the Hills

She kept finding arrowheads
when she walked to Flower Mountain
and shards of ancient pottery
drawn with brown and black designs—
cloud ladders, lightning stairs and rainbirds.

One day
she took a shovel when she walked that way
and unburied fist-axes, manos, scrapers,
stone knives and some human bones,
which she kept in her collection
on display in her garden

She said that it gave her
a sense of peace to dig and remember
the women who had cooked and scrubbed
and yelled at their husbands
just like her. She liked, she said,
to go the spot where she'd found
those things and remember the women
buried there.

It was restful, she said,
and she needed rest . . .
from her husband's quiet alcohol
and her son who walked around dead.

Rain for Ka-waik

Out the back window the sky is dead. Rain
promises the garden its grave relief, its
promise buried in furrowed hearts

SHIWANNA
SHIWANNA
old footsteps echo on the southern hills.
To the west, over the village, the sky is bright

(Paitamo, set us at rest.)

Last night under the yellow light we moved
bright things, speaking of sleep, trying to renew
old firelight dreams. Like the old ones we sat
gathering fragments of long since broken hearts
(Bring tomorrow.)

Today the rain comes. It gleans
powers of light on a slant, releases
blossoms in the shape of pity and ancient grace
(Grandfather, give us yesterday.)

Rain today coming from the east. Tomorrow
from another hill, the Shiwanna will send again
a token for our hearts to drink,
a wakening.

(San Ysidro, Cabezon)

We went up the pass, she and I,
to see the mountain turning,
watched it discover
its golden light
rejoicing
we followed a rutted road
center blooming and filled with rocks,
yellow, magenta and pale brown,
that kept us twisting, unable to see
what was ahead, climbing
until the valley opened wide below
fading into simple blue as the sky,
revealing distance to our astounded eyes.
We were reminded of an old wanderer's dream,
a stream fizzing and bubbling among the hills,
the blooming, smokable trees—
the kind and perfect ease anyone would wish for,

going so unbelieved.
I want to tell you this:
the notion of how it ought to be,
name of an Eskimo god who sits,
content, grinning. He understands.
And so do you, and I,
if only we could remember
the banks are steep,
the peaks so far away,
but in between
a careful space of perfect springs
and all we'd ever need,
and swift winds on the peaks
where the light is clear.

Kopis'taya

(A Gathering of Spirits)

Because we live in the browning season
the heavy air blocking our breath,
and in this time when living
is only survival, we doubt the voices
that come shadowed on the air,
that weave within our brains
certain thoughts, a motion that is soft,
imperceptible, a twilight rain
soft feather's fall, a small body
dropping into its nest, rustling, murmuring,
settling in for the night.

Because we live in the hardedged season,
where plastic brittle and gleaming shines
and in this space that is cornered and angled,
we do not notice wet, moist, the significant
drops falling in perfect spheres
that are the certain measures of our minds;
almost invisible, those tears,
soft as dew, fragile, that cling to leaves,
petals, roots, gentle and sure,
every morning.

We are the women of daylight; of clocks and steel
foundrys, of drugstores and streetlights,
of superhighways that slice our days in two.
Wrapped around in glass and steel we ride
our lives; behind dark glasses we hide our eyes,
our thoughts, shaded, seem obscure, smoke
fills our minds, whisky husks our songs,
polyester cuts our bodies from our breath,
our feet from the welcoming stones of earth.
Our dreams are pale memories of themselves,
and nagging doubt is the false measure of our days.

Even so, the spirit voices are singing,
their thoughts are dancing in the dirty air.
Their feet touch the cement, the asphalt
delighting, still they weave dreams upon our
shadowed skulls, if we could listen.
If we could hear.
Let's go then. Let's find them. Let's
listen for the water, the careful gleaming drops
that glisten on the leaves, the flowers. Let's
ride the midnight, the early dawn. Feel the wind
striding through our hair. Let's dance
the dance of feathers, the dance of birds.

The Bearer of the Sun Arises

There was a man who had come into her life, into her, feeding her, feeding on her. She told him about magic, and the mystery she knew about. But he, Judah, didn't believe. Said that was why she was there on the tatami raised a foot above his apartment floor, in the center of the room.

He talked pleasantly, not looking at her mostly, just talked hypnotically. He cooked supper as the long sun set over San Francisco, talked as they ate seated on the tatami. They talked and drank, she talked about magic and he talked about his work. They ate food he cooked on a brazier, Japanese style. "I'm Nesei," he said. "There are these: Essei, Nesei, Sensei, Yonsei. They are generations in America. The Essei are the old ones. I am Nesei. We are the only people who count the generations," he said.

She remembered her own clan, descended of Iyatiku, Earth Woman, Corn Woman. There were four corn clans, then her clan. "I am Oak," she said. "The fifth. My uncle, Oak Man, helped Iyatiku in the beginning. He assisted her in laying down the orders, the rules. The way the people would live. How they would be. He was the first War Captain, the first outside chief. We begin to count from the time the people came here from the last world, just like you."

When it was late, when the sun had long set and the fog was thick against the glass he undressed her like a doll and took her to bed on the tatami altar where they had eaten. He transformed the table into a bed. He laid her down upon it. He entered her, slowly, mastering his time, fucked her, his face gone from her, intent on his own straining to appease something unspoken within him, something far away and deep inside that he did not acknowledge with even a flicker of his eyes, not even a flicker of a look in her directions, he fucked her like a doll, and lay beside her, and went to sleep.

She looked at him then. His small body. His brown skin rippling still as the muscles went slack. As slack as such muscles could. The sheen of his skin she gazed at, for a long long time.

She wondered as she watched him sleep safe in his own place far from her why she thought only of hurt. When she was near him, why did she cry. His lovemaking was good. Solid and certain. Unfumbling. Free, somehow clean. Like his neat apartment. Like his clean food. It was good, and though her body responded to him, he was very far from her, from any place she usually lived. His eyes, open or closed in sleep, did not touch her, and while he fucked he said so little, nothing at all really addressed to her, just the formula utterances he'd rotely learned to say as he was getting off. And when he was through he turned and slept and waking took her home. Politely. Smoothly. And she cried. She didn't know what to make of this. Of his confidence. His desire. His isolated sureness. Like Stephen, he refused to make her real.

Maybe he was a spirit-man. Maybe both he and Stephen were spirit men. Maybe they were in her life like others were in her dreams. Significant. Laden. Pointing to or away. From sleep to sleep, from shadow to shade, from need to need. Down in the arroyo that runs alongside Guadalupe she had learned to dig useless yellow clay and shape it into bowls for the sun to eat. Coiling the ropes, smelling the sweet smell of earth, she had shaped clay forms with Elena beside her in the tall shadows the high arroyo walls cast. Digging, she had gathered the earth. Smoothing, she had made it. Alone in a place that had few shadows, she was alone and she was afraid. Riding the high wind on a sunspun morning she went out and came in, wondering. And in the darkness of late night, when the children were long asleep, she lay, eyes huge in the shadows, feeling his pain. Judah, she would say, testing it on her tongue. Yoshuri. Nesei man. And, rubbing her palms against the satinedge of the blanket, she would lay in the shadows of that northern night, coiling her mind into sleep.

And dream. Of walking down corridors in a museum. Where no one recognized her, no one acknowledged. Walking down endless corridors, marble shining and gold leaf trimmed, halls where people walked, shadowed faces turning away if her eyes met theirs, turning toward the wall rather than face her, look at her, see her. In these halls she wandered, unable to find the way out. Not the way she had come, not the way she was going, a silent scream rising up in her always rising but never uttered in those silent, marble halls. No one ever spoke to her there.

In her dreams she would sometimes enter a room full of people, would sit with them and await the speaker, the film, whatever was being offered for enjoyment or instruction there. And would find herself unable to stay, needing to orient herself, to still the panic that had a voice saying over and over, you are not here, you are not. And would leave to once again walk the corridors where walls appeared in the place that a doorway had been, where stairs that had led down now only rose, where she searched for someone she could not find. And she would awaken, aware only of the cold coiling terror in her belly, the trembling of her veins as the blood tried to make its way through their branches. Branches branching like the tree that had stood outside her windows in that other place, the one she had left.

In one of those dreams she saw her mother, walking along the corridor near the wall. Agnes and Ben were with her. They were talking and laughing as they walked swiftly along. Ephanie tried to cross the corridor to them, but there were too many people and they were all walking toward her. She called to her mother, but she didn't look in Ephanie's direction. She called Agnes, she called Ben, but they kept walking toward her and never looked her way. Then they were past her. She turned, looked after them, tried to go after them but they had vanished as though they had not been there at all. She woke then, tears pouring from her eyes. Nobody knows my name, she thought. And arose in the fog-chilled early light to enter a kitchen she did not recognize, to wander through a flat she did not recognize, to stare at bowls and cups, pottery and photographs she did not recognize, to gaze long into the bathroom mirror under the hard, brittle light at a face she did not know.

Therapist's Notes. July 26, 1976

Dream: "I am in a huge building somewhere. It's made of marble. I think it's a museum. There are a lot of rooms and all sorts of people. I can't find my way out. I'm looking for someone, I don't know who, but I get more and more lost and I never find them. As I walk the people coming toward me turn away as I pass. They turn all the way toward the wall sometimes so they won't have to look at me. They are all strangers. Now I see my mother coming toward me. She's with the kids and they're walking on the other side of this big corridor we're in. It seems like everyone is going one direction but me. I call to my mom and Ben and Agnes, but they don't act like they can hear me or see me. They just keep going, in the direction opposite mine, talking and looking around. They're looking around but they don't see me even though I wave at them to get their attention. They walk on past me and I try to turn and go after them but as I turn around I can't see them anywhere. It's like they vanish into thin air."
Therapist: "Be the people."
Ephanie: "Okay. I'm the people. We're walking down the hall at the museum. We're on our way somewhere, and it's almost time. There's an important lecture and tour going on, and we don't want to miss it. There's this woman going the wrong way, but we don't pay any attention to her. She's not going the same way. Some of us have to go out of our way to avoid her, and that slows us down. We don't like that, but we're not going to let her interfere with our purpose. We have something important to do and she's not going with us. We don't know who she is, only that she's going the wrong way."
Therapist: "Be Ben."
Ephanie: "Okay. I'm Ben Atencio. I'm twelve years old. My grandma is taking me and my sister to see a show at the museum. This is a special show that she wants us to see. We're hurrying so that we won't be late,

and Grandma is telling us about what we're going to see. She keeps telling us to keep up so we won't miss anything. I'm feeling excited about the show because she's been talking to us about it for a long time. It was hard to get in here, and we have a long way to walk before we get to the place where the show's going on. I wish there weren't so many people. They scare me. They all walk so fast and they're tall and I can't see much except Agnes's face, she's acting like a girl right now so she's not laughing and fooling around like she usually does. I'm scared and excited and kinda mad because I don't want to walk so fast. I want to stop and look at some near things that are in cases along the walls. And I want to look out the windows we go by. Grandma says we have to get a good seat, so we have to hurry. She's holding my hand so I don't get lost in this crowd."

Therapist: "Be Agnes."

Ephanie: "I'm Agnes Atencio. I'm fourteen. I'm walking with Grandma and Ben down a long hall. It's a very wide and beautiful hall with big windows and cases with beautiful things in them. It's the museum where they put special things for everyone to look at and admire. I admire the things. There's dishes and bowls, there's things made of gold and jade from China and Egypt, things from Africa and South America and Mexico and Europe. Paintings and statues, carpets and hangings. I'm all dressed up. I have on new boots with almost high heels and a nice plaid wool coat. I have a hat that's made of fur and it's soft and it looks really good on me. It makes me look like women in the magazines. Grandma and Ben and I are walking in a hurry with all the people who are going to the show. It's a display of ancient things, with a film. They've made everything just like it used to be, Grandma says, and we're really lucky to be going to see it. I'm glad she treats me like a grown-up. She helped me fix my hair and she bought me this fur hat. I wish my mother would treat me like Grandma does. Take me places and talk about hairdos and makeup and clothes. Sometimes she does, but she's not very interested in them. I wish she was going to the show with us. She'll be sorry to miss it. She has to work all the time, and she's always so busy and so tired."

Therapist: "Be the mother."

Ephanie: "I'm Saichu Kawemie. I'm taking my grandchildren to see a special show that's here at the museum. They're like my own children. I keep them for my daughter a lot of the time. I wish she could make more money, and that she could be here with us today. They're good kids, though. She does the best she can, and I'm glad to help her with them. I miss the kids when they're gone, and having little ones around keeps me young. They have so much energy and they're so curious about things. They help out a lot around the place too, so my husband and I like to have them. I don't like this crowd though. The people are all pushing and hurrying. I want to see the show, and I want Ben and Agnes to see it too. Agnes is growing up. She's so smart. She'll go a long ways, that one. Her grandfather always says that. We have to make sure that Agnes gets a good education, he says. She'll make something of herself. That's what he says. I hope we get there pretty soon. We've been walking down hallways for a while. I feel lost in this crowd of white people. Everyone is dressed so nice. I wonder why nobody smiles or talks. I guess that's how they are in the big city. I wonder if my daughter remembers the time we took her to that play from New York when she was a little one. Maybe she does, and that's why she moved here. It's not as far as New York, but a lot goes on here. I hope she comes home sometime, though. I miss her when she's gone."

Therapist: "Be the museum."

Ephanie: "I'm the museum. I'm huge and imposing. I'm square and shining and clean. All these people walk around in me and admire me. They see how tall and big I am, how full of special things. I have almost everything anyone would care to see. From everywhere in the world. Lots of the things here aren't on display. There is much more hidden away in me, in vaults and storage rooms than is ever put out for people to see. I have a huge staff of people who work here and keep things running smoothly. I am a bulwark. A strength. Half of what is stored in me is unrecognized by the people who work here. They can't begin to understand the knowledge and the treasures that I hold in me. But I keep these things safe, for sometime when there will be those who can understand, who can recognize what the artifacts and treasures I keep are worth. They think that things are about money or history. They think they will put them away because of their beauty. They are afraid that the beauty will be lost. But I know the truth of the matter, a truth that is carefully kept in the records that are filed carefully away. Someday they will be read and understood."

Therapist: "Be Ephanie."

Ephanie: "I am Ephanie Atencio. Ephanie Kawemie Atencio. I'm wandering in the great museum and I am hopelessly lost. I recognize nothing. I can't find my way. I can't see anything because I don't have time. I have to meet someone here, but I can't find them. They aren't here. There's a lot of people here, they are shadows. They won't look at me. I don't recognize anyone here. I am walking against the traffic. I am lost and frightened. They look so threatening, so alien. They won't look at me. They're all in a hurry and they just walk by me, moving aside to get out of my way. They won't touch me or look at me and I'm afraid to stop anyone to ask where they're going or how to find the way out. The walls are so high, so smooth. I don't belong in a place like this. It scares me. I'm scared of it because it's so big and so alien, so strange. I don't understand anything I see here. Why do they put those things in a big building? Doesn't anyone use them? What are they for? I feel so stupid, so helpless. I see my mother and my kids. They're walking along the corridor. They don't see me. I call them, I wave at them, but they just keep walking on by like I'm not even here. I am so frightened here, and nobody even cares."

Therapist: "Tell them that, Ephanie."

Ephanie: "You don't care! I'm so frightened here. I'm lost and frightened and you don't even care." (Voice barely audible)

Therapist: "Louder, say it like you mean it."

Ephanie, shouting: "You don't even care! I'm lost and you won't even look at me! I am so scared and you don't even care. You dumb stupid idiots, quit looking away from me. Look at me, goddammit! Look at me!" (Starts strong, ends almost whispering)

Therapist: "Louder!"

Ephanie: "Look at me! Look at me! Look at me!" (Said in a stronger voice)

Below on the Lower Hills He Strides

One late night after Ephanie had gone to bed, after the children were long asleep, somebody knocked at the door. It was Judah. He came in. She did not turn on the lights. They sat in the streetlight-lit front room of her flat and talked in quiet tones. She wondered why he was there. He said he needed to see her. He began to kiss her, almost desperately. He fumbled in his clothes, unzipped his pants. He dropped them slightly and pushed her down on the couch. She protested. "No, Judah. Not now. I can't right now." She couldn't say she was having her period. Shyness, inarticulate fear rose in her at the thought. "Please," he was muttering so low she could barely hear. "Please." There was the sound almost of a sob in his voice.

She let him push her down. She let him lie on her. He pushed her gown up, reached for her panties, thin, nylon briefs. With one pull he had torn them, pushed them aside. He was moaning, saying her name. "Ephanie, oh Ephanie, I love you," he was saying, "Oh, please let me, Ephanie," and with his strong brown fingers between her legs he touched her, slid a finger inside her, found the tampax and took it out, spread her legs farther, saying more and more strongly, like a chant, like a drum, "Let me, Ephanie, let me. Let me Ephanie, let me."

And with his hand he pushed his half flaccid penis into her, almost sobbing, "Damn thing," he cursed, moaning, "Damn thing."

And cursing, breathing with sobbing breaths, he held her shoulder pinned against the couch. He buried his face in her breasts and he wept.

And in the dim light from the blinded windows he arose and straightened his clothes. He pulled his pants over his slim, firm hips and zipped them with his strong brown hands. He buckled his belt and then looked down at her torn face. That had gone silent and remote in the dim half light. He reached down and touched her hair. He pulled her gown over her legs. He went out into the night, the darkness of the city night that was never complete. He closed the door.

And left her there to ponder the pain of him, of her. "I don't want to live," she whispered to the shadows that waited quietly in the room. "I don't want this to go on. I can't make it stop." She said that, whispering so the children wouldn't hear her, so she wouldn't hear. "I don't want to live this anymore." And after a while she arose and slowly, whispering the words that came, she returned to her room and got into her bed.

You Be My Snag, I'll Be Your Snagaroo. A '49

Two nights later she went to the Indian bar. She went early and it was almost empty. There were a couple of men she didn't recognize at the bar, talking together in low tones. They wore work shirts and heavy silver and turquoise jewelry. The bartender looked up as she sat on a tall stool. "Hi, Ephanie," he said. "Gimme a Bud," she replied, speaking quietly so no one would notice her. She didn't want to see anyone right now. She just wanted to sit in whatever comfort was available here. Sit and not think about anything at all.

The man brought her her beer. He was a Miwok man, tall and heavy framed. His black hair fell in a line over his forehead. His huge hands sported several large heavy Navajo rings. He went back to his place at the other end of the bar after he served her, and picked up the girlie magazine he had been looking at, his impassive face eerily lit by the dim bar lights.

She looked around at the scarred bar, the simple kitchen tables by the window. She didn't want to look into the mirror that faced her. Restless, she got up, went over to the pool table that took up most of the room and began to shoot. She didn't bother to set up, just shot the balls that were left from the last players.

A man and a woman came in. He was very large, and so was she. They got a couple of drinks and went over to the other pool table. They were pretty drunk, Ephanie could see, so warily, she laid down the cue stick and went to sit at the bar's one table that was crammed against the plate glass window.

It was getting toward late evening. The fog was settling down over the city. She sipped her beer and smoked her cigarettes, staring out at the sidewalk, at the street.

The man and woman began to talk in loud voices, and suddenly the woman exploded into a rage. Ephanie turned to look their way. The woman was yelling in earnest now. She was screaming. "You bastard," she yelled. "You rotten son of a bitch. I'll show you, you lousy lying bastard." And she began to hurl the balls at him. He ducked and she kept pelting him. The mirror over the bar shattered. No one moved. The bartender and the two men had turned to watch. They were silent. She threw the balls with enormous force. Ephanie froze for a few moments, then ducked under the table as the wildly pounding billiard balls began to come toward her. The plate glass of the window she had been staring out of broke, glass flying everywhere. She crouched under the table, holding her head in her arms. The only sound was of the breaking glass, the thuds as the billiard balls hit the wall, hit the tables, the woman's cursing voice, shouting her pain and her rage.

She threw all of the balls, then hurled the cue sticks. Storming and raging, she threw everything within reach, then ran out the door, shattering its heavy glass as she slammed it behind her.

Slowly the people in the bar began to move. Slowly Ephanie came out from under the table, looking at her hands, her arms, to see if she was bleeding. Slowly the men began to talk, laughing, they began to pick up the billiard balls and the cue sticks. The bartender began to sweep up the glass. "Bar's closed tonight, folks," he said. "Sam, you son of a gun, don't you bring that woman in here drunk again."

Sam, his brown face ashen, nodded drunkenly. "No, Jake," he said. "I'm not gonna bring that woman anywhere, drunk or sober." And he began drunkenly to laugh as the other two men slapped him on the shoulder. "It's okay, Jake," they said. "Want another beer?"

Ephanie went into the ladies' room, splashed some water on her face. She looked into the mirror at eyes that were squinted into glittering slits: "Right on, sister," she said. "I know just what you mean."

She Makes a Clean Sweep

It was the most amazing thing. The whole place, the marble and the gold plate, the huge spaces uncluttered by so much as a bench, the marble staircases rising and falling out of sight, leading godknowswhere, footsteps unheard in the long marble corridors, the shadowy rotunda. People walked purposefully, carefully somber, eyes down, showing no amazement at all.

But it was truly an amazing place, this monument to established authority, one where only purposefulness was a suitable pose, where nothing of the street or the great grimy reaches of the city, the homes and the ordinary cares of the everyday, the informal, the familiar could enter. In one great room, marbled spacious, where the walls soared almost out of sight overhead to the gold-leafed, fleur-de-lysed corners, the gold letters proclaimed: HALL OF RECORDS. Ephanie thought for a moment of the legends of a secret brotherhood, saw her name in a secret file containing the most private records of her inmost heart, where she would find the secret of her purpose here in this time and space, and she wished that the lost could be so stored and retrieved, even in this awesome institutional costume hall.

Up the spiraling stairs: surely Alice fresh out of Wonderland would have been awed, intimidated by this show of massive authority. The serene presence of the state, the faceless shadow of authority, of power, of those who controlled because they had seen fit to entomb themselves and their sacred honor in the vast caverns of city hall. No swaggering politicians, slightly rumpled from their labors, stood around these halls gossiping like they did at home. None such stood or sat along creaking benches trading favors, gossiping, guffawing. No young or funky hung out among the tasteful echoes. Only file clerks and secretaries scurried silent here and there, and men with briefcases swinging manfully at their sides, properly dwarfed in the silent vastness, insignificant.

Ephanie finally found her lawyer. He was waiting for her where the gold-leafed dome arched overhead. She had lost much of her sense of herself in her wanderings through the marbled halls, but she could see that the whole thing was a carefully constructed set, designed to create an illusion of unbreakable, everlasting power. In its own way it was a masked dance. Its priests and shamans wore different costumes, made different motions, but its intended effect was the same. She felt profoundly disoriented, an appropriate enough state considering the occasion.

Her lawyer raised a hand, signalling her. Modishly suited, mustached and fashionably grizzled, he was trying to create an impression of ease and elegance, to cast some glow of personal dignity against the cold white walls and floors of this inhuman place. But his thin figure and his bare maturity made his effort, like hers, futile. "Hello," he said, smiling.

"This place is amazing," Ephanie said, grinning at him.

He peered at her, eyes coming almost unglazed for a second, then shaded again with businesslike glinting. "You haven't been here before?" he asked, appearing nonchalant, pretending she was saying a tourist thing instead of another sort of thing entirely. Which was a difficult pretense to maintain, she thought, considering the way she was dressed. She wore the flower-emblazoned, silk fringed shawl she had brought from home and worn habitually since being in the city. It covered a purple shirt and ranch-style levis. She wore moccasins. Not expensive, cool ones, but the simple ones she had gotten from the trading post near her home. "No, I haven't been here until now," she said, resisting the urge to pull her shawl over her head and face. "I think it's one of the strangest places I've seen yet!"

They went to the elevator and entered it. The small, dingy-carpeted box was framed by gold-tinged metal doors.

"The judge will be here soon," the lawyer said. He straightened his tie carefully. Something about judges set him off, Ephanie thought. "He'll ask you some questions," the young man continued, "but it shouldn't take long."

"Here's the piece of paper with the property disposition and signatures you wanted," Ephanie said, handing him a single sheet of cheap, unlined paper. I sound very matter-of-fact, she thought, considering the barely controlled anger and my terror at getting this written and getting Judah to sign it. Considering Judah's real or imagined rage at the whole thing. He hadn't wanted the divorce, she knew that, though he'd left her to run around with other women. He also wanted to keep the pot boiling at home. Well, she thought, the fire went out. I don't really want to pay his bills while he has a bang-up time, so to speak. And grinned wryly at her own unconscious punning.

"The property is divided more or less evenly, isn't it?" The lawyer gazed at her, expressionless.

She bit her lip. "Not really."

"Oh?" He looked surprised.

"Considering I pay the bills and he gets the goodies," she shrugged and tightened her shawl across her shoulders and breasts.

"Oh." The mustached young man gazed down the round hole in the floor. They leaned against the polished brass rail that encircled the shaft of the rotunda. "But, aside from that," he said, looking stubbornly determined to get through this.

"Sure," she said. "It's okay."

"And you understand that by waiving support payments now you're waiving them forever. You can't ever come and ask for them."

She nodded. Judah should support us when we're divorced when he didn't while we were married, she thought. Out loud she cried, "Yeah. I understand that." Her voice was deep and scratchy.

"It's okay," the lawyer said, "since you're . . ."

"More than able to support myself," she finished his thought for him in a flat tone of voice. And him and the kids and whoever else comes along, she thought. I pay for my loving and I refuse to pay when they refuse to love. Shit.

She smiled coolly at the lawyer.

They went into the courtroom. Waited for the judge. The lawyer was nervous. She was nervous. She held her jaws tightly clenched. She wanted to smoke, but smoking wasn't allowed in the courtroom. You can't be overawed and terrorized when relaxed with a cigarette in your hand, she thought.

A fiftyish woman with too much makeup over her pasty white skin came into the room. She looked fatter and older than she needed to because of the makeup and the neat, fashionless secretary's dress and pointed-toe shoes she wore. The lawyer went up to her and said something Ephanie couldn't hear. "Nine o'clock," the woman said, folding papers busily.

The bailiff, also old, also sickly white, yawned.

A man in a suit came in and sat down in front of the steno machine. He was toothless, his lips caved in against his gums. His washed-out grey suit matched his dingy skin.

Ephanie waited, hands folded in her lap, her moccasined feet dangling from the bench. Damn they always make the benches for Texans, she thought. Indians are short. At least my kind are.

"You'll go up there," her lawyer said. "All the way next to the judge." He pointed to the witness chair that sat forlorn and tiny beside the judge's massive desk at the other end of the long room from where they sat waiting. The chair looked isolated and humble. There was a microphone in front of it.

"All the way up there," she said, voice mechanical.

"Yeah." The lawyer smiled at her fleetingly. Bared his teeth at her, actually. He kept worrying about the judge. "I don't know what he's likely to ask, today. Judge Mather is one of the few intelligent ones," he continued, striving to reassure her with his knowing tone of voice, "but he gets picky. If he's gotten up feeling grouchy."

Ephanie's stomach felt twisted up. She kept wanting to laugh. Or tell the young man beside her that this whole thing was ridiculous and walk out. She picked up a newspaper lying on the long bench they sat on and began to read the front page.

"The court will rise. Case Number 651079." The lawyer read the number stamped on the documents in his hand. "Yoshuri versus Yoshuri." He motioned her to walk through the gates, past the tables where the stenographer and the secretary sat, past the empty jury box, up the steps to sit beside the judge's high desk.

Ducking her head and pulling her shawl tighter, she obeyed. She was conscious of the soft shooshing sound her moccasins made on the floor as she walked the long way to the steps, climbed them and sat down. Her fringes swayed as she moved, like at the Squaw Dance. Her lawyer followed her and stood in front of her at a safe distance. He droned the questions they'd rehearsed.

She answered each one in a strong, clear voice, surprising herself with her control. The judge, a large grey man, didn't look up from the papers in front of him. Ephanie's disorientation was almost total. She was so dizzy, the edges of her vision were blurred and dark. She fixed her eyes on the judge, who, like the bailiff, stenographer and secretary, was well into his prime, very nearly beyond it. He didn't look up the whole time. She noticed that she, her lawyer, another client—a pretty Chicana—and her lawyer were the only people under sixty. She wondered if that was significant. She and the Chicana were the only nonwhites in the huge echoing room.

"The court grants the interlocutory. File the papers in Room 317," the older man told the younger. The stenographer pushed buttons silently, unseeing.

"You can go," the judge said to her.

She walked down the steps, past the over-aged secretary, past the long, empty tables, past the gates, looking at the blond modish lawyer who was signalling his client toward the witness chair at the other end of the long long room as her case was called. "Pacheco versus Pacheco" the bailiff announced. The tiny, dark woman walked the long way up to the tiny, isolated witness chair, through the huge, almost empty hall, as Ephanie closed the courtroom door behind her.

Diane Burns

Our People

Our people
slit open the badger
to see the tomorrows
in its blood.

Now
look at me
and see what our
tomorrows hold.

We lie together
Souls slit open raw
            and bleeding
We embrace
And rub
        the wounds
                together.

On Lac Court Orreilles
the ice is breaking up
melting
succumbing to April.
The Canadian geese
are flying
home.

Uncle Waynaboozhoo and Grandpa
are making little birchbark baskets
and whittling spigots
(they burned through the veins
        of young branches with
            a hot coat hanger)
Waiting on the maple trees
who are waiting on the
sun in late April.

But
in Washington Square Park
the trees are showing
tips of green
and youngblackmenin Armygreenjackets

advertise their ailments and medicinals
("Loose joints,
        Loose joints," they whisper)

And I sit on a bench and wait
for the sun.
I can smell how clean the air is
back home;
I can feel electricity in the air.

My wrist twinges
from the change in weather
and I tighten the black leather brace
that keeps my knife hand steady.

Big Fun

I don't care if you're married I still love you
I don't care if you're married
After the party's over
I will take you home in my One-Eyed Ford
Way yah hi yo, Way yah hi you!

Modene!
    the roller derby queen!
She's Anishinabe,
    that means Human Being!
That's H for hungry!
and B for frijoles!
        frybread!
        Tortillas!
        Watermelon!
        Pomona!
Take a sip of this
and a drag of that!
At the rancheria fiesta
It's tit for tat!
Low riders and Levis
go fist in glove
Give it a little pat
a push or a shove

Move it or lose it!
Talk straight or bruise it!
Everyone
has her fun
when the sun
is all done
We're all one
make a run
hide your gun
Hey!
I'm no nun!
'49 in the hills above
                Ventura
Them Okies gotta drum

I'm from Oklahoma
I got no one to call my own
if you will be my honey
I will be your sugar pie, way hi yah,
Way yah hey way yah hi yah!

We're gonna sing all night
bring your blanket
or
be that way then!

For Carole

rodeo rider

cowgirl

pointy toes and a pink hat
won at a race
fringe dripping from elbows
                wrists
                breasts
                legs
prancing spotted pony
glitter glued discreetly
to cardboard rowels

A smile that knocks 'em dead
at two hundred paces,
Dust you churn up around the barrels
    hasn't a chance
    to settle before
you are home

One day
   she's wearing her pink suit into the tavern
   down the road a piece
she's just eighteen and it's morning
   & she's a young Indin rodeo star.
Folks buy her beers & afore she knows it,
it's afternoon and the rodeo's starting
But she doesn't care there in the gloom
   & glow & starring around.
. . . Some hundreds of beers later the pink hat
   gets lost
   the fringe goes gray & rots off the satin shirt.
The glittered spurs scraped off some brass rail—

   and leavin' the bar one afternoon
she spots a young Indin cowboy trainin' his horse
   and she hears the flags snappin' in the breeze
     hands clappin'
     folk cheering
"Friend, let me take a spin on your pony"
He looks closely "Lady you sure you know how to ride?"
"Young feller, I was the only pole bender this county ever produced!"
He doesn't know what pole benders were
   reluctantly hands her the reins
Her knees creak like old saddle leather as she rises in stirrups
   surprised and out of breath she sits
   then
   chirrups
   & whips the reins
   rides around a tree &
   decides to show off a bit as
   gone-by moments roar in rodeo memories
   standing the bay pony on one stocking foot &
   falls
   off.

Startled by the impact of the ground she thinks

It's been ten years
since I missed
my last
rodeo

Houston and Bowery, 1981

Sometimes those crazy drunks on the corner
scream
like they're being sliced up or something,
except when they're really sliced up they never scream.
sometimes just for the hell of it
they throw their heads back
and holler.
They sit on the curb and talk
    honky this and honky that
    nigger this and nigger that.
I get disgusted.
Their ol'ribbon shirts tore up
    & crusty
And they talk like they're Tecumseh come back
while they booze it up
all day.
Sheeeit.
            Other times
I see them on the corner
walking straight
and standing tall.
I see those greasy ol'ribbon shirts
& I get a lump
swelling in my throat
I know
there's a wolf, a lugarou
inside me too.
There's a voice
that scorches stars
and withers starlings on the wing
A voice that
sings '49s on rooftops

and drives back demons and talks with spirits
One that blows like plutonium dust
over the rez.
Inside the ribbon shirts
coyote laughs/wolf waits
The village cryers hang out on the corner.

Gladys Cardiff

Long Person

Dark as wells, his eyes
Tell nothing. They look
Out from the print with small regard
For this occasion.
Dressed in neat black, he sits
On a folded newspaper
On a sawhorse in front of his blacksmith shop.
Wearing a black suit and white, round-brimmed hat,
My father stands on one side, his boy face
Round and serious. His brother stands
Like a reflection on the other side.
They each hold a light grasp on the edge
Of their daddy's shoulder, their fingernails
Gleaming like tiny moons on the black wool.
Each points his thumb up at the sky,
As if holding him too closely, with their whole hand,
Would spur those eyes into statement.
Coming out of a depth known as dream—
Or is it memory?
I can see inside the door where the dim shapes
Of bellows and tongs, rings and ropes hang on the wall,
The place for fire, the floating anvil,
Snakes of railroad steel, wheels in heaps,
Piled like turtles in the dark corners.
Oconoluftee, Long Person,
You passed a stone's throw away from his door.
Your ripples are Cherokee prayers.
River, Grandfather,
May your channels never break.

Tsa'lagi Council Tree

This is a story my father told to me
when I was a girl.

Hilahi', long ago,
before the whites,

hilahi'yu, long, long ago
in buckskin days,
the old men and women of the people
met at the place of the Principal Wood.
The elders held council,
some sitting in the branches
of this *u'tanu ata'ya*.
They smoked the old tobacco
in a whitestone pipe.
The pipe had seven bores, one for each.
They spoke of many mysteries
and matters of law
words that were pleasing to all
who heard them.
Here, trails from every direction met.
Tsa' nadiska, they say
the rustling leaves sang green enchantments,
red and yellow songs,
reminding always to honor *ela e'ladi*,
the earth below, the place of roots.

Now we burn the wood of oak trees,
and do not believe that bugle weed
will necessarily make our children
eloquent. But this is what the old man
said to him when he was a boy,
hilahi', *hilahi'yu*, long ago.

Tlanusi'yi, The Leech Place

Surely it is death to come here.
This rock overhang
opens a shadowy well in the river
to give me a deep look.
I am hungry for fish.
I forget the woman tossed up
downstream,
her face without nose or ears.
I never saw
the baby that disappeared,
the quiet sleeper.

"I'll tie red leech skins upon my legs
and wear them for garters."
My song scythes over wet fields
parting the water like braids
wound with foam feathers,
wound with sunperches, snakes, and green turtles.
"I'll tie red leech skins upon my legs
and wear them for garters."
Its breath is like milk.
Young as I am, I am
old in a striped ahunwogi,
girded in red and in water,
Young as I am I know
the secret caverns of the Hiwassee,
that the river is eating the land.
I was hungry for fish.
I was from Birdtown.
I am dressed in a whirlpool of leech skins.

Grey Woman

A woman coming down the snowy road
in moccasins, a basket on her arm
her back bent by ninety Indian winters,
here to pick inside the garbage bins below
the porches on the Cheyenne reservation,
well-known among her people

Called Grey Woman. Finding a tin of sour
butter, she makes her way between the lines
of sheets that hang in rigid squares; each step
dependent on a frame less surely pinned
than frozen cloth cold-soldered to a wire.
She takes a rancid gob to eat.

Once the red Wyoming sun fell to her feet.
Young when the young men reeled, tied to the sun
and bringing it down, she watched one dance alone
on thongs sewn in his breast, his breath in blasts
that shook the twirling feathers on his pipe.
She hears the echo of her chirping heart,

The sound of day outlasted. The night she died,
following the old belief, all doors were locked
until, after the manner of her ancestors,
she found *Maheo* and a final place.
*The hand has turned to horn, and obdurate
Her spirit stands unhoused before my door.*

Outer Space, Inner Space

Expecting no miracles, we walked
beside the water, resting in
ourselves and a vacant stretch
of sand along Puget Sound.
At the edge of a tide pool a green
iridescent worm wound
in slow grace its segmented
length over fields of black
cobblestone dollars, crabs, both
purple and brown, blue
mussels, snails, kelp
in ribbons of red and green.
You walked ahead while I,
sprawled on a tangle of wood,
feeling heavy and loose, ripe
as a vegetable among club fern,
dandelions, broom, and wild roses,
looked back where our footsteps went
in pocks, two lines parallel.

A gull, screeching like iron
in an old hoist, patrolled
where you stood and waited for me.
You had found a nest, pink
with tumbling baby shrimp.
We watched them tuck and burrow.
With care, you lifted their rock,
swaddled in kelp and venerable
in studded barnacles,
and placed it as you'd found it.

We saw the urchin stars
that ringed its base unfold
and take their colors.

Night came with deeper gray
and settled in, turning
the clam shells white as thoughts.
Pointing to the pale shell
of moon you said, "Those three
are on their way home now,"
and I pointed to Venus,

Remembering how it was
watching the hump-backed shrimp
wriggling in unaccustomed light,
each carapace pink and delicate,
almost transparent. I dreamt of hands
swimming in new air
before eyes that take their color
from the slate-blue shades of the sea.
Heading back, we saw our tracks,
in two lines, parallel.
They stretched until they seemed
to converge where we began.

Where Fire Burns

I.

Where fire burns in the hollow sycamore,
    smoke like a vague feather lift-
    ing up from the island,
    and the world is cold,
    where all the animals wait
    on the river's edge
    while Water Spider weaves
    a *tusti* bowl, and steals
    across the waves,
    where in the little crucible
    she carries on her back
    an orange piece of the Thunders gift,

there all the fires
of hearth and harvest,
the conflagrations to come,
everlasting fire of the sacred mounds,
leap into being.

II.

Where fire burns in the Carolinas
      sweeping up the hillsides
      in a red and gold combustion
      of blossoming azaleas,
      and blue smoke rises above
      immovable mountains,
      and it is 1898
      sixty years after
      the Trail of Tears when
      Going Snake heard peal after peal
      of thunder in a cloudless sky,
      and you were four and hiding in the mountains,
      you Suate, the Chosen One,
      your face like last year's apple,
      will speak to Sunday's congregation
      of Wasi and God's voice
      in a burning bush,
      but today
      you are telling stories
      while the man from Washington
      writes in his book
      "The rabbit was the leader of them all
      in mischief."

III.

Where the fires of generation have brought me here
      to the opposite end of the land,
      to work late at night
      while my husband and children sleep,
      where out from the yellow pages
      the tongues of fire ignite
      and wily rabbit dances
      into the broom-grass
      tricking the wolf again,
      it is like gathering nuts

after the leaf-burning,
stirring and sifting
through ashes and husks,
cracking the vowels and consonants
of a language I need to know,
trying to get the taste of them.
Because of our son
with hair blacker than soot,
and eyes that become darker every year
and more impenetrable,
for our daughter with hair as orange
as fire on the hill,
her eyes the color of smoke,
I gather the names and places,
these nutmeats sweetened
with the char of fire,
these inextinguishable seeds,
that they may hold wherever they go
the interior kernels
of recognition and remembrance
saying *tsita'ga*, "I am standing,"
da nita'ga, "They are standing
together as one."

Leaves like Fish

Cottonwood, willow and brier,
Night air billows in the dark grove,
hauls the alders over, their leaves

Jumping, spilling silver-bellied on the lawn.
The lighted wind is running with a flood
of green fish, phosphorescent and wild

On the winter grass, breaking like struck matches,
without warmth or place, random as green minnows.
Above the clouds the sky waits, one-celled,

Expanded over tides and winds, loving
the south wind as much as the north,
schooling the planets in discretion and form.

Simples

Healing Arnica,
astringent birthroot trillium,
the "sprint bitters" sassafras and dandelion root,
yarrow for dancing on fire,
dill, a field of fire,
quieting monkshood, blood-staunching nettles,
fleabane, Scarlet Gilia, Black Haw for the French disease,
poultices made with jam, Bag Balm, Black Draught,
Pine Tar, Bay Rum, Karaya Gum,
Glover's Imperial Sarcoptic Mange Cure,
Calamine, Diuril, Co-Pyronil, Quinidine,
Valium, Doriden, Seconal,
Digitoxin, Filaxis, Alka-
Butazoliden, Tal-
Win

Nora Dauenhauer

Winter Developing

Bathing in inversion:
negative
at night.
Inversion on positive:
over-exposure
by day.
Dissolve inversion,
positive appears.

Skiing on Russian Christmas

Southeast at low tide:
how the frosted trees
are heavy with herring eggs.

Branches in water:
how the birds fly to them
spawning their roe.

Frosted alders:
shapes of coral
clawing outward.

Breech Birth

Reluctant Sh Kaxwul.aat, "Being
Troubled About Herself," baby
with her foot hanging out,
testing the world.

Pregnant Image of "Exaggerating the Village"
(A Poem on Two Tlingit Names)

Under her
exaggerated hair
lying on
her exaggerated belly
lies
"Lying There."

Jessy

Trying to write
about you is like dragging
a fishing line through bushes.
I go a short distance
and my line hooks
on underbrush.

Seal Pups

As if inside
a blue-green bottle
rolling with the breakers.

Kelp

Ribbons of iodine
unrolled by the hands
of the waves.

Rookery

Under its brown fur
the beach twitches with life.

Voices

We sound like crying bullheads
when we sing
our songs.

Granddaughters dancing,
blossoms
swaying in the wind.

Genocide

Picketing the Eskimo
Whaling Commission
an over-fed English girl
stands with a sign
"Let the Whales Live."

Tlingit Concrete Poem

```
                              t'a  n
                            a        i
                          a    k
          x'aax'x'aax'x'aax'x'aax'x'aax
           aax'x'aax'x'aax'x'aax'x'aax'x'aax'x
          'x'aax'x'aax'x'aax'x'aax'x'aax'x'aax'x'a
         x'x'aax'x'aax'x'aax'x'aax'x'aax'x'aax'x'aax
        aax'x'aax'x'aax'x'aax'x'aax'x'aax'x'aax'x'aax'
       'aax'x'aax'x'aax'x'aax'x'aax'x'aax'x'aax'x'aax'x
      x'aax'x'aax'x'aax'x'aax'x'aax'x'aax'x'aax'x'aax'x'
     'x'aax'x'aax'x'aax'x'aax'x'aax'x'aax'x'aax'x'aax'x'
     'x'aax'x'aax'x'aax'x'aax'x'aax'x'aax'x'aax'x'aax'x'a
     'x'aax'x'aax'x'aax'x'aax'x'aax'x'aax'x'aax'x'aax'x'a
    x'x'aax'x'aax'x'aax'x'aax'x'aax'x'aax'x'aax'x'aax'x'a
    x'x'aax'x'aax'x'aax'x'aax'x'aax'x'aax'x'aax'x'aax'x'a
    x'x'aax'x'aax'x'aax'x'aax'x'aax'x'aax'x'aax'x'aax'x'a
    x'x'aax'x'aax'x'aax'x'aax'x'aax'x'aax'x'aax'x'aax'x'a
     'x'aax'x'aax'x'aax'x'aax'x'aax'x'aax'x'aax'x'aax'x'a
     'x'aax'x'aax'x'aax'x'aax'x'aax'x'aax'x'aax'x'aax'x'
     'x'aax'x'aax'x'aax'x'aax'x'aax'x'aax'x'aax'x'aax'x'
      x'aax'x'aax'x'aax'x'aax'x'aax'x'aax'x'aax'x'aax'x'
       'aax'x'aax'x'aax'x'aax'x'aax'x'aax'x'aax'x'aax'x
       'aax'x'aax'x'aax'x'aax'x'aax'x'aax'x'aax'x'aax'
        aax'x'aax'x'aax'x'aax'x'aax'tl'ukwx̲'aax'x'aax'
         ax'x'aax'x'aax'x'aax'x'aax'x'aax'x̲'aax'x'aax
          x'x'aax'x'aax'x'aax'x'aax'x'aax'x'aax'x'aa
          'x'aax'x'aax'x'aax'x'aax'x'aax'x'aax'x'a
           'aax'x'aax'x'aax'x'aax'x'aax'x'aax'x
            ax'x'aax'x'aax'x'aax'x'aax'x'aax
            'x'aax'x'aax'x'aax'x'aax'x'a
             'aax'x'aax'x'aax'x'aax'x'
              'x'aax'x'aax'x'aa
               'x'aa
```

Akat'ani = stem
x'aax' = apple
tl'ukwx̲ = worm

Charlotte de Clue

the underside of trees

color of leaves
fading into shadows
branches opening
for the sun

limbs becoming forests

shade
becoming the other side
becoming our dreams
our loneliness

the undersides of trees
are the undersides of turtles
the bellies of the great fish
the puma nursing her young
all that stays
when bones turn to chalk

where everything drops
dried and bloodless
and returns
to the roots

to become

other trees

61

*So the spirits dance
the devil's step, and are kept
from riding the winds to the sea.*
—ETHERIDGE KNIGHT

I.

In early fall, along the Salt Fork,
the red clay and water mingled
like honey and butter. And the cottonwoods
stood in the glistening flats

like horns on the great elk.
Summer lingered in our limbs
as blood pulses feverishly
in a dying animal.
   I walked home, my hands
greasy from fists of bacon fat
we used to catch the crawdad.
The sun sank across the plains,
burning the edges of fields;
burning a path through a world
of crayon etchings
waiting for tomorrow for their meaning.

II.

   Coldness came without warning,
like a knife tearing into me, as I
saw the black car parked in the road.
My instincts sharpened
like soft wood whittled to a fine point.
It always meant trouble.
A woman would be left alone,
crying. A family made poorer.
A child would have to give up
being a child.
   And I knew, as the trap springs,
the dying animal must face its hunter.
The sheriff's men had come
to take my father away.
   The doors shut, the car
pulled away.
When the pleading stopped,
the road was empty.

III.

   (Prisons, I know little of,
but letters saying: I am afraid.
And grey walls, and grey faces,
and hands that reach across the table
but cannot touch. And hatred
that has no words.)

IV.

     When spring came the river rose
to wash the deadness of winter
from the roots of trees.
I shook the coldness from my mind,
for now it was becoming inhabited
with dreams of women.
And buried a child in the soft dust
that swirls and dances
in the south wind.

Healing

their hands
passing thru the darkness,
pulling from the earth
life's force.
eyes hollowed
and star-filled,
gazing gently
to a place
where there is no pain.
their faces are fire,
blood red,
burning it out,
burning deep.

shaking,
shaking,
ah,
sickness can be stubborn.

                      here is a sign,
                      taught me by a friend
                      who lives in a world
                      where there is no sound

gently press your thumb
against your cheek.
curve your fingers
drawing an arc
for the passing day.

                              it means gathon ihn don . . . . tomorrow.

Morning Song.

          Grey is the color of time
          when all things stretch
          in the four directions
          and nothing is touched
          with defeat.
Niki nonk'on
Owononk'on ieh
          Dawn is the child
          wet with birth.
Owononk'on ieh
          Sky pulls its sheets back
          and nurses the clouds,
          tickles their bellies,
          and they run.
          And the sun warms the feathers
          of the washinga.
          Earth-maker reminds us
          things are not the same.
Niki wathon
          Song goes out
          across the space
          between night and day
          telling us
          we have slept
          while the spirits walked
          the earth.
Niki wathon
Niki nonk'on
          And oh,
          what is it to be awakened from life

Yesterday, Robin spoke to me.
My hands were tied, twisted together
with strings of gut,
loosened with sweat, and dried with sleep.
And yet I could hear,
but the words twisted my hands tighter.
And she spoke and laughed at me,
and danced in the pale, watery air.
Can you free my hands, I asked her.
And they dropped to my lap,
my fingers separating.
I counted them, wein . . . thonba . . . thabathin . . .
while she sat
balanced in the wind.
Who has come to play with me, I asked.
Is it you?
The branch snapped.
Winter's heart, you will not make it
through the spring, she cried.
I will catch you, ShinKu KuGe,
I said. I will catch you and cut your heart out.

Today, Robin barely lifts herself
from the ground.
I watch her,
my arms falling lightly to my side
circling 'round my back, spreading
gently in the wind.

Tomorrow,
she will die.

Place-of-Many-Swans.

I sit on the ground
in the path of the little spider, Tesehchobe
Like the great grey fish,
the clouds dip their heads
in their watery sky.
When the sun leaves unnoticed

and hints of daylight for someone else,
the poet waits for the moon.
But i am somewhere in between
making the shadows my friends,
giving them faces i have seen before,
ancient and wise,
and crying.

The people that lived here
came from the trees
and were proud in the way they stood.
But they were whittled away.
first their limbs,
then their center,
and left bare.

Tesehchobe walks across my feet
and darts in and out of the shadows.
I think she limps
from an old wound.
Are you lonely without them, Tesechobe?
Will you cry when I leave?

Who weeps over fallen trees?

In Memory of the Moon. (A Killing.)

the hated dog sits
in the blackest part of the night
where the edges of earth will never turn to day.
his eyes are red, for they see only the Moon
and the blood.
he slept alone
under the tables and between the stools
licking his hunter's boots,
thinking about the afternoon sun chasing him
through the open door.
it made him angry.

the Moon walked out of her house and down an empty road.
and the hated dog
with the taste of his master's boots in his mouth,
followed her.

and the sun fell to its knees
and buffed the sky with a bloody haze.
the wind blew once more, then cold.

the hated dog killed the Moon.

Ijajee's Story

When you are traveling
and find yourself alone,
it is not wise
to think of yourself as ignorant.
Because when you travel alone
you have no one to depend on
but yourself.
And would you trust someone
you thought to be ignorant?

Just say, "I do not understand."
These things that you do not
understand . . . . . .
put them into a bag
and carry them over your shoulder.
As time goes on,
the bag will get empty.

To the spirit of Monahsetah
and to all women who have been
forced to the ground.

(from the banks of the Konce.)

there is death in this river
you can hear it speak.

the people fishing
or watching the great birds
nest in shallow coves

cannot hear it.
they have not been made to listen.

i have seen the eagles
and cast for fish

and there is something else here.
the Mystery that speaks
of life and death
and rebirth
has been stretched to its limits.
violence has imposed
new conditions.

if i could
i would pull the death from this river.
if i could
i would fling it to the sky.
but today the clouds hang
bruised and battered
as if saying
they too have had enough.

for downstream
a woman's body was found

delivered naked and nameless
into the river's lap.

my fingers claw wet clay
    touch earth touch earth.
if you get lost
    touch earth.
if the wind changes directions
or you are caught midstream
    touch earth.

when violence hits you
    touch deep
for that is where it strikes.
the place
the moment
when the killer and his instrument
become one.

cold lifeless metal
held to my throat.
hand digging into pain.

i close my eyes to push
back the memory
but there is no stopping it.
no force of mind
no threat of retaliation.
(victims are stripped of will.)

only the sheer nothingness
of a star breaking
into a million pieces
falling scattering.
and the sound
that only those who have heard
a star fall
can hear.

if i could
i would heal you Ushuaka
Woman's-self.
and we would walk again
without fear
without stumbling.

we would walk together
you and i
and talk about this and that.
(but not about what we have in common.)

we could forget
and the river would be as it once was.

                   at night
                   the river flows silently
                   past my bed
                   while the full moon
                   echoes across my floor

                     be whole again
                     little one.
                     be whole.

Diary.

Moon of the Hiding Doe.

  skin pulsates
to the touch of a lover's fingers
like water rippling
with moon and wind

and rain.
the last breath of summer
gives way in a sigh

i awoke to darkness
wanting to breathe life
into my dry mouth.
asking,
have i kissed death once too often?
i reek with sorrow.

The Deer Break Their Horns.

  poverty
spits from my mouth,
a bitterness,
like a snake
that cannot shed its skin.
it clings to our ribs
when our stomachs are empty

and leaves
immutable memories.

it becomes,
once again,
the narrowing eye
of disillusionment.
(it is not the stuff of poetry.)

Black Bear's Moon.

  (Dino and Gary Butler,
still imprisoned,
still awaiting trial.)

the bowwood snaps
and cracks in the hungry air,
scratching thorns against
frozen windows.

today,
walking on thin ice of pain,
anger suspends me.

but here,
they shove your anger in your face.

Solitary Moon.

   this morning the sun
was shining,
but it was too late.

this morning a tree broke
under the weight
of too many days
of cold,
cloudless
silence.

and i held my breath
as i heard it fall.

this morning i wept.

Louise Erdrich

Jacklight

The same Chippewa word is used both
for flirting and hunting game, while
another Chippewa word connotes both
using force in intercourse and also
killing a bear with one's bare hands.
—DUNNING 1959

We have come to the edge of the woods,
out of brown grass where we slept, unseen,
out of knotted twigs, out of leaves creaked shut,
out of hiding.

At first the light wavered, glancing over us.
Then it clenched to a fist of light that pointed,
searched out, divided us.
Each took the beams like direct blows the heart answers.
Each of us moved forward alone.

We have come to the edge of the woods,
drawn out of ourselves by this night sun,
this battery of polarized acids,
that outshines the moon.

We smell them behind it
but they are faceless, invisible.
We smell the raw steel of their gun barrels,
mink oil on leather, their tongues of sour barley.
We smell their mother buried chin-deep in wet dirt.

We smell their fathers with scoured knuckles,
teeth cracked from hot marrow.
We smell their sisters of crushed dogwood, bruised apples,
of fractured cups and concussions of burnt hooks.

We smell their breath steaming lightly behind the jacklight.
We smell the itch underneath the caked guts on their clothes.
We smell their minds like silver hammers
cocked back, held in readiness
for the first of us to step into the open.

We have come to the edge of the woods,
out of brown grass where we slept, unseen,
out of leaves creaked shut, out of our hiding.
We have come here too long.

It is their turn now,
their turn to follow us. Listen,
they put down their equipment.
It is useless in the tall brush.
And now they take the first steps, not knowing
how deep the woods are and lightless.
How deep the woods are.

Balinda's Dance

Sometimes when I dance
I break away from the shores of men's eyes
and float alone down the river of my own hair.

Below the surface, my face, a pale heart-shaped leaf
fills slowly as a lung
breathing deeper of the cool water.

I pull the dark from my body into waves all around me,
drifting lower, until I know it is impossible to return

to the men's arms stretched across the bar like piers
rocking and trembling in my current.

The Lady in the Pink Mustang

The sun goes down for hours, taking more of her along
than the night leaves her with.
A body moving in the dust
must shed its heavy parts in order to go on.

Perhaps you have heard of her, the Lady in the Pink Mustang,
whose bare lap is floodlit from under the dash,
who cruises beneath the high snouts of semis, reading
the blink of their lights. *Yes. Move Over. Now.*
or *How Much.* Her price shrinks into the dark.

She can't keep much trash in a Mustang,
and that's what she likes. Travel light. Don't keep
what does not have immediate uses. The road thinks ahead.
It thinks for her, a streamer from Bismark to Fargo
bending through Minnesota to accommodate the land.

She won't carry things she can't use anymore,
just a suit, sets of underwear, what you would expect
in a Pink Mustang. Things she could leave anywhere.

There is a point in the distance where the road meets itself,
where coming and going must kiss into one.
She is always at that place, seen from behind,
motionless, torn forward, living in a zone
all her own. It is like she has burned right through time,
the brand, the mark, owning the woman who bears it.

She owns them, not one will admit what they cannot
come close to must own them. She takes them along,
traveling light. It is what she must face every time
she is touched. The body disposable as cups.

To live, instead of turn, on a dime,
one light point that is so down in value.
Painting her nipples silver for a show, she is thinking
You out there. What do you know.

Come out of the dark where you're safe. Kissing these
bits of change, stamped out, ground to a luster,
is to kiss yourself away piece by piece
until we're even. Until the last
coin is rubbed for luck and spent.
I don't sell for nothing less.

The Strange People

The antelope are strange people . . .
they are beautiful to look at, and yet
they are tricky. We do not trust them.
They appear and disappear; they are
like shadows on the plains. Because
of their great beauty, young men

sometimes follow the antelope and are
lost forever. Even if those foolish ones
find themselves and return, they are
never again right in their heads.
                    —Pretty Shield

All night I am the doe, breathing
his name in a frozen field,
the small mist of the word
drifting always before me.

And again he has heard it
and I have gone burning
to meet him, the jacklight
fills my eyes with blue fire;
the heart in my chest
explodes like a hot stone.

Then slung like a sack
in the back of his pick-up,
I wipe the death scum
from my mouth, sit up laughing
and shriek in my speeding grave.

Safely shut in the garage,
when he sharpens his knife
and thinks to have me, like that,
I come toward him,
a lean grey witch,
through the bullets that enter and dissolve.

I sit in his house
drinking coffee till dawn,
and leave as frost reddens on hubcaps,
crawling back into my shadowy body.
All day, asleep in clean grasses,
I dream of the one who could really wound me.

When he comes, more quiet
than the others,
I take him away with me.
On his head
fix the simple, cleft prongs.
I make him come with me to the trees and lie down.

Wind cries like a cat.
The leaves cut where they touch
and we curl from our wet flesh like smoke,
leaving the light of our hunger in the bones
that will burn till dew falls
in the ashes.

When you pass
these grey forms
that flake and shiver in the wind,
Do not touch them, turn back.
Human, frail human,
Lope toward your own dark shelter.

Snow Train

The body keeps spilling its sweet, heavy freight
as the night goes.
The morning brings heavier snows
that settle around us, drifts in blind corners,
and a wind that recovers what falls.

Refusing to give up any part of my load,
I push it before me until the world fills
with voices *Stop, let it go, now.*
I keep moving
although the weight makes me slow.

Tunnels that the body strikes open in air.
Bridges that shiver across
every water I come to.
And always the light
I was born with, driving everything before it.

Here is the charge I carried, the ballast
I chose to go down with,
the ponderous soul.
Here is the light I was born with, love.
Here is the bleak radiance that levels the world.

Painting of a White Gate and Sky

For Betsy

There is no one in the picture
so you must enter it.
Your dress held together with bent pins.
You must enter
with your heart of grey snow.

There is no one in the blank left corner
so you must stand there
You with your wrists chained
with your stomach locked up,
You with emptiness tapping
sorrow's code
in its cage of bone.

The steps are grown over with sharp blades.
No one has been there.
You are the first one.
Desperate, proper,
your heels leave deep punctures.

You with breath failing.
You with your mother's ring.
With your belt undone.
You with your mind of twisted ferns.

There is no one at the gate
So you must stand there.
You with your picked over heart.
You with shoulders of cracked glass.
With hands falling open.
You with nobody.

It is a gate no one ever pushed open,
a gate that stands alone,
swung shut before the stars
were strung up in the black net.

There is no one beyond the gate.
There is no one to watch you.
There is no one to see grief unloading like train cars.

Go there you chained one
You heels that leave wounds
You sister
You heart of grey snow.

Dear John Wayne

August and the drive-in picture is packed.
We lounge on the hood of the Pontiac
surrounded by the slow-burning spirals they sell
at the window, to vanquish the hordes of mosquitoes.
Nothing works. They break through the smoke-screen for blood.

Always the look-out spots the Indians first,
spread north to south, barring progress.
The Sioux, or Cheyenne, or some bunch
in spectacular columns, arranged like SAC missiles,
their feathers bristling in the meaningful sunset.

The drum breaks. There will be no parlance.
Only the arrows whining, a death-cloud of nerves
swarming down on the settlers
who die beautifully, tumbling like dust weeds
into the history that brought us all here
together: this wide screen beneath the sign of the bear.

The sky fills, acres of blue squint and eye
that the crowd cheers. His face moves over us,
a thick cloud of vengeance, pitted
like the land that was once flesh. Each rut,
each scar makes a promise: *It is
not over, this fight, not as long as you resist.*

Everything we see belongs to us.
A few laughing Indians fall over the hood
slipping in the hot spilled butter.
The eye sees a lot, John, but the heart is so blind.
How will you know what you own?
He smiles, a horizon of teeth
the credits reel over, and then the white fields

again blowing in the true-to-life dark.
The dark films over everything.
We get into the car
scratching our mosquito bites, speechless and small
as people are when the movie is done.
We are back in ourselves.

How can we help but keep hearing his voice,
the flip side of the sound-track, still playing:
Come on, boys, we've got them
where we want them, drunk, running.
They will give us what we want, what we need:
The heart is a strange wood inside of everything
we see, burning, doubling, splitting out of its skin.

Turtle Mountain Reservation

For Pat Gourneau

The heron makes a cross
flying low over the marsh.
Its heart is an old compass
pointing off in four directions.
It drags the world along,
the world it becomes.

My face surfaces in the green
beveled glass above the wash-stand.
My handprint in thick black powder
on the bedroom shade.
Home I could drink like thin fire,
that gathers
like lead in my veins,
heart's armor, the coffee stains.

In the dust of the double hollyhock,
Theresa, one frail flame eating wind.
One slim candle
that snaps in the dry grass.
Ascending tall ladders
that walk to the edge of dusk.

Riding a blue cricket
through the tumult of the falling dawn.

At dusk the grey owl walks the length of the roof,
sharpening its talons on the shingles.
Grandpa leans back
between spoonfuls of canned soup
and repeats to himself a word
that belongs to a world
no one else can remember.

The day has not come
when from sloughs, the great salamander
lumbers through snow, salt, and fire
to be with him, throws the hatchet
of its head through the door of the three room house
and eats the blue roses that are peeling off the walls.

Uncle Ray, drunk for three days
behind the jagged window
of a new government box,
drapes himself in fallen curtains, and dreams that the odd
beast seen near Cannonball, North Dakota,
crouches moaning at the door to his body, the latch
is the small hook and eye

of religion. Twenty nuns
fall through clouds to park their butts
on the metal hasp. Surely that
would be considered miraculous almost anyplace,

but here in the Turtle Mountains
it is no more than common fact.
Raymond wakes,
but he can't shrug them off. He is looking up
dark tunnels of their sleeves,
and into their frozen armpits,
or is it heaven? He counts the points
of their hairs like stars.

One by one they blink out,
and Theresa comes forth
clothed in the lovely hair
she has been washing all day. She smells
like a hayfield, drifting pollen
of birch trees.

Her hair steals across her shoulders
like a postcard sunset.

All the boys tonight, goaded from below,
will approach her in The Blazer, The Tomahawk,
The White Roach Bar where everyone
gets up to cut the rug, wagging everything they got,
as the one bass drum of The Holy Greaseballs
lights a depth
charge through the smoke.

Grandpa leans closer to the bingo.
The small fortune his heart pumps for
is hidden in the stained, dancing numbers.
The ping pong balls rise through colored lights,
brief as sparrows.
God is in the sleight of the woman's hand.

He walks from Saint Ann's, limp and crazy
as the loon that calls its children
across the lake
in its broke, knowing laughter.
Hitch-hiking home from the Mission, if he sings,
it is a loud, rasping wail
that saws through the spine
of Ira Comes Last, at the wheel.

Drawn up through the neck ropes,
drawn out of his stomach,
by the spirit of the stones that line
the road and speak
to him only in their old agreement.
Ira knows the old man is nuts.
Lets him out at the road that leads up
over stars and the skulls of white cranes.

And through the soft explosions of cattail
and the scattering of seeds on still water,
walks Grandpa, all the time that there is in his hands
that have grown to be the twisted doubles
of the burrows of mole and badger,
that have come to be the absence
of birds in a nest.
Hands of earth, of this clay
I'm also made from.

Scales

for I.G. & B.P.

I was sitting before my third or fourth Jellybean—which is anisette, grain alcohol, a lit match, and a small, wet explosion in the brain. On my left sat Gerry Nanapush of the Chippewa Tribe. On my right sat Dot Adare of the has-been, of the never-was, of the what's-in-front-of-me people. Still in her belly and tensed in its fluids coiled the child of their union, the child we were waiting for, the child whose name we were making a strenuous and lengthy search for in a cramped and littered bar at the very edge of that Dakota town.

Gerry had been on the wagon for thirteen years. He was drinking a tall glass of tonic water in which a crescent of soiled lemon bobbed, along with a maraschino cherry or two. He was thirty-six years old and had been in prison, or out of prison and on the run, for exactly half of those years. He was not in the clear yet nor would he ever be; that is why the yellow tennis player's visor was pulled down to the rim of his eyeglass frames. The bar was dimly lit and smoky; his glasses were very dark. Poor visibility must have been the reason Officer Lovchik saw him first.

Lovchik started toward us with his hand on his hip, but Gerry was over the backside of the booth and out the booth before Lovchik got close enough to make a positive identification.

"Siddown with us," said Dot to Lovchik when he neared our booth. "I'll buy you a drink. It's so dead here. No one's been through all night."

Lovchik sighed, sat, and ordered a blackberry brandy.

"Now tell me," she said, staring at him, "honestly. What do you think of the name Ketchup Face?"

It was through Gerry that I first met Dot, and in a bar like that one, only denser with striving drinkers, construction crews in town because of the highway. I sat down by Gerry early in the evening and we struck up a conversation, during the long course of which we became friendly enough for Gerry to put his arm around me. Dot entered at exactly the wrong moment. She was quick-tempered anyway, and being pregnant (Gerry had gotten her that way on a prison visit five months previous) increased her irritability. It was only natural then, I guess, that she would pull the barstool out from under me and threaten my life. Only I didn't know she was threatening my life at the time. I didn't know anyone else like Dot, so I didn't know she was serious.

"I'm gonna bend you out of shape," she said, flexing her hands over me. Her hands were small, broad, capable, with pointed nails. I used to do the wrong thing sometimes when I was drinking, and that time I did the wrong thing even though I was stretched out on the floor beneath her. I started laughing at her because her hands were so small (though strong and determined looking, I should have been more conscious of that). She was about to dive on top of me, five-month belly and all, but Gerry caught her in mid-air and carried her, yelling, out the door. The next day I reported to work. It was my first day on the job, and the only other woman on the construction site besides me was Dot Adare.

The first day Dot just glared toward me from a distance. She worked in the weighshack and I was hired to press buttons on the conveyor belt. All I had to do was adjust the speeds on the belt for sand, rocks, or gravel, and make sure it was aimed toward the right pile. There was a pyramid of each type of material, which was used to make hot-mix and cement. Across the wide yard, I saw Dot emerge from the little white shack from time to time. I couldn't tell whether she recognized me and thought, by the end of the day, that she probably didn't. I found out differently the next morning when I went to the company truck for coffee.

She got me alongside of the truck somehow, away from the men. She didn't say a word, just held a buck knife out where I could see it, blade toward me. She jiggled the handle and the tip waved like the pointy head of a pit-viper. Blind. Heat-seeking. I was completely astonished. I had just put the plastic cover on my coffee and it steamed between my hands.

"Well I'm sorry I laughed." I said. She stepped back. I peeled the lid off my coffee, took a sip, and then I said the wrong thing again.

"And I wasn't going after your boyfriend."

"Why not!" she said at once. "What's wrong with him!"

I saw that I was going to lose this argument no matter what I said, so for once, I did the right thing. I threw my coffee in her face and ran. Later on that day Dot came out of the weighshack and yelled "Okay, then!" I was close enough to see that she even smiled. I waved. From then on things were better between us, which was lucky, because I turned out to be such a good button presser that within two weeks I was promoted to the weighshack, to help Dot.

It wasn't that Dot needed help weighing trucks, it was just a formality for the State Highway Department. I never quite understood, but it seems Dot had been both the truck-weigher and the truck-weight-inspector for a while, until someone caught wind of this. I was hired to actually weigh the trucks then, for the company, and Dot was hired by the State to make sure I recorded accurate weights. What she really did was sleep, knit, or eat all day. Between truckloads I did the same. I didn't even have to get off my stool to weigh the trucks, because the arm of the scale projected through a rectangular hole and the weights appeared right in front of me. The standard back dumps, belly-dumps, and yellow company trucks eased onto a platform built over the arm next to the shack. I wrote their weight on a little pink slip, clipped the paper in a clothes-pin attached to a broom handle, and handed it up to the driver. I kept a copy of the pink slip on a yellow slip that I put in a metal filebox—no one ever picked up the filebox, so I never knew what the yellow slips were for. The company paid me very well.

It was early July when Dot and I started working together. At first I sat as far away from her as possible and never took my eyes off her knitting needles, although it made me a little dizzy to watch her work. It wasn't long before we came to an understanding though, and after this I felt perfectly comfortable with Dot. She was nothing but direct, you see, and told me right off that only three things made her angry. Number one was someone flirting with Gerry. Number two was a cigarette leech (someone who was always quitting but smoking yours). Number three was a piss-ant. I asked her what that was. "A piss-ant," she said, "is a man with fat buns who tries to sell you things, a Jaycee, an Elk, a Kiwanis." I always knew where I stood with Dot, so I trusted her. I knew that if I fell out of her favor she would threaten me and give me time to run before she tried anything physical.

By mid-July our shack was unbearable, for it drew heat in from the bare yard and held it. We sat outside most of the time, moving around the shack to catch what shade fell, letting the raw hot wind off the beetfield suck the sweat from our armpits and legs. But the seasons change fast in North Dakota. We spent the last day of August jumping from foot to numb foot before Hadji, the foreman, dragged a little column of bottled gas into the shack. He lit the spoked wheel on its head, it bloomed, and from then on we huddled close to the heater—eating, dozing, or sitting blankly in its small radius of warmth.

By that time Dot weighed over 200 pounds, most of it peanut-butter cups and egg salad sandwiches. She was a short, broad-beamed woman with long yellow eyes and spaces between each of her strong teeth. When we began working together, her hair was cropped close. By the cold months it had grown out in thick quills—brown at the shank, orange at the tip. The orange dye-job had not suited her coloring. By that time, too, Dot's belly was round and full, for she was due in October. The child rode high, and she often rested her forearms on it while she knitted. One of Dot's most peculiar feats was transforming that gentle task into something perverse. She knit viciously, jerking the yarn around her thumb until the tip whitened, pulling each stitch so tightly that the little garments she finished stood up by themselves like miniature suits of mail.

But I thought that the child would need those tight stitches when it was born. Although Dot, as expecting mother, lived a fairly calm life, it was clear that she had also moved loosely among dangerous elements. The child, for example, had been conceived in a visiting room at the state prison. Dot had straddled Gerry's lap, in a corner the closed circuit TV did not quite scan. Through a hole ripped in her pantyhose and a hole ripped in Gerry's jeans they somehow managed to join and, miraculously, to conceive. When Dot was sure she was pregnant, Gerry escaped from the prison to see her. Not long after my conversation with Gerry in the bar, he was caught. That time he went back peacefully, and didn't put up a fight. He was mainly in the penitentiary for breaking out of it, anyway, since for his crime (assault and battery when he was eighteen) he had received three years and time off for good behavior. He just never managed to serve those three years or behave well. He broke out time after time, and was caught each time he did it, regular as clockwork.

Gerry was talented at getting out, that's a fact. He boasted that no steel or concrete shitbarn could hold a Chippewa, and he had eel-like properties in spite of his enormous size. Greased with lard once, he squirmed into a six-foot thick prison wall and vanished. Some thought he had stuck there, immured forever, and that he would bring luck like the bones of slaves sealed in the wall of China. But Gerry rubbed his own belly for luck and brought luck to no one else, for he appeared suddenly at Dot's door and she was hard-pressed to hide him.

She managed for nearly a month. Hiding a six-foot-plus, two hundred and fifty pound Indian in the middle of a town that doesn't like Indians in the first place isn't easy. A month was quite an accomplishment, when you know what she was up against. She spent most of her time walking to and from the grocery store, padding along on her swollen feet, astonishing the neighbors with the size of what they thought was her appetite. Stacks of pork-chops, whole fryers, thick steaks disappeared overnight, and since Gerry couldn't take the garbage out by day, sometimes he threw the bones out the windows, where they collected, where dogs soon learned to wait for a hand-out and fought and squabbled over whatever there was.

The neighbors finally complained, and one day, while Dot was at work, Lovchik knocked on the door of the trailerhouse. Gerry answered, sighed, and walked over to their car. He was so good at getting out of the joint and so terrible at getting caught. It was as if he couldn't stay out of their hands. Dot knew his problem, and told him that he was crazy to think he could walk out of prison, and then live like a normal person. Dot told him that didn't work. She told him to get lost for a while on the reservation, any reservation, to change his name and, although he couldn't grow a beard, to at least let the straggly hairs above his lip form a kind of mustache that would slightly disguise his face. But Gerry wouldn't do that.

He simply knew he did not belong in prison, although he admitted it had done him some good at eighteen, when he hadn't known how to be a criminal and so had taken lessons from professionals. Now that he knew all there was to know, however, he couldn't see the point of staying in a prison and taking the same lessons over and over. "A hate-factory," he called it once, and said it manufactured black poisons in his stomach that he couldn't get rid of, although he poked a finger down his throat and retched and tried to be a clean and normal person in spite of everything. Gerry's problem, you see, was he believed in justice, not laws. He felt he had paid for his crime, which was done in a drunk heat and to settle the question with a cowboy of whether a Chippewa was also a nigger. Gerry said that the two had never settled it between them, but that the cowboy at least knew that if a Chippewa was a nigger he was sure also a hell of a mean and lowdown fighter. For Gerry did not believe in fighting by any rules but reservation rules, which is to say the first thing Gerry did to the cowboy, after they squared off, was kick his balls.

It hadn't been much of a fight after that, and since there were both white and Indian witnesses Gerry thought it would blow over if it ever reached court. But there is nothing more vengeful and determined in this world than a cowboy with sore balls, and Gerry soon found this out. He also found that white people are good witnesses to have on your side, since they have names, addresses, social security numbers, and work phones. But they are terrible witnesses to have against you, almost as bad as having Indians witness for you.

Not only did Gerry's friends lack all forms of identification except their band cards, not only did they disappear (out of no malice but simply because Gerry was tried during powwow time), but the few he did manage to get were not interested in looking judge or jury in the eye. They mumbled into their laps. Gerry's friends, you see, had no confidence in the United States Judicial System. They did not seem comfortable in the courtroom, and this increased their unreliability in the eyes of judge and jury. If you trust the authorities, they trust you better back, it seems. It looked that way to Gerry anyhow.

A local doctor testified on behalf of the cowboy's testicles, and said his fertility might be impaired. Gerry got a little angry at that, and said right out in court that he could hardly believe he had done that much damage since the cowboy's balls were very small targets, it had been dark, and his aim was off anyway because of three, or maybe it was only two, beers. That made matters worse, of course, and Gerry was socked with a heavy sentence for an eighteen-year-old, but not for an Indian. Some said he got off lucky.

Only one good thing came from the whole experience, said Gerry, and that was maybe the cowboy would not have any little cowboys, although,

Gerry also said, he had nightmares sometimes that the cowboy did manage to have little cowboys, all born with full sets of grinning teeth, stetson hats, and little balls hard as plum pits.

So you see, it was difficult for Gerry, as an Indian, to retain the natural good humor of his ancestors in these modern circumstances. He tried though, and since he believed in justice, not laws, Gerry knew where he belonged (out of prison, in the bosom of his new family). And in spite of the fact that he was untrained in the honest life, he wanted it. He was even interested in getting a job. It didn't matter what kind of job. "Anything for a change," Gerry said. He wanted to go right out and apply for one, in fact, the moment he was free. But of course Dot wouldn't let him. And so, because he wanted to be with Dot, he stayed hidden in her trailerhouse even though they both realized, or must have, that it wouldn't be long before the police came asking around or the neighbors wised up and Gerry Nanapush would be back at square one again. So it happened. Lovchik came for him. And Dot now believed she would have to go through the end of her pregnancy and the delivery all by herself.

Dot was angry about having to go through it alone, and besides that, she loved Gerry with a deep and true love—that was clear. She knit his absence into thick little suits for the child, suits that would have stopped a truck on a dark road with their colors—bazooka pink, bruise blue, the screaming orange flagmen wore.

The child was as restless a prisoner as his father, and grew more anxious and unruly as his time of release neared. As a place to spend a nine-month sentence in, Dot wasn't much. Her body was inhospitable. Her skin was slack, sallow, and draped like upholstery fabric over her short, boardlike bones. Like the shack we spent our days in, she seemed jerry-built, thrown into the world with loosely nailed limbs and lightly puttied joints. Some pregnant women's bellies look like they always have been there. But Dot's stomach was an odd shape, almost square, and had the tacked-on air of a new and unpainted bay window. The child was clearly ready for a break and not interested in earning his parole, for he kept her awake all night by pounding reasonlessly at her inner walls, or beating against her bladder until she swore. "He wants out, bad," poor Dot would groan. "You think he might be premature?" From the outside, anyway, the child looked big enough to stand and walk and maybe even run straight out of the maternity ward the moment he was born.

The sun, at the time, rose around seven and we got to the weighshack while the frost was still thick on the gravel. Each morning I started the gas heater, turning the nozzle and standing back, flipping the match at it the way you would feed a fanged animal. Then one morning I saw the red bud through the window, lit already. But when I opened the door the shack was empty. There was, however, evidence of an overnight visitor—cigarette stubs, a few beer cans crushed to flat disks. I swept these things out and didn't say a word about them to Dot when she arrived.

She seemed to know something was in the air, however; her face lifted from time to time all that morning. She sniffed, and even I could smell the lingering odor of sweat like sour wheat, the faint reek of slept-in clothes and gasoline. Once, that morning, Dot looked at me and narrowed her long, hooded eyes. "I got pains," she said, "every so often. Like it's going to come sometime soon. Well all I can say is he better drag ass to get here, that Gerry." She closed her eyes then, and went to sleep.

Ed Rafferty, one of the drivers, pulled in with a load. It was overweight, and when I handed him the pink slip he grinned. There were two scales, you see, on the way to the cement plant, and if a driver got past the state-run scale early, before the state officials were there, the company would pay for whatever he got away with. But it was not illicit gravel that tipped the wedge past the red mark on the balance. When I walked back inside I saw the weight had gone down to just under the red. Ed drove off, still laughing, and I assumed that he had leaned on the arm of the scale, increasing the weight.

"That Ed," I said, "got me again."

But Dot stared past me, needles poised in her fist like a picador's lances. It gave me a start, to see her frozen in such a menacing pose. It was not the sort of pose to turn your back on, but I did turn, following her gaze to the door that a man's body filled suddenly.

Gerry, of course it was Gerry. He'd tipped the weight up past the red and leapt down, cat-quick for all his mass, and silent. I hadn't heard his step. Gravel crushed, evidently, but did not roll beneath his tight, thin boots.

He was bigger than I remembered from the bar, or perhaps it was just that we'd been living in that dollhouse of a weighshack so long I saw everything else as huge. He was so big that he had to hunker one shoulder beneath the lintel and back his belly in, pushing the doorframe wider with his long, soft hands. It was the hands I watched as Gerry filled the shack. His plump fingers looked so graceful and artistic against his smooth mass. He used them prettily. Revolving agile wrists, he reached across the few inches left between himself and Dot. Then his littlest fingers curled like a woman's at tea, and he disarmed his wife. He drew the needles out of Dot's fists, and examined the little garment that hung like a queer fruit beneath.

" 'S very, very nice," he said, scrutinizing the tiny, even stiches. " 'S for the kid?"

Dot nodded solemnly and dropped her eyes to her lap. It was an almost tender moment. The silence lasted so long that I got embarrassed and would have left, had I not been wedged firmly behind his hip in one corner.

Gerry stood there, smoothing black hair behind his ears. Again, there was a queer delicacy about the way he did this. So many things Gerry did might remind you of the way that a beautiful woman, standing naked before a mirror, would touch herself—lovingly, conscious of her attractions. He nodded encouragingly. "Let's go then," said Dot.

Suave, grand, gigantic, they moved across the parking lot and then, by mysterious means, slipped their bodies into Dot's compact car. I expected the car to belly down, thought the muffler would scrape the ground behind them. But instead they flew, raising a great spume of dust that hung in the air a long time after they were out of sight.

I went back into the weighshack when the air behind them had settled. I was bored, dead bored. And since one thing meant about as much to me as another, I picked up her needles and began knitting, as well as I could anyway, jerking the yarn back after each stitch, becoming more and more absorbed in my work until, as it happened, I came suddenly to the end of the garment, snipped the yarn, and worked the loose ends back into the collar of the thick little suit.

I missed Dot in the days that followed, days so alike they welded seamlessly to one another and took your mind away. I seemed to exist in a suspension and spent my time sitting blankly at the window, watching nothing until the sun went down, bruising the whole sky as it dropped, clotting my heart. I couldn't name anything I felt anymore, although I knew it was a kind of boredom. I had been living the same life too long. I did jumping jacks and push-ups and stood on my head in the little shack to break the tedium, but too much solitude rots the brain. I wondered how Gerry had stood it. Sometimes I grabbed drivers out of their trucks and talked loudly and quickly and inconsequentially as a madwoman. There were other times I couldn't talk at all because my tongue had rusted to the roof of my mouth.

Sometimes I daydreamed about Dot and Gerry. I had many choice daydreams, but theirs was my favorite. I pictured them in Dot's long tan and aqua trailerhouse, both hungry. Heads swaying, clasped hands swinging between them like hooked trunks, they moved through the kitchen feeding casually from boxes and bags on the counters, like ponderous animals alone in a forest. When they had fed, they moved on to the bedroom and settled themselves upon Dot's kingsize and sateen-quilted spread. They rubbed together, locked and unlocked their parts. They set the trailer rocking on its cement block and plywood foundation and the tremors spread, causing cups to fall, plates to shatter in the china hutches of their more established neighbors.

But what of the child there, suspended between them. Did he know how to weather such tropical storms? It was a week past the week he was due, and I expected the good news to come any moment. I was anxious to hear the outcome, but still I was surprised when Gerry rumbled to the weighshack door on a huge and ancient, rust-pocked, untrustworthy-looking machine that was like no motorcycle I'd ever seen before.

"She asst for you," he hissed. "Quick, Get on!"

I hoisted myself up behind him, although there wasn't room on the seat. I clawed his smooth back for a handhold and finally perched, or so it seemed, on the rim of his heavy belt. Fly-like, glued to him by suction, we rode as one person, whipping a great wind around us. Cars scattered, the lights blinked and flickered on the main street. Pedestrians swiveled to catch a glimpse of us—a mountain tearing by balanced on a toy, and clinging to the sheer northwest face, a young and scrawny girl howling something that dopplered across the bridge and faded out, finally, in the parking lot of the Saint Francis Hospital.

In the waiting room we settled on chairs molded of orange plastic. The spike legs splayed beneath Gerry's mass, but managed to support him the four hours we waited. Nurses passed, settling like field gulls among reports and prescriptions, eyeing us with reserved hostility. Gerry hardly spoke. He didn't have to. I watched his ribs and the small of his back darken with sweat, for that well-lighted tunnel, the waiting room, the tin rack of magazines, all were the props and inevitable features of institutions. From time to time Gerry paced in the time-honored manner of the prisoner or expectant father. He made lengthy trips to the bathroom. All the quickness and delicacy of his movements had disappeared, and he was only a poor weary fat man in those hours, a husband worried about his wife, menaced, tired of getting caught.

The gulls emerged finally, and drew Gerry in among them. He visited Dot for perhaps half an hour, and then came out of her room. Again he settled; the plastic chair twitched beneath him. He looked bewildered and silly and a little addled with what he had seen. The shaded lenses of his glasses kept slipping down his nose. Beside him, I felt the aftermath of the shockwave, traveling from the epicenter deep in his flesh, outward from part of him that had shifted along a crevice. The tremors moved in widening rings. When they reached the very surface of him, and when he began trembling, Gerry stood suddenly. "I'm going after cigars," he said, and walked quickly away.

His steps quickened to a near run as he moved down the corridor. Waiting for the elevator, he flexed his nimble fingers. Dot told me she had once sent him to the store for a roll of toilet paper. It was eight months before she saw him again, for he'd met the local constabulary on the way. So I knew, when he flexed his fingers, that he was thinking of pulling the biker's gloves over his knuckles, of running. It was perhaps the very first time in his life he had something to run for.

It seemed to me, at that moment, that I should at least let Gerry know it was all right for him to leave, to run as far and fast as he had to now. Although I felt heavy, my body had gone slack, and my lungs ached with smoke, I jumped up. I signaled him from the end of the corridor. Gerry turned, unwillingly turned. He looked my way just as two of our local police—Officers Lovchik and Harris, pushed open the firedoor that sealed off the staircase behind me. I didn't see them, and was shocked at first that my wave caused such an extreme reaction in Gerry.

His hair stiffened. His body lifted like a hot-air balloon filling suddenly. Behind him there was wide, tall window. Gerry opened it and sent the screen into thin air with an elegant, chorus-girl kick. Then he followed the screen, squeezing himself unbelievably through the frame like a fat rabbit disappearing down a hole. It was three stories down to the cement and asphalt parking lot.

Officers Lovchik and Harris gained the window. The nurses followed. I slipped through the fire exit and took the back stairs down into the parking lot, believing I would find him stunned and broken there.

But Gerry had chosen his window with exceptional luck, for the officers had parked their car directly underneath. Gerry landed just over the driver's seat, caving the roof into the steering wheel. He bounced off the hood of the car and then, limping, a bit dazed perhaps, straddled his bike. Out of duty, Lovchik released several rounds into the still trees below him. The reports were still echoing when I reached the front of the building.

I was just in time to see Gerry Nanapush, emboldened by his godlike leap and recovery, pop a wheelie and disappear between the neat shrubs that marked the entrance to the hospital.

Two weeks later Dot and her boy, who was finally named Jason, like most boys born that year, came back to work at the scales. Things went on as they had before, except that Jason kept us occupied during the long hours. He was large, of course, and had a sturdy pair of lungs he used often. When he cried, Jason screwed his face into fierce baby wrinkles and would not be placated with sugar tits or pacifiers. Dot unzipped her parka halfway, pulled her blouse up, and let him nurse for what seemed like hours. We could scarcely believe his appetite. Dot was a diligent producer of milk, however. Her breasts, like overfilled innertubes, strained at her nylon blouses. Sometimes, when she thought no one was looking,

Dot rose and carried them in the crooks of her arms, for her shoulders were growing bowed beneath their weight.

The trucks came in on the hour, or half hour. I heard the rush of air-brakes, gears grinding only inches from my head. It occurred to me that although I measured many tons every day, I would never know how heavy a ton was unless it fell on me. I wasn't lonely now that Dot had returned. The season would end soon, and we wondered what had happened to Gerry.

There were only a few weeks left of work when we heard that Gerry was caught again. He'd picked the wrong reservation to hide on—Pine Ridge. At the time it was overrun with Federal Agents and armored vehicles. Weapons were stashed everywhere and easy to acquire. Gerry got himself a weapon. Two men tried to arrest him. Gerry would not go along and when he started to run and the shooting started Gerry shot and killed a clean-shaven man with dark hair and light eyes, a Federal Agent, a man whose picture was printed in all the papers.

They sent Gerry to prison in Marion, Illinois. He was placed in the control unit. He receives his visitors in a room where no touching is allowed, where the voice is carried by phone, glances meet through sheets of plexiglass, and no children will ever be engendered.

Dot and I continued to work the last weeks together. Once we weighed baby Jason. We unlatched his little knit suit, heavy as armor, and bundled him in a light, crocheted blanket. Dot went into the shack to adjust the weights. I stood there with Jason. He was such a solid child, he seemed heavy as lead in my arms. I placed him on the ramp between the wheel-sights and held him steady for a moment, then took my hands slowly away. He stared calmly into the rough, distant sky. He did not flinch when the wind came from every direction, wrapping us tight enough to squeeze the very breath from a stone. He was so dense with life, such a powerful distillation of Dot and Gerry, it seemed he might weigh about as much as any load. But that was only a thought, of course. For as it turned out, he was too light and did not register at all.

Rayna Green

Mexico City Hand Game

the perpetual rebozo man
spreads his arms for me
holding the shawl to fold me in

the chicle niña
and her chicharrones madre want to feed me
and the Indian beggar wants me to feed her

the lottery ticket seller
presses chances with roses
into my hands
He loves his job

but the rebozo is cheap white nylon
street food will keep me from the street
and I won't be here
for the roll
on the wheel of chance

still, these Indians are everywhere
tiny, our ladies of sorrow
tiny, los hombres de las sombras
tiny, these hands that reach
to fold me in with the roses
                              chiles
                                      chicharrones
                                                chicle

all
into white shawl sorrows
and old nightmare shadows

stop the wheel that turns
                         and turns
and turns

these Indians tilt the odds
in a lottery
you can't buy tickets for

When I Cut My Hair

when I cut my hair
at thirty-five
Grandma said she'd forgive me
for cutting it
without her permission

but I cried out everytime
I touched my head

years from then
and Grandma dead
it came back to me last night when
you said you wanted it all

your rich body grounding me safe
the touch of your hair
took me out
I saw pigeon feathers
red wool
and fur

and it wrapped me
with the startled past
so sudden
your hair falling all around us

I touched center
and forgave myself

Nanye'hi (Nancy Ward), the Last Beloved Woman of the Cherokees, 1738–1822

a woman in Oklahoma makes tobacco, sending her dream of our
    Ghigau out
in the smoke
she calls for her, our elder sister, waiting
to gossip with her and make her mad enough to come home again
tribeswomen come to her house

          and sing in secret
          making tobacco magic again
          while Thunder hides their voices

from the men

          plotting the return of the women
          plotting the power of the women
          making the women all come home

to Adair County
Toppling the men is what they're up to
back there
and our Ghigau will set it right

          so they set about making magic
          to make her hear

to make the Councilmen sick

          and they laugh and sing some more

when one falls dead in the middle of a meeting
They know Nancy's de-horned him
One is as good as another
when you hunger for the old ways

They knew she came from North Carolina with them
even though her grandson said she'd died
and a light flew from her body toward Chota

          but the women knew better

They figure she's somewhere running things like always
raising cattle like she taught the people
a meat baron in Texas maybe
or trading gold on Wall Street
taking it from whites who took it from her

          getting her revenge

when they said she wasn't needed anymore
when they said the women might as well go home
when white men taught them to act like white men

To run things was what the women were about

          and having no job
          made them take to magic
          and worse

So they wait for her plane to land in Tulsa

tall as Tseg'sin
and just as rough
She'll haul them out of the Osiyo Club
and take them down to the river

> while the women file back
> in the Council room
> to do their jobs again

At night, while the seven fires burn
in Adair County
this is what the women think

Their silence all these years
doesn't fool anyone

Coosaponakeesa (Mary Mathews Musgrove Bosomsworth), Leader of the Creeks, 1700–1783

for Joy Harjo

what kind of lovers could they have been
these colonists

good enough to marry them everyone
or was it something else that made her take them on

all woman
part swamp rat
half horse
she rode through Georgia
It was hers and the Creeks'
and Oglethorpe wanted it all

But she rolled with him too
and kept them at bay
for too long
'til they said
she'd sold out for the goods

the money and velvet was what she loved
sure enough
but Ossabaw and Sapelo and Savannah more

so she fought them with sex and war
and anything that worked
until they rolled over her

The Creeks say Mary came back as Sherman
just to see what they'd taken away
burned to the ground
and returned to her once more

The Creek girls in Oklahoma
laugh like Mary now
wild and good
they'll fight you for it
and make you want everything all over again

no deals this time though
it's all
or nothing

Another Dying Chieftain

he was a braids-and-shades dog soldier
AIM all the way

reduced to telling white women
about coup counting
in a hotel room
late

where they wanted his style
and he wanted the reporters
back again

so he seduced them with lectures
on the degrees of Sioux adoption
trying to make the talk
pass for battle

when the others came in
Indian women and not his tribe
they knew what kind of war was being fought

and one asked
when he was finished
what degree were you adopted in

when he shook his fist at her
it didn't make headlines
there's no good day to die
in these wars

Old Indian Trick

I thought she was white
but she missed her calling
really Indian and fooled me
with all that talk
Not one silence the whole
evening filled
no place to rest my head
All the tequila didn't shut her up
or the crazy ride home either

I thought maybe the danger
would stop her voice
and make her show respect
for the possibilities
there on the road

But she won
making me think she was white
I forgot to shield myself
and she got inside my silence

a good disguise, little sister

hide your thoughts with words
like white girls
so blood, crushed bone, burned flesh
terrify only as ghosts
of brown women's lives

Indian silence
leaves no room to hide
except in dreams
visions of light and spirit
to wipe terror away

Road Hazard

the car-tape machine
plays the music I want
and it is pow-wow trash, a forty-nine
nothing sacred
still, the drums have a way

I forget the other cars
and I am on another highway
north of Talihina
going to the Choctaw all-night sing

Grandma relished
that Choc singing
brush arbor Christian music

and so I stay up all night
and drive for no reason
but the singing
to get somewhere
with the singing
to be out there
in the singing

it's not the booze or pick-ups
that will kill me
on this road

Palace Dancer, Dancing at Last

she wanted to be a dancer
on the Palace stage
always dressed to kill
she'd play whorehouse songs on the piano
or sad ones
that made us cry and beg for more

she said she knew Bonnie and Clyde
in the old West Dallas days

and told how
Clyde broke his mother's heart
and how Belle Starr's Indian husband
might have been related to us
in some way

on that summer porch then
she could have been anything
we'd believe
living in her ruby pleasures

oh, she glittered then

but seven husbands and
too many five-and-dime jobs later
she'd had all she could take
and still wanted the Palace stage

that never done,
she died, dressed to kill
leaving a ragtime, gospel tune
and stories no books
but hearts could hold

dancing across that summer porch
dancing the stories
that made us dream over her
shattered breath

High Cotton

Is everything a story? Ramona asked her.

It is if a story's what you're looking for—otherwise, it's just people telling lies and there's no end to it. Grandma waited to see how she took that and she started in again, smoothing out the red-checked oilcloth on the kitchen table as she talked. Ramona watched the purple cockscombs she could see through the kitchen door.

You don't have to hear anything, not about the white ones or the red—nothing about any of them, and you can call 'em all lies if you want. In a way, they are all lies just like them Thunder stories Gahno tells you or like the Bible—something that happened too far back for anyone to see and too close for anyone to deny. You listen to her stories much more and you won't want to know the difference. Still, there's always choices. It's like the time Gahno was out in the cotton field—right here at the old home place, just beyond this door. We was just girls, all of us—her and me and Rose and Anna—and there was Poppa, the meanest old German bastard that ever lived. He had us out chopping cotton in the worst heat of the day. He treated Indian and white alike—you might say just like we was niggers—well, that's what Anna used to say when she had sense, but some might dispute that she ever had any at all. Anyway, a big old black snake run acrost Gahno's foot out there in the high cotton. And she commenced to screaming and run up to the house. Lord, she throwed down that hoe and hollered loud enough to make us all run up from the field.

Snake, she hollered, snake.

But Poppa had seen the blacksnake come acrost the field and he didn't put no store at all in running from snakes. He liked to kill 'em, you know, and nail their skins up on the barn door yonder.

Goddammit, he yelled, you scheisskopf Indin', ain't one ting but one blacksnake an' he don't hurt you.

That was his way of talking when he got mad and he never could talk good English anyway. Well, we all commenced to laughing and screaming at the sight of Poppa all puffed up and Gahno scared to fits—and her no better at English than him any day. She was so damn mad she about near spit at Poppa.

Jesus no, Jesus no, he maybe not hurt me, but dat damn snake he make me hurt myself.

And then we all went to laughing like as not to stop—and she started to giggle too that way she has even now. Poppa swole up even more like a toad and marched off into the house for Momma to soothe his hurt feelings, and Gaȟno threw down that hoe for good. She left Tahlequah and went to Dallas and she never came back—and I follered her the next year and Rose ten years later. Poppa never forgive any of us and Gaȟno wasn't even his kin—but he acted like she was—so he had one heart spell too many when your Momma married her son. Betrayal was bad enough, but race mixing was worse. Marrying Indians was a damn sight worse to him. I guess he thought she'd stay and slave for him forever just like he thought we would. But he was wrong. Grandma paused for breath and then stopped, watching Ramona get up and head toward the old ice box near the sink.

I know there's another story here, Ramona said. Are you going to tell it now or should I get you more ice tea to get through it? You want me to doctor yours with some of Baby Dee's finest so you don't get hoarse?

She saw assent in Grandma's eyes so she opened the flour bin where Rose always kept the drinking whiskey—remembering Aunt Anna who always called it her heart medicine when she took it by the tablespoon ten times a day.

It's Rose I want to tell you about—and Will—and that snake wadn't just a side story. Yes, get me some of Baby Dee's good whiskey. It never hurt me nor anybody else who drank it with a clear heart. He got the trick of it from those Cherokee hill climbers you stem from, I'll say that. But your Uncle Will, he was white and he drank white whiskey. It kilt his sense and will and left nothing but feeling. Baby Dee's whiskey makes me want to go file my teeth and whip up on Andy Jackson. Just bring the jar and a bite of that ham on the sideboard, and I'll tell you the real story.

Ramona set the Mason jar of clear liquid in front of her grandmother, with the bowl of rock candy and mint leaves she favored for her particular brew. And she poured herself some into the blue enamel cup she always used when she came down home to Aunt Rose's.

To heart medicine, she said.

God knows it ain't head medicine you need, Grandma told her. You had too big a dose of that from your Daddy—thinking is the family disease.

Honey, your Uncle Will, he was just like that snake, and the Baptist Church, it was like him—they was made for one another. But he was a drinking man, and he was when Rose married him. When he couldn't get whiskey from the white bootleggers, he got it from the black ones. He never drank no Indian whiskey—not like everybody else—'cause he believed they boogered it just like Baby Dee does in truth. And that whiskey made him crazy anyway. He got worse. He didn't have nothing but the whiskey and the whiskey had him. For ten years he poured the whiskey down.

Rose got all the church women to pray and pray over him, week after week, and they kept poor Jesus awake yelling about Will's sinful state. The more they prayed and hollered over him, the more he cussed and drank. And that made them pray more. You know how them prissy Baptist women is, honey—wouldn't say shit if they had a mouthful—and they like to drove everyone to the ginmills and shake dance parlors before long. But everyone was more disgusted with Will. He'd run everybody's patience out, and if he'd been on fire, not a soul would have pissed on him to save him. He raved and carried on when Rose and Bubba took the truck from him—they hid it out in Dadáyi's barn over yonder at Lost City—but he stole the tractor and drove it to the bootlegger's anyway.

Well, then one night, he put the harrow on and run that tractor over thirty acres of good lake bottom cotton, and Rose finally pitched a fit. She and Bubba tied that old drunk to the bedposts and left him there to piss and shit all over hisself and he done it—they left him for two days and more.

Thirty acres might not sound like much to you now, but it was something then. They tied him to the bed right there in that room yonder and he thrashed and cussed and rolled for three days. He threatened and begged and done damn near everything he could to get them to turn him loose. But Rose's heart had hardened—even to the point of letting her spotless house stink of drunkard's shit. On the third night, he was worse than ever before, yelling and carrying on. And Rose finally come in from the front parlor where she'd tried to sleep these nights while he was cutting up. She come in and stood at the foot of his bed.

Sister, give me just another bite of that ham and some of Gaĥno's bean bread before I go on. I could piece all day on that ham and never set down to a meal. There's nothing like funerals for good eating.

You better hurry with the story or they're all going to be back from the funeral parlor and hear the worst, Ramona told her. I'm going to have just a little bite myself to keep my strength up. I may need a whole ham the way you're going.

Baby Sister, I never knew you to let your strength get endangered. You're both your Grandmas' child, that's for certain.

Well, Rose come into the bedroom trying to breathe in the stench and keep from laughing at the old bastard's misery at the same time. She loved seeing him as wretched as she'd been all these years. So she stood at the foot of the bed, all dressed in an old white flannel gown—the same old one she'd worn for ten years and the one she would wear today if they hadn't bought that silly blue town dress just to go to the boneyard. So there she stood in that ruffled white flannel gown, and Will, crazy with having the whiskey took from him, thought it was Jesus come to take him away. He seen the ghosts and boogers of his worst drunk dreams and commenced to bleat and call out to Jesus. Guilty through all the whiskey boldness, he called out to Jesus and begged Him not to take him now.

Jesus, I been bad I know, but I'll be good tomorrow. Jesus, I'm not ready now, but give me another chance to serve you. Jesus, I'll praise your name tomorrow and never take another drop of drink.

Well, sir, he went on like that 'til Rose got tickled and you know what a cut-up she is when she gets provoked. So, she started to laugh for all those ten years of suffering with that drunken worthless farmer, and she begin to shake that white gown and talk to him. So, she made out to him like she was Jesus. Well, if he could give up his sins, she reasoned, why couldn't she take some up since there'd be room left in the emptiness.

Oh, Will, she said, talking deep, I've got plans for you. I need a sober man, a righteous man, a just man. I've got plans for your life, but you'll have to promise me to quit drinking and whoring and treating your good wife so bad.

Oh, Jesus, I will, I will do it, he yelled. Jesus, I'm the one to do it.

Will, she said, waving her arms and standing on tiptoe in the kerosene light—her gown all cloudy and white around her—I want you to come out of that piss and shit, out of the hog wallow you've fallen in, and I want you to preach my word.

Oh, Jesus, he promised, I'm the one.

Well, she damn near kilt herself laughing, but she went on until they was both worn out with it and he promised to preach Jesus' word until he died. When she'd calmed herself, Will was still a-raving about Jesus. But she looked at that piece of stinking flesh on the bed and thought about murder. She picked up the jonny pot from under the bed and tried to break his head with it. She picked up the pissy sheets and tried to strangle him around his turkey neck, and she offered to smother him with the last of her good feather pillows.

But Jesus had him no matter what she done, and he lived and praised her, thinking all the time it was Jesus putting him to the test. And well it might have been. But wanting to kill him so bad and Jesus saving him made her hate the church on the spot. She thought if he did wake up and fulfill his promise to preach, it was a church she didn't want nothing to do with it anyway. Well, the Devil didn't offer her a solution and the little son-of-a-bitch didn't die. So, she took off that white gown and threw it into the bed with him.

It ain't Jesus, you damned old fool, she up and screamed at him, it's your crazy wife and be damned to the both of you.

She boiled up water for the hottest bath she'd ever had and sat buck naked at the parlor pump organ all night, playing every shake dance tune she knew, and she was sitting there when Baby Dee come to start plowing in the morning. She was laughing and singing and happy like he's never seen her, and he couldn't believe his ears when she asked him if he'd ever thought of taking his whiskey making skills to Dallas. They was gone before Will come to, and when he did, he took her leaving for the punishment he deserved. He cleaned himself up and went right uptown to the preacher to confess his sins and sign up for the Jesus Road.

Rose and Baby Dee went right to Dallas with Gaĥno and the other Indians that had left before, and that's where we all ended up—that is, until Will died fifteen years ago as sober as when he was born. But she'd had the good time and he'd paid for what he done to her by living a strict and righteous life. She'd takened away the only thing he loved, and ended up making her living selling it.

And Jesus done it all, she would tell people.

There's a white flannel salvation that comes to drunks in the dark and makes 'em change. So she wondered when it would come to her. She got Baby Dee to booger his whiskey too, so wouldn't nobody get saved on it and tot up more souls for Jesus. She used to tell him—we're in the whiskey business, not the salvation business. Jesus looked like an Arab and dressed like a woman and that ain't what we're about. And they'd go on up to the stomp dances in the hills after they'd come back here to live, never drinking one drop of the whiskey they made, 'cause she'd turned Indian just as sure as she'd turned away from Christians, and that would have driven a nail into Poppa's heart too. She always figured, just like Gahno, that snakes was meant to warn you, and she took the warning.

Well, that's the story and there's no end to it. There's more than one thing that will make you hurt yourself and more than one that'll save you.

Jesus, Ramona said.

Yes, Jesus, Grandma said.

There's the picture of Poppa and Will on the wall, where they belong—in stockmen's suits and French silk kerchiefs. And here's the rest of us—you and Momma and Baby Dee and Gahno and me—gone to the Indians or to Dallas or to some of those strange places you favor. Except for Rose, who's laying dead up town. At least we won't have no one preach over her. She can take that comfort. We can just sing and tell lies when they all come back to the house, and the Indians can bury her the right way to-morrow. You and Baby Dee can do it right. Maybe Baby Dee will take a drink of his own whiskey today.

More stories? Ramona asked.

Snakebite medicine, Grandma said.

Joy Harjo

Early Morning Woman

early morning woman
rising   the sun
        the woman
bending and stretching
with the strength of the child
that moves
in her belly

early morning makes her
a woman that she is
the sun
is her beginning
it is the strength
that guides her child

early morning woman
she begins that way
        the sun
        the child
are the moving circle
beginning with the woman
in the early morning

The Blanket around Her

maybe it is her birth
which she holds close to herself
or her death
which is just as inseparable
and the white wind
that encircles her is a part
just as
      the blue sky
hanging in turquoise from her neck

oh woman
remember who you are
woman
it is the whole earth

Conversations between Here and Home

Emma Lee's husband beat her up
this weekend.
His government check was held
up, and he borrowed the money
to drink on.
Anna had to miss one week of work
because her youngest child
got sick,
she says, "it's hard sometimes, but
easier than with a man."
"I haven't seen Jim for two weeks
now," his wife tells me on the phone
(but I saw him Saturday with that Anadarko
woman).

angry women are building
houses of stones
they are grinding the mortar
between straw-thin teeth
and broken families

I Am a Dangerous Woman

the sharp ridges of clear blue windows
motion to me
from the airport's second floor
edges dance in the foothills of the sandias
behind security guards
who wave me into their guncatcher machine

i am a dangerous woman

when the machine buzzes
they say to take off my belt
and i remove it so easy
that it catches the glance
of a man standing nearby
(maybe that is the deadly weapon
that has the machine singing)

i am a dangerous woman
but the weapon is not visible
security will never find it
they can't hear the clicking
of the gun
         inside my head

There Was a Dance, Sweetheart

It was a dance.
Her back against the wall
at Carmen's party. He was alone
and he called to her—come here come here—
That was the first time
she saw him and she and Carmen
later drove him home and all the way
he talked to the moon to stars and to
other voices riding in the backseat
that she and Carmen didn't hear.

And the next time was either a story
in one of his poems or what she had heard from crows
gathered before snow caught
in the wheels of traffic silent
up and down Central Avenue.
He was two thousand years old.
She ran the bars with him,
before the motion of snow
caught her too, and he moved in.
It was a dance.

In the dance were mesas winding
off the western horizon, the peak
of Mount Taylor that burned up every
evening at dusk light.
And in rhythm were Sandia mountain curves
that she fell against every night looking up
looking up. She knew him then, or maybe it had been
the motion of crows against the white cold and power lines.
The voice that was him moved into her rocked
in her and then the child small and dark
in the dance dance dance of the dance.

There was no last time she saw him
He returned with stars, a certain moon
and in other voices like last night.
She heard him first. Screen door slammed
against the wall. Crows outside the iced-tight windows.
Which dance. Locked and echoed and sucked
the cliffs of her belly in.
She picked up their baby from the crib,
more blankets to tuck them in.
Loud he called—come here come here—

It was a dance.

Someone Talking

they watch the glittering moon
from the front porch in Oxford, Iowa.
Which reservation
in this river of star motion?
The man of words sits next to
Noni Daylight
listening this time.

           Tequila, a little wine
           and she remembers some Old Crow
           yellow in a fifth on the drainboard.
           She thinks of him
           in Oklahoma, how he drank with her
           the summer powwow in Anadarko.
           Where is the word for a warm night
           and how it continues to here,
           a thousand miles from that time?
Milky Way.
And there are other words
in other languages. Always
in movement. He touches
her back where her hair
reaches to the middle. There
is that gesture and the
cricket's voice beginning.
all in the same circle of space.

Maybe the man of words speaks
like the cricket.
Noni Daylight
hears him that way.

> It is along the Turner Turnpike
> between Tulsa and Oklahoma City,
> tells him
> where they have all those signs:
> Kickapoo, Creek,
> Sac and Fox.
> Dating the beginning and end
> of the United States recognition
> of tribal histories.
> And hell
> where is he now
> when she needs, and
> tastes the Old Crow.
> Yellow fire all the way into
> her belly.
> The way they meant it.

They have maps
named after Africa and the blue oceans.
Sky circles the other way
but she doesn't feel dizzy.
Stars in the dark are clear,
not blurred, and the earth's movement
is a whirring current in the grass.
The man of words outlines wet islands
with his lips
on Noni Daylight's neck.

> She got stopped outside
> of Anadarko once.
> Red lights.
> and you must be Indian, said
> the Oklahoma Highway Patrol
> Of course they knew the history
> before switching on the lights.
> And when they rolled open the truck
> in the moist night,
> she was only going home
> she said.

What voice
in the warm grass of her belly,
What planet?

There Are Oceans

Where could I meet you
that would be outside of our conversations?
I want no escape, no edge
that I would not recognize myself
within or without you.
I swim into the sensual ache
that this longing arranges.
A soft ocean of wanting
you against me. Gently more
gently so that I have already
created the motions.
Your hair, the eyes, horizon of the breast,
curved to the very center. Yes,
I have touched you already
in the oceans of air between us.
It is the connecting secret.
Ultimate bone. Water.
The current ours.

Fire

a woman can't survive
by her own breath
                    alone
she must know
the voices of mountains
she must recognize
the foreverness of blue sky
she must flow
with the elusive
bodies
of night wind women
who will take her into
her own self

look at me
i am not a separate woman
i am a continuance
of blue sky
i am the throat
of the sandia mountains
a night wind woman
who burns
with every breath
she takes

Obscene Phone Call #2

Oh baby
You can't have armies charging in here.
Phone crawling around my arm
your voice rising and falling
and sex marching towards me from the other end.
Oh baby
The last phone call like this
I was in Oklahoma City
Frankie answered it in Albuquerque
"No, she isn't home but would you like to leave a message?"
And you did.
She wrote it out. Handed me the exhibitionist's list
of four letter words and breathing when I returned.
Said you would call back.
Oh baby.
I can't believe it.
Voice strung around my ears tied like combat boots.
The firing line and I would not be yours
for two minutes on the phone.
Oh baby.
You can't have armies charging in here.
None of your voices is enough
to fill this woman up.

She Was a Pretty Horse

She was a pretty horse.
Long black-shiny-crow-hair
eyes slanted and dark her
mother was from Chinle
you know the dusty wind plain
out of the Chuska Mountains
west slope down into
66 Bar in Flagstaff
where this pretty horse
was just waiting,
you know flashed those eyes
she said, baby
do you want a ride
put her arm around me
and then that smile
we rode all the way to
Albuquerque on.

A Scholder Indian Poem

I saw that guy in Oklahoma
the last time I went home.
He was broken and put back together
in San Francisco the first time.
          (PHS stitched and tied
          his brown skin together
          with remnants of orange, green and blue.)
The second time, in Reno
he shouldn't have got off the Greyhound bus.
Beaten by too much wine
and some mistaken Kiowas
he now wears a crooked smile
of yellow around his lips.
He is hiding out
waiting for the last time
in Carnegie, Oklahoma.

He drinks any color of paint,
now,
sips it patiently
between his silver-mirrored teeth.

It's the Same at Four A.M.

He's half Creek, half plains.
I'm part Creek and white.
"Which part do you want tonight?"
    I ask him.

The forty-nine singers are drumming
Creek stomp dance songs on the hood
of someone's car.
I pull his arm
"Come on, let's dance."

But he wants the other half

The Last Song

how can you stand it
he said
the hot oklahoma summers
where you were born
this humid thick air
is choking me
and i want to go back
to new mexico

it is the only way
i know how to breathe
an ancient chant
that my mother knew
came out of a history
woven from wet tall grass
in her womb

and i know no other way
than to surround my voice
with the summer songs of crickets
in this moist south night air

oklahoma will be the last song
i'll ever sing

Morning Once More

the sun over the horizon
a sweating yellow horse
our continuance
        the uncountable distance
that sweeps through our hands
the first prayers
        in the morning
it is this that i believe in
the galloping sun
and my whole life
        a rider

Origins

Noni Daylight left the morning
at Bluewater Lake.
She got out and drove west
into the shiny side of the earth.
Where stars have come down into rocks
between Sanders and Flagstaff.
Orange nova cliffs,
glinting, and the whole earth cracked.

Noni heard
that the Hopi say that Grand Canyon
is the birthplace of their people, but
she thinks most of the world
must have originated
from that point.

And this afternoon in the vague horizon
she thought she could see
the earth's motion,
formed
> of wind
> of sunrise
> of sandbrook.

And she thinks
she must still be traveling from there.
Holbrook, Seattle.
Oklahoma and Winslow.

But not very far at all.

Remember

Remember the sky that you were born under,
know each of the star's stories.
Remember the moon, know who she is. I met her
in a bar once in Iowa City.
Remember the sun's birth at dawn, that is the
strongest point of time. Remember sundown
and the giving away to night.
Remember your birth, how your mother struggled
to give you form and breath. You are evidence of
her life, and her mother's, and hers.
Remember your father, his hands cradling
your mother's flesh, and maybe her heart, too
and maybe not.
He is your life, also.
Remember the earth whose skin you are.
Red earth yellow earth white earth brown earth
black earth we are earth.
Remember the plants, trees, animal life who all have their
tribes, their families, their histories, too. Talk to them,
listen to them. They are alive poems.
Remember the wind. Remember her voice. She knows the
origin of this universe. I heard her singing Kiowa war
dance songs at the corner of Fourth and Central once.
Remember that you are all people and that all people
are you.

Remember that you are this universe and that this
universe is you.
Remember that all is in motion, is growing, is you.
Remember that language comes from this.
Remember the dance that language is, that life is.
Remember
to remember.

Your Phone Call at Eight A.M.

Your phone call at eight a.m. could
have been a deadly rope.
All the colors of your voice
were sifted out. The barest part flew
through the wires. Then tight-roped
into the comfort of my own home,
where I surrounded myself with smoke
of piñon, with cedar and sage.
Protected the most dangerous places,
for more than survival, I always
mean. But what you wanted, this morning
you said, was a few words
and not my heart. What you wanted . . .
But the skeleton of your voice
clicked barely perceptible,
didn't you hear it?
And what you said you wanted
was easy enough, a few books
some pages, anything, to cancel
what your heart ever saw in me that you didn't.
But you forgot to say that part.
Didn't even recognize it when it
came winging out of you—
the skeleton's meat and blood,
all that you didn't want to remember
when you called at eight a.m. . . .
But that's all right because
this poem isn't for you
but for me
after all

Talking to the Moon

Moon, my mother opened up
and dropped me here.
Tulsa, Oklahoma.
Where is that, moon?
I am afraid of who
I might be.
I am two months early
out of my mother's belly
and moon, into this terror
of humming metal and numbers
and odd lights.
This life is your fault, moon
You pulled me here and
I am coughing, my voice
barely coming through and
they say I am fighting
for my life but it is you,
moon, that I am looking for
and not my breath.
I am afraid, moon.
I am not my mother, or my
drunk father and moon
I have only you around me
in this clear box. Cradle
me in your hands.
Take me home, away
from these burning lights
and this breathing machine.
Only the arms of your moist
tight ocean will free me
from this terror,
                    moon.

Moonlight

I know when the sun is in China
because the night shining other-light
crawls into my bed. She is moon.

Her eyes slit and yellow she is the last
one out of a dingy bar in Albuquerque—
Fourth Street, or from similar avenues
in Hong Kong. Where someone else has also
awakened, the night thrown back and asked,
Where is the moon, my lover?
And from here I always answer in my dreaming,
"the last time I saw her was in the arms
of another sky."

Talking to the Moon #002

Moon
you lift your white skirts
over your thighs.
I want you this way,
soft river
in the dark.

Cuchillo

cuchillo
    sky
       is blood filling up my belly

cuchillo
    moon
       is a white horse thundering down
       over the edge
       of a raw red cliff

cuchillo
    heart
       is the one who leaves me
       at midnight
       for another lover

cuchillo
>dog
>>is the noise of chains and collar
>>straining at the neck to bite
>>the smell of my ankles

cuchillo
>silver
>>is the shell of black sky
>>spinning around inside
>>my darker eyes

cuchillo
>dreams
>>are the living bones that want out
>>of this voice dangling
>>that calls itself
>>>knife
>>>(cuchillo).

Two Horses

     I thought the sun breaking through Sangre de Cristo
Mountains was enough, and that
                         wild musky scents on my body after
  long nights of dreaming could
                  unfold me to myself.
    I thought my dance alone through worlds of
odd and eccentric planets that no one else knew
  would sustain me. I mean
               I did learn how to move
                    after all
and how to recognize voices other than the most familiar.
  But you must have grown out of
                 a thousand years dreaming
   just like I could never imagine you.
     You must have
             broke open from another sky
to here, because
        now I see you as a part of the millions of

other universes that I thought could never occur
        in this breathing.
                        And I know you as myself, traveling.
In your eyes alone are many colonies of stars
                        and other circling planet motion.
                And then your fingers, the sweet smell
                of hair, and
                                your soft, tight belly.
My heart is taken by you
        and these mornings since I am a horse running towards
    a cracked sky where there are countless dawns
                                breaking simultaneously.
There are two moons on the horizon
and for you
            I have broken loose.

Ice Horses

These are the ones who escape
after the last hurt is turned inward;
they are the most dangerous ones.
These are the hottest ones,
but so cold that your tongue sticks
to them and is torn apart because it is
frozen to the motion of hooves.
These are the ones who cut your thighs,
whose blood you must have seen on the gloves
of the doctor's rubber hands. They are
the horses who moaned like oceans, and
one of them a young woman screamed aloud;
she was the only one.
These are the ones who have found you.
These are the ones who pranced on your belly.
They chased deer out of your womb.
These are the ice horses, horses
who entered through your head,
and then your heart.
your beaten heart.

These are the ones who loved you.
They are the horses who have held you

so close that you have become
a part of them,
                    an ice horse

galloping into
               the fire.

Noni Daylight Remembers the Future

"We are closer than
blood," Noni Daylight
tells her. "It isn't
Oklahoma or the tribal
blood but something that
we speak."

(The otherself knows
and whispers
to herself.)

The air could choke, could
kill, the way it tempts
Noni to violence, this
morning. But she needs
the feel of danger,
                    for life.

(It helps her remember.)

Noni Daylight knows
there is meaning in all
of it,
       but it isn't easy.
She smokes cigarettes
watches the grey dawn
from a room in Albuquerque.
She dreams her otherself
next to her.

She feels the sky
tethered to the changing
earth, and her skin
responds, like a woman
to her lover.

It could be days, it could
be years, White Sands
                or Tucson.

She asks,
        "Should I dream you afraid
        so that you are forced to save
        yourself?

        Or should you ride colored horses
        into the cutting edge of the sky
        to know

        that we're alive
        we are alive."

The Blood-Letting

It is the morning after
the morning after.
Your voice echoes like a broken
bottle muffled into my skin.
I won't let you do this
to myself, as for you
you can always do
what you want.
                Again.
How am I to stop you with
stark words, promises
glued together with blood,
or with the smell of love
a distant memory?
Will it drive in to save us
once more? Or will the smell
be dried and baked into ribbons
against a rusty knife?
I know it was meant in beauty,
but inside there are voices
urging me on to another distance
to a place that is even more
intimate than this one.

It, too, is another morning
made of blood, but it is sunlight
on a scarlet canyon wall in
early winter.
It does not scatter the heart,
but gathers the branches tenderly
into a slender, dark woman.

She Had Some Horses

She had some horses.

She had horses who were bodies of sand.
She had horses who were maps drawn of blood.
She had horses who were skins of ocean water.
She had horses who were the blue air of sky.
She had horses who were fur and teeth.
She had horses who were clay and would break.
She had horses who were splintered red cliff.

She had some horses.

She had horses with long, pointed breasts.
She had horses with full, brown thighs.
She had horses who laughed too much.
She had horses who threw rocks at glass houses.
She had horses who licked razor blades.

She had some horses.

She had horses who danced in their mothers' arms.
She had horses who thought they were the sun, and their
bodies shone and burned like stars.
She had horses who waltzed nightly on the moon.
She had horses who were much too shy, and kept quiet
in stalls of their own making.

She had some horses.

She had horses who liked Creek stomp dance songs.
She had horses who cried in their beer.
She had horses who spit at male queens who made
them afraid of themselves.

She had horses who said they weren't afraid.
She had horses who lied.
She had horses who told the truth, who were stripped bare
of their tongues.

She had some horses.

She had horses who called themselves, "horse."
She had horses who called themselves, "spirit," and kept
their voices secret and to themselves.
She had horses who had no names.
She had horses who had books of names.

She had some horses.

She had horses who whispered in the dark, who were afraid to speak.
She had horses who screamed out of fear of the silence, who
carried knives to protect themselves from ghosts.
She had horses who waited for destruction.
She had horses who waited for resurrection.

She had some horses.

She had horses who got down on their knees for any savior.
She had horses who thought their high price had saved them.
She had horses who tried to save her, who climbed in her
bed at night and prayed as they raped her.

She had some horses.

She had some horses she loved.
She had some horses she hated.
These were the same horses.

New Orleans

This is the south. I look for evidence
of other Creeks, for remnants of voices,
or for tobacco brown bones to come wandering
down Conti Street, Royale, or Decatur.
Near the French Market I see a blue horse
caught frozen in stone in the middle of
a square. Brought in by the Spanish on

an endless ocean voyage he became mad
and crazy. They caught him in blue
rock, said
          don't talk.

I know it wasn't just a horse
                    that went crazy.

Nearby is a shop with ivory and knives.
There are red rocks. The man behind the
counter has no idea that he is inside
magic stones. He should find out before
they destroy him. These things
have memory,
          you know.

I have a memory.
                It swims deep in blood,
a delta in the skin. It swims out of Oklahoma,
deep the Mississippi River. It carries my
feet to these places: the French Quarter,
stale rooms, the sun behind thick and moist
clouds, and I hear boats hauling themselves up
and down the river.

My spirit comes here to drink.
My spirit comes here to drink.
Blood is the undercurrent.

There are voices buried in the Mississippi
mud. There are ancestors and future children
buried beneath the currents stirred up by
pleasure boats going up and down.
There are stories here made of memory.

I remember DeSoto. He is buried somewhere in
this river, his bones sunk like the golden
treasure he traveled half the earth to find,
came looking for gold cities, for shining streets
of beaten gold to dance on with silk ladies.

He should have stayed home.

                    (Creeks knew of him for miles
                    before he came into town.
                    Dreamed of silver blades
                    and crosses.)
And knew he was one of the ones who yearned

for something his heart wasn't big enough
to handle.
               (And DeSoto thought it was gold.)

The Creeks lived in earth towns,
                           not gold,
        spun children, not gold.
That's not what DeSoto thought he wanted to see.
The Creeks knew it, and drowned him in
        the Mississippi River
            so he wouldn't have to drown himself.

Maybe his body is what I am looking for
as evidence. To know in another way
that my memory is alive.
But he must have got away, somehow,
because I have seen New Orleans,
the lace and silk buildings,
trolley cars on beaten silver paths,
graves that rise up out of soft earth in the rain,
shops that sell black mammy dolls
holding white babies.

And I know I have seen DeSoto
                    having a drink on Bourbon Street,
                    mad and crazy
                    dancing with a woman as gold
                    as the river bottom.

What Music

      I would have loved you then, in
the hot, moist tropics of your young womanhood.
Then
        the stars were out and fat every night.
They remembered your name
                    and called to you
as you bent down in the doorways of the whiteman's houses.
You savored each story they told you,
and remembered
                    the way the stars entered your blood
                                    at birth.

Maybe it was the Christians' language
                              that captured you,
or the bones that cracked in your heart each time
you missed the aboriginal music that you were.
I don't know. But then,
                              you were the survivor of the births
of your two sons. The oldest one hates you, and the other
wants to marry you. Now they live in another language,
in Los Angeles
              with their wives.
And you,
          the stars will return every night to call you back.
They have followed your escape
          from the southern hemisphere
                                    into the north.
Their voices echo out from your blood and you drink
the Christians' brandy and fall back into
      doorways in an odd moonlight.
                              You sweat in the winter in the north,
and you are afraid,
                  sweetheart.

The Woman Hanging from the 13th Floor Window

She is the woman hanging from the 13th floor
window. Her hands are pressed white against the
concrete moulding of the tenement building. She
hangs from the 13th floor window in east Chicago,
with a swirl of birds over her head. They could
be a halo, or a storm of glass waiting to crush her.

She thinks she will be set free.

The woman hanging from the 13th floor window
on the east side of Chicago is not alone.
She is a woman of children, of the baby, Carlos,
and of Margaret, and of Jimmy who is the oldest.
She is her mother's daughter and her father's son.
She is several pieces between the two husbands
she has had. She is all the women of the apartment
building who stand watching her, watching themselves.

When she was young she ate wild rice on scraped down
plates in warm wood rooms. It was in the farther
north and she was the baby then. They rocked her.

She sees Lake Michigan lapping at the shores of
herself. It is a dizzy hole of water and the rich
live in tall glass houses at the edge of it. In some
places Lake Michigan speaks softly, here, it just sputters
and butts itself against the asphalt. She sees
other buildings just like hers. She sees other
women hanging from many-floored windows
counting their lives in the palms of their hands,
and in the palms of their childrens' hands.

She is the woman hanging from the 13th floor window
on the Indian side of town. Her belly is soft from
her childrens' births, her worn levis swing down below
her waist, and then her feet, and then her heart.
She is dangling.

The woman hanging from the 13th floor window hears voices.
They come to her in the night when the lights have gone
dim. Sometimes they are little cats mewing and scratching
at the door, sometimes they are her grandmother's voice,
and sometimes they are gigantic men of light whispering
to her to get up, to get up, to get up. That's what she wants
to have another child to hold onto in the night, to be able
to fall back into dreams.

And the woman hanging from the 13th floor window
hears other voices. Some of them scream out from below
for her to jump, they would push her over. Others cry softly
on the sidewalks, pull their children up like flowers and gather
them into their arms. They would help her, like themselves.

But she is the woman hanging from the 13th floor window,
and she knows she is hanging by her own fingers, her
own skin, her own thread of indecision.

She thinks of Carlos, of Margaret, of Jimmy.
She thinks of her father and of her mother.
She thinks of all the women she has been, of all
the men. She thinks of the color of her skin, and
of Chicago streets, and of waterfalls and pines.
She thinks of moonlight nights, and of cool spring storms.
Her mind chatters like neon and northside bars.
She thinks of the 4 a.m. loneliness that has folded

her up like death, discordant, without logical and
beautiful conclusion. Her teeth break off at the edges.
She would speak.

The woman hangs from the 13th floor window crying for
the lost beauty of her own life. She sees the
sun falling west over the gray plane of Chicago.
She thinks she remembers listening to her own life
break loose, as she falls from the 13th floor
window on the side of Chicago, or as she
climbs back up to claim herself again.

Anchorage

for Audre Lorde

This city is made of stone, of blood, and fish.
There are Chugatch Mountains to the east
and whale and seal to the west.
It hasn't always been this way, because glaciers
who are ice ghosts create oceans, carve earth
and stone, and shape this city here by the sound.
They swim backwards in time.

Once a storm of boiling earth cracked open
the streets, threw open the town.
It's quiet now, but underneath the concrete
is the cooking earth,
                        and above that, air
which is another ocean, where spirits we can't see
are dancing joking getting full
on roasted caribou, and the praying
goes on, and extends outward.

Nora and I
go walking down 4th Avenue and know
it is all happening.
On a park bench, we see someone's Athabascan
grandmother, folded up, smelling like 200 years
of blood and piss. Her eyes are closed against some
unimagined darkness, where she is buried
in an ache in which nothing makes
                              sense.

We keep on breathing, walking, but softer now,
the clouds whirling in the air above us.
What can we say that would make us understand
better than we do already?
Except to speak of her home and claim her
as our own history, and know that our dreams
don't end here, two blocks away from the ocean
where our hearts still batter away at the muddy shore.

And I think of the 6th Avenue jail, of mostly Native
and Black men, where Henry told about being shot at
eight times outside a liquor store in LA, but when
the car sped away he was surprised he was alive,
no bullet holes, man, and eight cartridges strewn
on the sidewalk all around him.

Everyone laughed at the impossibility of it,
but also the truth. Because who would believe
the fantastic and terrible story of all our survival,
those who were never meant
                              to survive?

For Alva Benson, and for All Those Who Have Learned to Speak

And the ground spoke when she was born.
Her mother heard it. In Navajo she answered
as she squatted down against the earth
to give birth. It was now when it happened,
now giving birth to itself again and again
between the legs of women.

Or maybe it was the Indian Hospital
in Gallup. The ground still spoke beneath
mortar and concrete. She strained against the
metal stirrups, and they tied her hands down
because she still spoke with them when they
muffled her screams. But her body went on
talking, and the child was born into their
hands, and the child learned to speak
both voices.

She grew up talking in Navajo, in English,
and watched the earth around her shift and change
with the people in the towns and in the cities
learning not to hear the ground as it spun around
beneath them. She learned to speak for the ground
the voice coming through her like roots that
have long hungered for water. Her own daughter
was born, like she had been, in either place
or all places, so she could leave, leap
into the sound she had always heard,
a voice like water, like the gods weaving
against sundown in a scarlet light.

The child now hears names in her sleep.
They change into other names, and into others.
It is the ground murmuring, and Mt. St. Helens
erupts as the harmonic motion of a child turning
inside her mother's belly waiting to be born
to begin another time.

And we go on, keep giving birth and watch
ourselves die, over and over.
And the ground spinning beneath us
goes on talking.

Linda Hogan

red clay

Turtle, old as earth
his slow neck has pushed aside
to bury him for winter.

His heart beats slow.
And the fish
are embedded in ice.

I photograph you
at the potter's wheel, the light
and the dark of you.

Tonight the turtle is growing
a larger shell, calcium
from inside deep.

The moon grows
layer on layer
across iced black water.

On the clay your fingertips
are wearing away
the red soil.

We are here, the red earth
passes like light into us
and stays.

calling myself home

There were old women
who lived on amber.
Their dark hands
laced the shells of turtles
together, pebbles inside
and they danced
with rattles strong on their legs.

There is a dry river
between them and us.
Its banks divide up our land.
Its bed was the road
I walked to return.

We are plodding creatures
like the turtle
born of an old people.
We are nearly stone
turning slow as the earth.
Our mountains are underground
they are so old.

This land is the house
we have always lived in.
The women,
their bones are holding up the earth.
The red tail of a hawk
cuts open the sky
and the sun
brings their faces back
with the new grass.

Dust from yarrow
is in the air,
the yellow sun.
Insects are clicking again.

I came back to say good-bye
to the turtle
to those bones
to the shells locked together
on his back,
gold atoms dancing underground.

Leaving

Good-bye, divisions of people:
   those hickory-chopping,
   the hump hunters,

skunk people
dung people
people who live under trees
who live in broken houses
and parts of houses.
Their house worn out people
are the meanest of all.

My house-cut-off people, I'm saying good-bye
to that person behind me.
She's the one
who tried to please her father,
the one an uncle loved for her dark hair.

White coyote behind me
light up your eyes, your white shadows,
your white round mouth
in its cage of black trees, a moon
running from branch to branch.
Moon that lives in the water,
snapping turtle that crawled out
at me.

Good-bye shooting horse
    above a dead man's grave.
Let that blessed rain
where fish descended from the sky
                  evaporate.

Silver lures, minnows
in that river who is the moon
living in a broken house,
who is the coyote
dwelling among the blackjack broken off
people, the turtle
who lives in its round white shell,
        I can tell you good-bye.

Good-bye to the carved bone beads
I found by the river. They can grow back
their flesh,
    their small beating hearts,
    air in the bones
    and gray wings they fly
    away from me.

Good-bye to the milky way
    who lives in his old worn out place,
    dog white
    his trail.

All my people are weeping
when I step out of my old skin
like a locust singing good-bye,
feet still clinging
to the black walnut tree.
They say I've burned all my brown sticks
for telling time
and still it passes away.

Song for My Name

Before sunrise
think of brushing out an old woman's
dark braids.
Think of your hands
fingertips on the soft hair.

If you have this name,
your grandfather's dark hands
lead horses toward the wagon
and a cloud of dust follows,
ghost of silence.

That name is full of women
with black hair
and men with eyes like night.
It means no money
tomorrow.

Such a name my mother loves
while she works gently
in the small house.
She is a white dove
and in her own land
the mornings are pale,
birds sing into the white curtains
and show off their soft breasts.

If you have a name like this,
there's never enough water.
There is too much heat.
When lightning strikes, rain
refuses to follow.
It's my name,
that of a woman living
between the white moon
and the red sun, waiting to leave.
It's the name that goes with me
back to earth
no one else can touch.

Nativity

Old women
fire clay ovens.
There will be bread.

Six men
work on the church
lifting the cross.
The day is heat.

Lower your head
through the many eyes
that burn into flesh
and beyond.

White sun.
There are no shadows.
In the center of dust
a bridge crosses brief water.

A child stares into my face,
my eyes.
Guilty, I smile.

Bread.
The smell
comes from stone.

Blessings

Blessed
are the injured animals
for they live in his cages.
But who will heal my father,
tape his old legs for him?

Here's the bird with the two broken wings
and her feathers are white as an angel
and she says goddamn stirring grains
in the kitchen. When the birds fly out
he leaves the cages open
and she kisses his brow for such
good works.

> Work he says
> all your life
> and at the end
> you don't own even a piece of land.

Blessed are the rich
for they eat meat every night.
They have already inherited the earth.

For the rest of us, may we just live
long enough
and unwrinkle our brows,
may we keep our good looks
and some of our teeth
and our bowels regular.

Perhaps we can go live places
a rich man can't inhabit,
in the sun fish and jackrabbits,
in the cinnamon colored soil,
the land of red grass
and red people
in the valley
of the shadow of Elk
who aren't there.

> He says the damned earth is so old
> and wobbles so hard
> you'd best hang on to everything.
> Your neighbors steal what little you got.

Blessed
are the rich
for they don't have the same old
Everyday to put up with
like my father
who's gotten old,
            Chickasaw
            chikkih asachi, which means
they left as a tribe not a very great while ago.
They are always leaving,
those people.

Blessed
are those who listen
when no one is left to speak.

Oil

Men smile like they know everything
but walking in slant heel boots
their butts show they are tense.
Dark shirts.
Blue fire
puts out the sun. Rock bits
are clenched metal fists.

The earth is wounded
and bleeds.
Pray to Jesus.

An explosion could knock us all
to our knees

while the bosses stretch out,
white ridge of backbone
in the sun.

We're full of bread and gas,
getting fat on the outside
while inside we grow thin.

Heritage

From my mother, the antique mirror
where I watch my face take on her lines.
She left me the smell of baking bread
to warm fine hairs in my nostrils,
she left the large white breasts that weigh down
my body.

From my father I take his brown eyes,
the plague of locusts that leveled our crops,
they flew in formation like buzzards.

From my uncle the whittled wood
that rattles like bones
and is white
and smells like all our old houses
that are no longer there. He was the man
who sang old chants to me, the words
my father was told not to remember.

From my grandfather who never spoke
I learned to fear silence.
I learned to kill a snake
when you're begging for rain.

And grandmother, blue-eyed woman
whose skin was brown,
she used snuff.
When her coffee can full of black saliva
spilled on me
it was like the brown cloud of grasshoppers
that leveled her fields.
It was the brown stain
that covered my white shirt,
my whiteness a shame.
That sweet black liquid like the food
she chewed up and spit into my father's mouth
when he was an infant.
It was the brown earth of Oklahoma
stained with oil.
She said tobacco would purge your body of poisons.
It has more medicine than stones and knives
against your enemies.

That tobacco is the dark night that covers me.

She said it is wise to eat the flesh of deer
so you will be swift and travel over many miles.
She told me how our tribe has always followed a stick
that pointed west
that pointed east.

From my family I have learned the secrets
of never having a home.

Going to Town

For Donna

I wake up early while you sleep,
soft in that room whose walls
are pictures of blonde angels,
and set loose the fireflies.
Their lights
have flickered all night
on our eyelids.

Already you have a woman's hip bones,
long muscles
you slide your dress over
and we brush each other's hair
then step out into the blue morning.
Good daughters,
we are quiet
lifting empty milk cans,
silver cans into the wagon.
They rattle together
going to town.

We ride silent
because the old man has paid us
dimes not to speak
but the wheels of the wagon
sing and we listen,
we listen to ourselves singing
the silence of birds
and dust that flies up in our hair.

The dust moves closer to us,
the place is dark
where we have disappeared.
Our family returns to us
in the bodies of children, of dogs
stretched across the road,
cats who ran away from home.

What do we have left
except the mirage of sound,
frogs creaking over the night land.
The black walnut trees are gone,
stolen during the night
and transformed
into the handles of guns.

That song, if you sing for it
and pray it to come,
in the distance
it grows nearer.
Close your eyes and it comes,
the music of old roads
we still travel together, so far
the sound is all that can find us.

Daybreak.
My daughter sitting at the table,
strong arms,
my face in her eyes
staring at her innocence
of what is dark
her fear at night of nothing
we have created
light as a weapon against.
Dust floats
small prisms
red
blue
in her hair.
Light in her eyes, fireworks,
the smell of powder on her
is lilac

scenting narrow arms, thighs.
The cobalt light of her eyes
where yesterday a colt's thin legs
walked in a field
of energy.
Matter is transformed.
Her innocence is my guilt.
In her dark eyes
the children of Hiroshima
are screaming
and her skin is
their skin
falling off.
How quickly we could vanish,
your skin nothing.
How soft
you disappear confused
daughter
daughters
I love you.

The Women Are Grieving

for Sister Rosalie Bertell, M.D.

Light
Lumine
Our salvation
is a gold ring surrounding the eye
of a blackbird
and those red-winged birds
returned from war
wearing bloody feathers.
The women are grieving.

They dream cities
that are nothing in one moment.
Clouds opening like flowers.
They dream silence that doesn't break.
They light fat candles their hands molded
in the hopeful shape of children
who are thin.

In the night
a woman hears the blackbird on her roof.
Her dark neck,
her pale neck
her soft neck where the pulse moves
is mourning.
Hysteria, the doctors say of this pain,
from the womb.
And it is.
She watches while children disappear
in their own eyes.
That quickly you are not alive
and it is nothing
and she knows it.

Lumine.
Light pulls from the candles at the altar
you can pass a hand through
and pull back the wind
that blows through bodies
dancing the edges out of the earth.

Out of the earth
out in the wind
in the dancing rain and sun,
destroyed horses lose their light around them.
an aura of bleached fur
around the bones.

And women are grieving
the children of the world.
Through bloody feathers they are grieving,
through striking matches
and through the lanterns lighting eyes
they are grieving
down the long wick into bad water
they drink,
the luminous women
who have lost their bright children
say
Death is turning me around
Death is winning
Death is stealing from me
Death is dancing me ragged.

Black Hills Survival Gathering, 1980

Bodies on fire
the monks in orange cloth
sing morning into light.

Men wake on the hill.
Dry grass blows from their hair.
B52's blow over their heads
leaving a cross on the ground.
Air returns to itself and silence.

Rainclouds are disappearing
with fractures of light in the distance.
Fierce gases forming,
the sky bending
where people arrive
on dusty roads that change
matter to energy.

My husband wakes.
My daughter wakes.
Quiet morning, she stands
in a pail of water
naked, reflecting light
and this man I love,
with kind hands
he washes her slim hips,
narrow shoulders, splashes
the skin containing
wind and fragile fire,
the pulse in her wrist.

My other daughter wakes
to comb warm sun across her hair.
While I make coffee I tell her
this is the land of her ancestors,
blood and heart.
Does her hair become a mane
blowing in the electric breeze,
her eyes dilate and darken?

The sun rises on all of them
in the center of light
hills that have no boundary,

the child named Thunder Horse,
the child named Dawn Protector
and the man
whose name would mean home in Navajo.

At ground zero
in the center of light we stand.
Bombs are buried beneath us,
destruction flies overhead.
We are waking
in the expanding light
the sulphur-colored grass.
A red horse standing on a distant ridge
looks like one burned
over Hiroshima,
silent, head hanging in sickness.
But look
she raises her head
and surges toward the bluing sky.

Radiant morning.
The dark tunnels inside us carry life.
Red.
Blue.
The children's dark hair against my breast.
On the burning hills
in flaring orange cloth
men are singing and drumming
Heartbeat.

The Women Speaking

And the Russian women in blue towns
are speaking.
The flower-dressed women of India,
women in orange tents,
dark women
of the Americas
who sit beside fires,
have studied the palms of their hands
and walk toward one another.

It's time
to bless this ground.
Their hair is on fire
from the sun
and they walk narrow roads
toward one another.
Their pulses beat
against the neck's thin skin.
They grow closer.

Let us be gentle
with the fiery creature furnaces
smelling of hay and rum,
gentle with the veils of skin
that bind us
to the world.
Let us hold fierce
the soft lives of our children,
the light is inside them
and they are burning
in small beds of straw,
beds of scorched white sheets,
newspaper beds with words
wrapped against skin
the light burns through.

The women cross their hands
on their chests
and lie down to sleep a moment
along dust roads.

In the dark, Japanese women
light lanterns
the shape of children.
They blow gently
on the sides of hills,
the roads
illuminated by the bodies of children
that enter our eyes.

At night there are reflections on glass,
revelations of lucent skin
filled with muscle, lung,
nerve, that flash of dark and light skin,
shadows we love
that belong to us all.

Daughters, the women are speaking.
They arrive
over the wise distances
on perfect feet.
Daughters, I love you.

The Diary of Amanda McFadden

Amanda: My Song Remains

Here it speaks.
That song
the bird makes
of spring's green rain
and the blue rise of mountains
is mine.
It jumps to life
in the coils of your ears.
Swallowed grasshoppers
fly out of its mouth,
their clicking wings
whole again.
Listen, brave world, people
who read these words,
the stars are swallowing themselves
and men make war
on their bodies.
The ruin of empires
will sing from a bird's soft throat
that swallowed worms
my flesh tunneled through.

The Cup

In a hundred years
these words will return.
A mountain can be taken apart
and transformed into houses
and it is still the mountain.

I want to say
what we believe.
It is the cup,
to bend a woman's life
so that she fills the circumference,
not walls
but horizons.
And warmth that goes out where it will
and returns.

In a hundred years
these words will return.
The earth will rise up
out of its flesh
pushing up the sky
and the walls of houses
that hold you in
will have fallen away to earth
once again.

Amanda: For the Oneida Indians

I touch your trees for you
I follow the path of the fox
I eat fur it leaves like wisps on snow
to understand
and I open that pellet which passed
through its body.
Inside, what is beautiful
the fur and claws, small teeth.

I dreamed last night
of the Bear painted on walls
moving toward the edge
the walls no longer there
but in my mind, a people
I've not seen
living somewhere,
the light in this darkness of me
my words and dreams
when I see your moon,
breathe your air,
the dark shapes that moved away.

There is time.
This earth like an egg
grey-blue
is just beginning.

Harriet at Oneida: Death's Children

We plant our hearts
and small words that are prayers
and gauge distances to the sky.
Heaven is full of stars.
White things,
stones, shells.
Milk I think to hold back.

Today the fruit is shrouded in rain
and blue herons are legless
above water,
four of them, one for each child
lost to me
lost to air
and looking for all that water
like oval mists on a mirror.

The children buried
and cicadas who've grown new wings,
broken out of their bodies
to speak
Chirr, to the night.

I saw the herons fly past
their soft breasts rising,
the feathers like frost on windowpanes,
but warm.

Here child, hold this breath awhile,
a breath.
There are enough countries underground.
Hold
while I fill my womb with stones.

Woman Gardening

The glass works behind her,
opaque rubble
the sheets of air and sun.

She probes with her hands
the ground
of human blood,

laborers here before us
the women's lives
lost in birth.

So gentle
as if she were wearing a glove.
Her hands

reaching into the womb of earth
to define a land
by what it shapes.

Seeds underground
are beginning to break out of themselves.
Think of a snail,

a whorl of calcium
a cup containing the damp life.
A new order

that woman
in balance with the land,
things merged,

the new trees
and plants begging to grow
out of the decay of roots and leaves.

Think of the snail
spiralling to heaven.

The Women Quilting

Push the needle up into layers of cloth,
bring it back down.
As the sun
and the world
and the brief white stitches, birdsfeet
pacing a design into snow.
The spokes of a wheel.

Here is Harriet's dress
the red one
transformed,

a rose,
a part of her life
the lost children
nights with John
and smell of loves
and body so young
that wore it.

We sew rose petals
and lavender inside the cloth,
smells
which are the oldest love
and warm us at night
when an invisible wind rattles twigs
to kiss dark leaves.

Sisters,
this Tree of Life is shoved into knowledge
by Amanda's porcelain thimble
and fingers that hold words
she unlocks into ink each night.

In the branches
a cluster of grapes
a singing bird,
I know what it is singing,
I know.

Four Hundred Hands

The hair of women
men's eyes
moths
with their luminous wings
riding through space.
These are all hands
that touch us
dissolving into light.

Four hundred hands
hold our roof
against the stars
and reach out of sleep
for one another.

Outside, a peacock
spreads his feathers like night.
Behind him all the blue eyes
look into a far country.

In that land
powerful shapes,
a large tree breathing its work,
the windbones of birds
a blue fire
of wings.

Fossil of Eden,
Adam's five sons,
Eve's five daughters
sending out a voice
to take hold of the future,
the white tree in the center
blue rivers running their course,
a gesture of calm.

New Shoes

Even shaking the folds out of the sheet, Sullie formed questions in her head about the shoes. She looked as if she might divine answers from the whiteness of afternoon light in the fine weavings of cotton. The way an old woman might read the future inside a porcelain teacup.

Manny came in quietly, leaving her cart out on the balcony walkway of the motel. "Up where I come from, people read the newspapers instead of the sheets," Manny said, and then she went out the door, her legs two shadows inside her thin skirt.

Sullie tucked the sheets beneath the mattress and smoothed the worn green bedspread across them. It was the color of algae, mossy and faded. New motel guests would arrive soon to sleep between the sheets and the cotton was fragrant with the odor of laundry soap and the smell of scorch from the big mangle. Sullie's short hands tightened a wrinkle away. She watched herself in the dresser mirror as she folded a blanket. Some hair had fallen down the back of her neck. She pinned it up. Her dry and darkened elbows bent toward the ceiling and the pale blue smock rose up away from her hips. She watched the reflection of herself push the soiled bedclothes deep into the canvas bag that hung on the side of the metal cart. In the loneliness of the room, in the mirror with its distortion right at Sullie's forehead and another at her thighs, she saw herself the way others probably saw her, too serious, dark-eyed, her shoulders too heavy, but alive and moving, filling up the room that had never known a permanent tenant.

In the storeroom the black hands of the clock on the wall said 3:00. Already too late for the bus and Donna would be home ahead of her, sitting on the sofa listening for the sound of her mother's shoes, lazily turning the pages of an old magazine. Or perhaps she would have opened the metal wardrobe and stepped into one of Sullie's outdated dresses and stood before the mirror, turning herself this way and that, sticking her chest out a little too far, piling her own dark hair upon her head. With the one tube of dime-store lipstick Sullie bought and once treasured, Donna would paint little smudges on her cheekbones and smooth them out, darken her full lips that were still rosy from childhood. And she would step, barefooted, into the new shoes and stand at the full-length mirror inside the door of the wardrobe and look at the narrow lines of her hips curving out beneath the small of her back.

Sullie unsnapped the blue smock and hung it on the coathook. On its pocket in red thread were embroidered the words "The Pines Motel." The words hung there in the sky-blue cloth like writing from an airplane.

"There's only one pine in this entire vicinity," Manny said, "and it's that half-dead straggler over there across the street. Behind the white house."

Manny had already replaced her unused sheets on the shelves, had dropped the canvas bag of soiled linens into the corner for the laundry. "You going to walk?" she asked Sullie. "You ought to take the bus. How much money you figure you save walking those two miles?"

"I only walk in the morning."

"When your feet are still good?" She removed the safety pin from between her teeth and pinned her shirt from the underside. "Does it show?" Manny smiled and the rich gold of her eyes warmed Sullie. Manny with skin the color of earth, black hair straightened only enough to look smooth on the surfaces, like water where the undercurrents twist and pull beneath a seamless and laden skin. Manny's voice was slow, not full of fast chatter like the other maids, not talking about boyfriends and children, about whether to go dancing or save money for a car.

Manny made thirty-five cents an hour more than Sullie because she was colored instead of Indian. When Sullie got the nerve up to ask the manager about money, he said, "Don't gossip. I don't keep people on when they gossip. And take that chip off your shoulder."

The house with the pine stood alone and surrounded by a few shrubs, a small area of lawn, a remnant of farmland cut through with new streets and clouds of exhaust rising up from buses. In front of the house was a diner and Sullie's bus stop. It was all visible from the second-floor balcony of the motel. The dying tree bent by an invisible wind, shaped like a tired old woman reaching down to touch children.

Sullie seated herself on the bench that advertised used cars. Manny gestured with her head toward the diner. "Want some coffee?" But Sullie shook her head. "Suit yourself," said Manny and she walked toward the diner, slowly as if she were wearing green silk and gold bracelets instead of the thin printed shirt and skirt. She went into the diner, a converted house trailer that had an extra room built on the back side of it. The windows were slightly yellow from the grease of cooking. Behind them Sullie could see Manny sliding down into a seat behind the brown oilcloth and the little mustard jar vases with plastic flowers.

Sullie sat outside in the whirl of traffic, thinking of home, of large and slow-moving turtles migrating by the hundreds across the dirt roads, of silent nights when frogs leapt into water and the world came alive with the sounds of their swelling throats.

The wind began to blow off the street. With her hand Sullie covered her face from the dust and grit. Other women held down their skirts, their red and gold hair flying across their faces. A motion caught Sullie's eye.

Up in the sky, something white was flying like a large bird. In spite of the blowing sand, she looked up, but as she squinted at the sky, the bird lengthened and exposed itself as only a sheet of plastic churning and twisting in the wind. It stretched out like a long white snake and then lost its air current and began falling.

On the bus two elderly women sat in front of her. They were both speaking and neither one listened to the other. They carried on two different conversations the way people did in the city, without silences, without listening. Trying to get it all said before it was too late, before they were interrupted by thoughts. One of the women had steel-blue hair. The other one fanned herself with a paper as if it were hot and humid, talking to her own face in the window about her children, one in San Diego in the navy, one in Nevada running a gas station. She put the paper down on her lap and powdered her nose, squinting into the little circle of mirror that was caked pink with powder.

A man with dark hair in front of the women puffed hard on his cigarette. The powdered woman fanned away the smoke. Sullie watched it rise, nearly blue, into the light of the windows, drifting like a cloud in the air currents, touching the hair oil spot on the glass. It was like mist rising off a lake in the early morning. Steam from a kettle of boiling vegetables, squash, tomato, onion. It smelled good, the sweet odor of burning tobacco.

Buildings blurred past the window. The early shift men carried lunch pails to their cars and buses, all gliding past the window as if Sullie were sitting still and watching a movie, a large fast-moving film of people disappearing into the south. Even those people walking north were swept into it, pulled finally backwards across the window and gone.

Sullie stood and pulled the narrow rope. She felt exposed, the people behind her looking at her tied-back hair with its first strands of white, at her cotton dress wrinkled from sitting on the plastic seat, at the heaviness of her arm, bare and vulnerable reaching upward to ring the bell. She stepped out of the door and it hissed shut behind her.

Donna was not there. Her notebook was on the table and there was a dirty glass sitting beside the shiny new dish drainer Sullie had bought with her last paycheck. Sullie rinsed the glass and placed it, upside down, in the orange plastic drainer, then wiped the glass and the drainer both with a towel. Her shoes creaked the gray linoleum where it was bulging.

Donna's sweater was on the floor beside the sofa bed. Sullie picked it up and then, once again, she reached beneath the sofa and pulled out one of the sleek black shoes. New shoes. They were shiny, unworn. Patent leather with narrow pointed heels and a softly sculptured hole in each toe. Sullie brushed the dust from them with her skirt. She saw her face reflected in the shiny leather, her wide forehead in the roundness of leather. Her heart jumped in her chest again as it had when she first found the shoes.

They were prettier than the shoes Anna May had worn that summer when she came from Tulsa on the back of a man's motorcycle. And Anna May had worn them, dust-ridden, red leather, all the way from the city down the dirt roads, over the big gullies that washed into the soil. She wore them home, wearing also a red and blue dress flying out on the back of a motorcycle.

What a big to-do the family made, admiring the bright dress and shoes even before they welcomed Anna May and her thin-faced boyfriend. Sullie had polished the buckles of her sister's shoes, walked around the floor in the red shoes that were too big and wobbly, her dry and dirty legs rising out of them like old sticks and her ankles turning.

Sullie put Donna's new shoes back under the sofa. She lined them up and put them where they couldn't be seen from the table.

It was dark when Donna returned. Sullie's eyes wandered from Donna's face down the small shoulders held too high, the large hands that were always out of place, looking right down at her feet in the run-over saddle shoes. She glanced again at Donna's light-skinned face. "I've been worried," she said.

"I was at a friend's," Donna said.

"Hungry?"

"We ate."

Sullie opened the refrigerator and stood in the light. Steam rolled out the door and surrounded her. She took out the bologna and, sitting at the table, made herself a sandwich.

Donna looked at the window, watching their reflections on the glass. A woman and a girl like themselves sitting in the dark square of glass.

"What did you eat?"

"Meatloaf and potatoes." With her finger Donna traced the pattern of the black matrix in the gold-colored plastic table. "Look, this one is shaped like a hawk. See? There's its wing. See its beak? It's saying, the train is about to come by."

"I haven't had meatloaf in a hundred years," Sullie said. She reached across the table to touch Donna's arm. Donna pulled away, got up and filled the glass with water from the faucet. The water clouded and cleared.

"What do you really think a hawk would say, Mom?"

Sullie was quiet. She stood up and went over to fold the quilt Rena had made. She was careful with the quilt, removing it from the sofa back. Each patch was embroidered with stories of Sullie's life. If Rena had lived long enough, there would have been more stories to stitch, Sullie's life with Donna's father. That one would have contained a car and a man smoking cigarettes. There would have been a patch for the birth of Donna, the little light-skinned Indian who would someday wear black patent leather pumps on her bony feet. There would be a square containing the Pines Motel with Sullie standing on the balcony looking out at the yellowing pine tree that had lost most of its needles and looked like an old woman weeping. What else? A small coffin containing her dead son. Sullie taking the bus to Denver with little Donna crying and snuffling next to her. It was all like the great stained glass window, the quilt colors with light behind them. There was a picture for every special event of Sullie's childhood, a picture of Sullie's birth, the swarm of bees, little circles of gold, flying across the pale blue cotton, the old people all standing on the front porch of the old house. One of them, an old woman named Lemon, was wearing a yellow dress and holding the dark infant up to the sun. Her legs were red. There were indigo clouds.

The last patch had never been finished. Rena was working on it the summer she died. On it was the lake with golden fish stitched down across the quilted waves. And there were the two glorious red mules whose backs were outlined in yellow thread as if the sun shone down on them. Men in rafts and boats. A group of women sitting at a table and gossiping were just outlined in ink. Nothing solid to them. Nothing filled in or completed. They were like shadows with white centers.

Sullie folded the quilt and put it on the table beside the couch. "Help me pull out this sofa, will you, honey?" She looked at Donna. "You know, I really think the hawk would say, it shall come to pass that all the world will be laid bare by the doings of men."

Donna look at the quilt. "Can we sleep under it?"

"I'm saving it," Sullie told her once again.

"What for? When you get old and die?"

"No, honey, I just want to keep it nice. When you grow up, I'll give it to you."

Donna lay down between the sheets. Sullie sat next to her and ran her fingers down a loose strand of Donna's hair.

Saving things for old age. The very idea. Sullie reprimanded herself. Saving things when the girl wanted something pretty to hold now and to touch. No good. A mother and daughter alone in the city, no good. It was what happened when you married a man who drove up in the heat of summer after being gone two years and you had to tell him about the death of his son and then you wept and went away with the man, going anywhere just to get out of that desolate place and the heat. Just to get out of that place where your uncle had come home drunk and shot his wife, the place where your cousin sold off everything you owned one day just to buy a bottle and then tried to kiss your neck. Not that it was much to look at, but he sold it off to a young couple in a pickup truck that looked like they came from back east. And you went away with the white man and he went into the army. So the hawk would say.

It was better with him gone, with her husband gone. Even trying to earn a living. To mend socks and underwear for only two people. To not have to listen to that man bragging about what he used to be when he sang in bars or when he played baseball with some big team or other. Better to not even get any more of his letters or the snapshots, the shiny snapshots he sent of himself and his army friends sitting it out in bars with pretty oriental women smiling behind him. Still, Donna was growing up different. Like a stranger. She was going to be a white girl. Sullie could already see it in her. In her way of holding tension, of shaking her foot. In the hair she kept cutting. She was growing up with the noise of buses and cars, of GI's and red-dressed women laughing outside the window at night. She wasn't growing in the heat of woodstoves that burned hot even in the summer and the fireflies with their own little lanterns going on and off. Well, she wouldn't be picking cotton for the Woodruffs either like Sullie had done, feeling mad because Mrs. Woodruff was half Indian herself and spending that cotton money on silk dresses and luncheons at fancy places while Sullie was out there picking it from the dusty fields with her eyes watering. And she wouldn't be growing up laying down with men on the road at night like Anna May had done.

It must have been the quilt that moved her to dream of walking in the big lake at home. The water was warm against her legs. Silent except for the sound of water dripping off her, touching up against the shores in a slow rhythm like maybe it loved the land. And suddenly she was standing in the street by the diner, cars bearing down on her and she was paralyzed, unable to save herself.

Sullie woke up. It was cold. She covered Donna with her own half of the blanket and got up. The sky was growing lighter outside the window, beginning to light up the white cotton curtains with the rose colors of sunrise. Traffic picked up. Standing in her pale gown, her long hair loose and down around her waist, Sullie opened the curtains while the coffee water boiled. She called softly into the other room. And then she went over to pull back the covers. "Time to get up."

Outside, Donna stood at the end of the bench, waiting for the bus. Two young GI's slouched down on the bench. They wore olive drab, one with his military hat pulled down as if he were sleeping, one leg crossed over the other. His hands were folded loosely in his lap. Donna stood almost at attention.

A train passed over. It clattered and thundered along the trestle and it seemed to blow open Donna's tightly held sweater. It blew her hair in a blur of heat and exhaust, the heat waving up like a mirage, a summer field or highway. The soldier who sat straight up waved at an invisible conductor leaning off the platform between cars, and then he glanced at Donna. His eyes took in her thin body and chest. Under his gaze, she was stiff and unmoving. She stared straight ahead, but her body tightened inside her blue-gray sweater.

The train hurried past, carrying coal in the sweating black cars and speeding east on the vibrating track.

Donna was still. In the center of all the motion, the automobiles filled with people, the gold and red plastic streamers that waved and twisted about the used car lot, she was still, and then the train was gone.

Indoors, Sullie wiped the black shoes with a dish towel. She set them down on the table, on the speaking hawk laminated into plastic. She dried the dish drainer. It was pretty, the color of wildflowers at home. Bright orange like children's new toys and painted Mexican salt shakers, city swing sets. In the morning light, the entire kitchen shone, each item clear and full of its own beauty. The cereal bowls were dragonfly blue. The coffee cup was deep rich brown. It sat on the table beside the black shoes.

The shoes were small. Donna's size. Inside, in the place where Donna's delicate arch would touch and rise when she walked, were the words "Montgomery Ward." Monkey Wards, as Sullie's cousins called the large white department store on Broadway, the store with the wires going through the ceiling, across the desks, the little tubes of money sliding through air and stopping.

Sullie's own shoes were flat and worn, scuffed. The soles were worn down at the heels. Last week a nail had pushed into the heel of her foot.

Suppose Donna had stolen them, she wondered, standing back and looking at the new shoes. She sipped her coffee. Suppose Donna had stolen these woman shoes? Or stolen Sullie's money. Sullie picked up her handbag and unzipped the money compartment. Eighteen dollars and twenty-nine cents. It was all there.

Sullie imagined the fancy shoes on Donna's little horse legs. With the pink toes and jagged toenails protruding through the sculptured holes. Donna's thin calf muscles flexed above the high heels. Destitute and impoverished thin legs the color of cream and with fine and scraggly hairs and big knees all looking so much worse above the shining black shoes. And there were those young soldiers already looking at the little breasts and at the red-black hair moving unevenly across her shoulder blades. What would they think when they saw the girl walking at a slant, wearing them? Surely they wouldn't want to touch those pitiful small legs and thighs or cup their big hands over the bulges of her breasts.

Someone must have given them to her. The meatloaf friend.

Donna could not count money and she was shy with sales clerks, holding her handful of pennies too close to her own body and waiting for the clerks to reach over and count out what they needed from the moist palm. Donna's schoolteacher, Miss Fiedler, had herself told Sullie that Donna couldn't count money. She had visited their place and all the while Miss Fiedler spoke, her blue eyes darted around the room, never resting on Sullie, who believed the woman was looking for bugs and dust. Those cornflower blue eyes looking at the nailholes in the bare walls, at Donna's drawings taped on the kitchen wall next to the window, at the quilt with its needlework pictures of Sullie and her own mother standing surrounded by a field of green corn with a red turtle floating in the sky like a great sun and a yellow frog and curled scorpion in each corner.

"What's that?" Miss Fiedler pointed at the turtle and the scorpion. "Oh, a red turtle. It looks like it's swimming."

"The sky turtle. From an old story my father used to tell."

Miss Fiedler kept her feet square on the floor and her knees together. Sullie was aware of her own green blouse. It was ironed but growing thin beneath the arms. Sullie remembered to lean forward as she had seen other women do, to look at the teacher's face and occasionally at the pale yellow sweater and its softness and at the blonde curled hair. The teacher sat like a gold light in the center of the sofa that day, like a madonna in a church surrounded by a quilt of stained glass pictures.

Finally Miss Fiedler looked right at Sullie. "I was passing by and thought I might as well stop in. I thought it would be better than a letter."

"Oh?"

"Donna isn't ready to go on to seventh grade. It's out of the question. She doesn't even count money." She added, "She doesn't get along with the other girls."

And in a long silence following the words, the room brightened as the red turtle sun came out from behind a cloud. The teacher's hair lit up like brass. She expected Sullie to say something. Sullie watched the woman's face brighten. Then she said to the teacher, "She's good at art though, don't you think?" And Sullie went over to open the drawer and remove the collection of pictures she kept there. "See here? This is Lucy Vine. It looks just like her." And there was old Lucy wearing some plants in a sling of cloth on her back. She was bent, nearly white-headed, leaning over a fire. Behind her was a metal tub for washing and some men's shirts hanging along a fence like scarecrows and a raven flying overhead, its blue-black wings spread wide.

"Nice. That is nice."

Sullie looked up at the teacher and repeated, "She's good at art," and the teacher looked back at Sullie and said nothing.

Even remembering this Sullie felt ashamed and her face grew warm. She removed her apron and hung it on the doorknob that was heavy and crystal. The color of larva, with light pouring through it. Sullie lifted the apron and looked again at the doorknob, the room reflected in it a hun-

dred times, herself standing upside down and looking at the tiny replicas
of the motel apartment. She left it uncovered. She put the apron over the
back of the kitchen chair. The door knob was the nicest thing in the room
besides the quilt and Donna's pictures. The pictures were lovely. There
was one Donna had sketched of Sullie from the back, her shoulders soft
and round-looking, the hair unkempt, the heavy face just visible in pro-
file. And there was a picture of women dancing in a row. They wore
gathered skirts over their heavy hips, dresses with sewn patterns, the Dia-
mondback design, the Trail of Tears, the Hand of God. They were joined
hand to elbow. Their white aprons were tied in neat bows at the back.
"Funny dresses," Donna commented when she completed the picture.

Pretty as a picture postcard, Mrs. Meers was standing at the door with
her arms folded, the red and gold streamers flying behind her in the car
lot. There were flags on the antennae of a used Chevy that said $250 in
white soap on the windshield. Mrs. Meers, the manager, fidgeted with
her hair, one arm still crossed in front of her stomach. Sullie opened the
door.

"You got a phone call from the motel. They say you're mighty late
coming in today."

"The Pines? I'm not going in." Sullie didn't look surprised at the
message.

"You don't look sick to me." Mrs. Meers dropped both hands to her
hips. They were slim in white pants.

"I didn't say I was sick. Just tell them I'll be there tomorrow."

Mrs. Meers looked more seriously at Sullie. Like a doctor might do
when he discovered you were not just entertaining yourself by sitting in
his examining room. She squinted and sucked in her cheeks. "I don't
mean to step into your business, but to tell the truth I'm not good at
lying. You tell them. And tell them to quit calling me. Tell them you'll get
your own phone."

Sullie shrugged. "It's not lying." Only the hint of a shrug, so slight that
Mrs. Meers did not notice. And she continued talking more softly now.
"What's so important that you can't go in? What's worth losing your job
over?"

"Look there!" Sullie was pointing toward the street. "Look there. Is
that your little cat?"

Mrs. Meers looked impatient. "You know I don't keep cats."

"It'll get run down."

Mrs. Meers tucked in her red shirt. "Look, I know I ain't supposed to
be looking out for you tenants."

"Shows through," Sullie said.

"What?"

"Your shirt. It shows through your pants."

The landlady waved her hand in exasperation. "Listen to that. You worry about my shirt."

Sullie half-listened. She nodded. She was still watching the kitten stumble away from the wheels of one car and toward another.

"Okay. Okay, I'll tell them." Mrs. Meers went off grumbling, saying how was it these people could buy fancy black shoes like those there on the table and not ever go to work. Must be government dole or something. She herself could not afford shoes like those and she was running this place. She waved her arm as if to clear her mind, to get rid of Sullie and that sneaky quiet kid of hers. Deserved to lose her job, she mumbled. And all the while Sullie was out there in the street calling to the kitten, a scrawny little cat with greasy fur. "No pets!" Mrs Meers yelled at Sullie. "No pets allowed. We don't even let goldfish in."

After the cat coiled up on the sofa, Sullie washed her hands and returned her attention to the shoes. If they were stolen, they would have to be taken back. That would be the right thing to do, to hand the shoes to the sales clerk. She might be one of those older, efficient types who wore maroon suits and shirts that tied in bows at the neck. Pearl earrings. Or one of the tall ones in the thin dresses. If she were a young clerk, she would be nervous and call the manager. The managers were tight about the rules. They stuck with the rules. They might call in the police.

Sullie had never stolen anything. Just the thought of it sent her heart racing and made her knees weak. She had no courage against teachers, clerks, police, managers, and even now the fear came flying into her.

She put the shoes back where she found them.

It was a quiet day. Early afternoons were quiet. The traffic died down. The red and gold streamers were lifeless. A good day just for walking.

Sullie stepped across the railroad ties that smelled of creosote and the penny smell of oiled metal. She went across the vacant lot filled with weeds and a few spears of green that were irises. Behind the rows of houses, there was a lake, a few elm trees. She heard the doves in the mornings from her kitchen and she was hungry to look at the water, the blue sky lying down on its surface.

Two ducks swam there. The bright-colored male was showing off. He shook himself, ruffled his feathers, and paddled his orange feet. The female ignored him, diving under water with her backside exposed. Dipping and surfacing. A plane flew over and Sullie caught its light on the water.

An old man with a cane tipped his dark hat. He wore a heavy coat as if it were still winter and he had not noticed the change of seasons, the warm sun and the green dusty leaves on the few elms. A woman sat on a swing, her two children pushing at one another. The woman stared at the ducks. Her face looked bored and vacant, the look of mothers with young children. She would have spoken to Sullie if Sullie were thinner and looked different. If Sullie had worn a pair of slacks and a flowered blouse. The woman wanted to speak to someone. She greeted the old man.

When Sullie headed back, she had to wait at the tracks for a train to pass. It was a passenger train and the faces in the windows rushed past. One small boy waved at her. The wheels clattered, metal on metal. A man and woman stood on the platform, the wind in their hair and faces. His arm around her waist. The sounds roared in Sullie's ears and the earth beneath her feet rumbled and shook and then the train grew smaller in the distance, growing lighter, and she picked her way over the tracks and through the weeds of the field, out of the heat and cement and into the fresh smell of the grocery store. Cool. The banana odor, the laundry soap fragrance. There were cartons of eggs on the rack, tan and perfectly smooth and oval, red meats with their own fleshy odor. "How much?" she asked, pointing at the ground beef. The man in the white cap gestured to the marker. Sullie ordered a pound and he scooped it out and wrapped it in white butcher paper, wrote .31 on the top with black crayon.

Sullie left the store, walking slowly, her arms full of the large bag, her face to one side of it watching for cracks and settling in the sidewalk. Carrying milk and a small bag of flour, a half dozen eggs, an apple for Donna, two potatoes. And there was a small container of cinnamon inside the bag. A gold and green shaker holding in the sweet red odor of other countries, of islands with their own slow women carrying curled brown bark in baskets. The metal box was the color of their dresses, water green and sunlight color.

Sullie would make bread pudding out of it and fill the apartment up with the odors of islands and Mexico, warmth and spice and people dancing in bright colors and with looseness in their hips, at least as far as she imagined.

When Sullie arrived, there was another smell in the apartment, the wax and perfume smell of the lipstick Donna was wearing. The rouged cheeks and red lips made her look younger, against the girl's intentions. Her big dark eyes were innocent in contrast with the crimson lips. The lipstick paled her skin. All of her facial weaknesses were revealed by the rosy cheeks and the painted lips, as if her plainness normally strengthened her, camouflaged the self-consciousness of her expression and the awkwardness of her movements, the pensive bend of her shoulders. She looked away when people spoke to her and she did not look up into Sullie's eyes now while Sullie stood, her arms full of the brown paper bag. She stood one moment before putting the groceries down on the table, and Sullie said, "So." Nothing more or less, simply, "So."

The kitten slept in the child's lap. Its paws were twitching slightly. Down in the quick of it, beneath the smell of transmission fluid, the kitten was dreaming of something pleasant. Cream, perhaps. Or of stalking brilliant green flies. Lord, Lord, Sullie breathed, what things we put in our heads. All of us. Filling ourselves up with hopes. Looking out for an extra dollar or good job. Putting on these faces. Even the cats. And here it was, the kitten, all comfortable while Mrs. Meers over there was plotting how to get rid of it. No pets. All these dreams and hopes, and nothing out there but rules and laws. Even in the churchyards. Even in the big homes, the ones that smell like paint and god-fearing Sunday dinners. Even in the motel rooms, a sign on the door saying when to move on. A bible full of do and don't. A boss clocking you in. Red lights. And there was a girl with red lips whose eyes do not meet yours and her head filled up with pretty things and men who would someday love her right out of her loneliness for a few hours. Her head filled up with pearls, silk dresses, shining hair. Even in Paris perfume in the pretty blue bottles. All those thoughts flying around in there like crows circling over something down on the road.

Sullie was quiet as she put away the groceries. She removed her shoes and walked on the gray linoleum, her feet with a soft animal sound against the floor. She struck a match against the stove. The odor of sulphur and then of gas as she held it to the little hole inside the dark oven. All at once, as the fire took, there was the sound of burning, of the box-like oven opening up. She was going to cook meatloaf. Donna, holding the kitten, stood by the table and traced the black marbled patterns with her finger. "It's a monkey."

"Does it talk?"

"It says you got fired for missing work today."

Sullie put down a fork. "Who says that?"

"The monkey says Mrs. Meers told him."

"Monkeys lie. Besides, what's he doing hanging around women with black roots in their hair?"

"Did you ever hear of television? It's new. It's like a radio, only with pictures. And they move like in a movie." She was filled with amazement and the magic of it. Her eyes darkened. "I saw one."

"How do they get the pictures?"

"They come in the air."

"Pictures? You mean they are in the air?"

"Even in here and if we could turn on a button they'd show up. Yes, they would." And Donna saw the apartment peopled with men and women, animals, new places, all around her the black and white pictures of the rest of the world.

"I'll be. They think of everything, don't they? They just sit back up there in Washington with old Eisenhower and they think of everything." Sullie rubbed on the soap bar while she spoke and the bubbles foamed up in the dishwater. She smiled down at Donna. She dried her hands. "Sit there. Stay there." She went over to the couch. "Don't move." Donna remained at the table while her mother bent and reached underneath the couch for the shoes. Donna's hands tightened.

"Child," Sullie said, standing up. "I don't know where they come from but they are about your size." .

Donna was still. The light from the ceiling was on her hair and behind her, the small lamp burned an outline about her, like a small fire, like a burning match. Her delicate face was soft-looking even with the red lips.

"I found these. Here, put them on."

Donna stood and balanced herself by holding on to Sullie and then to the chair back. She put one small foot inside a shoe and then the other. She stood taller and thinner than before. She looked frail. The leg muscles tightened. She wobbled.

Sullie went to the wardrobe cabinet and opened the door to reveal the picture inside. "Look," she said and she was almost breathless. "Look. You're pretty."

Donna looked herself up and down. She looked into the depths of the mirror for the moving pictures of men who were flying through ordinary air, for the women selling Halo shampoo on the television. She heard their voices. She looked at the black patent leather shoes. She lifted one foot and polished the shoe against the back of her leg. She stood, turning herself in front of the mirror. Her skin looked moist, childlike in its warmth and lack of pores.

Sullie stood, her bare feet quiet, rocking a little, swaying in place. Donna could see her mother in the back of the mirror behind her, a dark woman, plain and dark and standing way back in the distance with her hair tied, her feet bare, a heaviness in the way she stood there in that air, that very air all the perfect white kitchens floated through, all the starched blonde women drifted into like ghosts. Sullie moved more fully into the mirror, her darkness like a lovely shadow beside the pale girl, her hand on the girl's narrow shoulder. "Pretty," she said, "You sure look pretty."

Wendy Rose

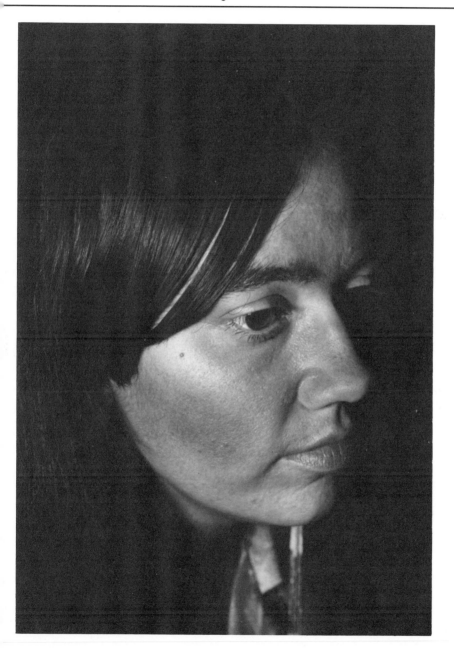

To some few Hopi ancestors

No longer the drifting
and falling of wind
your songs have changed;
they have become
thin willow whispers
that take us by the ankle
and tangle us up
with red mesa stone,
that keep us turned
to the round sky,
that follow us down
to Winslow, to Sherman,
to Oakland, to all the spokes
that have left earth's middle.
You have engraved yourself
with holy signs, encased yourself
in pumice, hammered on my bones
till you could no longer hear
the howl of the missions
slipping screams through
your silence, dropping dreams
from your wings.
             Is this why
             you made me
             sing and weep
             for you?

Like butterflies
made to grow another way
this woman is chiseled
on the face of your world.
The badger-claw of her father
shows slightly in the stone
burrowed from her sight,
facing west from home.

Walking on the prayerstick

When we go to the fields
we always sing; we walk
each of us at different times
on the world held
like a feathered and fetished prayerstick.
We map our lives this way: trace our lineage
by the corn, find our words in the flute,
touch the shapes that feed us with dry seed.
We grow as shrines grow from human belief;
we sing a penetration through our pottery bodies.
Nothing is old
about us yet;
we are
still waiting.

> Imagine you float
> to those white scar marks
> on the granite where water
> drains breaking open the rocks
> below, turning to ice
> and raining on in.
> This is where
> we first learned to sing
> on ancient mornings
> because our skin was
> red sand, because our eyes
> floated in flashflood water,
> because our pain was made
> of burdens bound in cornhusk,
> because our joy flowed
> over the land,
> because touching ourselves
> we touched everything.

The well-intentioned question

Here you are
asking me again
what is my Indian name

and this was the time
I promised myself
I'd tell the truth

and stand hard
and smooth
as madrone,

tight as mesquite
answering you.
My Indian name soars

in pinyon-wood flutes,
stopped at one end
by asphalt; my Indian name

catapults
like condors gliding inland
on the power of prayer;

my Indian name bumps
on the backs
of obsidian-hard women

sighting me with eyes
Coyote gave them;
my Indian name howls

around the black hats
of fullblood men
on Friday-night search

for fairness or failing that
for fullness;
my Indian name listens

for footsteps
stopping short of my door
then leaving forever.

Long division: A tribal history

Our skin loosely lies
across grass borders;
stones loading up
are loaded down with placement sticks,
a great tearing
and appearance of holes.
We are bought and divided
into clay pots; we die
on granite scaffolding
on the shape of the Sierras
and lie down with lips open
thrusting songs on the world.
Who are we and do we
still live? The doctor,
asleep, says no.
So outside of eternity
we struggle until our blood
has spread off our bodies
and frayed the sunset edges.
It's our blood that gives you
those southwestern skies.
Year after year we give,
harpooned with hope, only to fall
bouncing through the canyons,
our songs decreasing
with distance.
I suckle coyotes
and grieve.

Protecting the burial grounds

Womb-stolen woman, round woman:
the sad earth-stained leaves
that swallow your buckeye burden
are sterile in grinding-hole bedrock,
waylaid into deep-sea galaxy of obsidian.

Ohlone Woman, Costanoan Woman:
with saltwater I see you
cupping the coast live oak,
waking up the saproot shoots
to line your chin
with tattooed puberty,
a woman's badge
that from village to village
shadows your soul
with a thirst for names.

Abalone woman, obsidian woman:
it's you that's spawned
by grasshopper hands.
I am fat and honored
before you.

I expected my skin and my blood to ripen

When the blizzard subsided four days
later [after the Wounded Knee
Massacre], a burial party was sent to
Wounded Knee. A long trench was dug.
Many of the bodies were stripped by
whites who went out in order to get the
Ghost Shirts and other accoutrements
the Indians wore . . . the frozen bodies
were thrown into the trench stiff and
naked . . . only a handful of items
remain in private hands . . . exposure
to snow has stiffened the leggings and
moccasins, and all the objects show the
effects of age and long use . . . [Items
are pictured for sale that were gathered
at the site of the massacre:] Moccasins
at $140, hide scraper at $350, buckskin
shirt at $1200, woman's leggings at
$275, bone breastplate, at $1000.
—KENNETH CANFIELD, 1977 Plains
Indian Art Auction Catalog

I expected my skin
and my blood to ripen
not be ripped from my bones;
like fallen fruit
I am peeled, tasted, discarded.
My seeds open
and have no future.
Now there has been no past.
My own body gave up the beads,
my own hands gave the babies away
to be strung on bayonets,
to be counted one by one
like rosary-stones and then
tossed to the side of life
as if the pain of their birthing
had never been.
My feet were frozen to the leather,
pried apart, left behind—bits of flesh
on the moccasins, bits of paper deerhide
on the bones. My back was stripped of its cover,
its quilling intact; it was torn,
was taken away. My leggings were taken
like in a rape and shriveled
to the size of stick figures
like they had never felt the push
of my strong woman's body
walking in the hills.
It was my own baby
whose cradleboard I held—
would've put her in my mouth like a snake
if I could, would've turned her
into a bush or rock if there'd been magic enough
to work such changes. Not enough magic
to stop the bullets, not enough magic
to stop the scientists, not enough magic
to stop the money. Now our ghosts dance
a new dance, pushing from their hearts
a new song.

Three Thousand Dollar Death Song

Nineteen American Indian Skeletons
from Nevada . . . valued at $3000 . . .
—Museum invoice, 1975

Is it in cold hard cash? the kind
that dusts the insides of mens' pockets
lying silver-polished surface along the cloth.
Or in bills? papering the wallets of they
who thread the night with dark words. Or
checks? paper promises weighing the same
as words spoken once on the other side
of the grown grass and dammed rivers
of history. However it goes, it goes
Through my body it goes
assessing each nerve, running its edges
along my arteries, planning ahead
for whose hands will rip me
into pieces of dusty red paper,
whose hands will smooth or smatter me
into traces of rubble. Invoiced now,
it's official how our bones are valued
that stretch out pointing to sunrise
or are flexed into one last foetal bend,
that are removed and tossed about,
catalogued, numbered with black ink
on newly-white foreheads.
As we were formed to the white soldier's voice,
so we explode under white students' hands.
Death is a long trail of days
in our fleshless prison.

From this distant point we watch our bones
auctioned with our careful beadwork.
our quilled medicine bundles, even the bridles
of our shot-down horses. You: who have
priced us, you who have removed us: at what cost?
What price the pits where our bones share
a single bit of memory, how one century
turns our dead into specimens, our history
into dust, our survivors into clowns.

Our memory might be catching, you know;
picture the mortars, the arrowheads, the labrets
shaking off their labels like bears
suddenly awake to find the seasons have ended
while they slept. Watch them touch each other,
measure reality, march out the museum door!
Watch as they lift their faces
and smell about for us; watch our bones rise
to meet them and mount the horses once again!
The cost, then, will be paid
for our sweetgrass-smelling having-been
in clam shell beads and steatite,
dentalia and woodpecker scalp, turquoise
and copper, blood and oil, coal
and uranium, children, a universe
of stolen things.

Chasing the paper-shamans

Here I go drawing pictures again.
I illustrate a different world
as I chase the shamans who watch each day
to soak up the forming-eyes they had left
to be tended by me and be chased
onto paper. As I flatten them
their blood coagulates into legends of moss.
stories that split open in the shining stones
and the white peeled tamarack bark.

Within my skin Grandmother goes on laughing
and her eyes turn into distant black moons.
Her cells, handed down as surely as songs,
weave shapes as if tracing arroyos only to
color them with the airborne scent of sage.
I believe in them,
these hard-lined flat people
who are given life under my hand.
They are finished
as they direct the nervous spirit
on whose narrow back I ride.

Learning to understand darkness

Night has drawn its knees up
near me and settled in, singing its slow
and mysterious songs, keeping itself black.

Night must be threatened some
to shrink like that and fold itself so
into a cold ball that drops to touch earth.

I hear the dawn before I see it
and begin to understand with respect that
dark form crouching and covering itself

with the sound
of a thousand insects.

Detective work

Found the songs first
in little pieces
under a stone. Took all my strength
to gently roll the stone
and prod them out

but behind the yellow piss-pine
crouched the trickster, waiting
to put a mountain there.

For Mabel: Pomo basketmaster and doctor

Medicine song
moves air
into filaments
of skin; lets us
believe
we felt the storm

push our hands
into the redbud.
Grasses weep
upward into clouds,
grey and black
like tiny feathers,
tan and red
like baskets.
In monotone daylight
is the sound
　the sound
　　of healing bone.

The man who dreamt he was turquoise

From a dream by Arthur Murata

I know the man
who was the form
of turquoise lifted
into air and the man
who knew the artist's
feel, hands that rub
shapes into the form
and surround, search
and find. I know
the man who dreamt
he was turquoise,
laid in matrix,
waiting, following
the artist, finding
the form, chiseling
the night, loving him,
holding him, feeling
of him the red fingers,
peeling of him
along shell and
layers of loam
and the pressing
pounds. I know the man

who was held and
who felt the peeling
away. I know the man
who lay in the mountain
till the artist
was born who would
chip and fit, who
would hold, who would
set the form into
sandcast silver, who
would wear the form
in proud dreams.
I know the man
who believed in the man
who would love the form,
who would direct the
forming, who would
contain the form, who
would long for the
flowing. I know the man
who knows turquoise
from inside-out,
in a wholeness, who
becomes the shape
moving through the matrix
no different from
a cradle.
I know the man
who found his years
piled up under earth
and felt the earth
shift and change
around him, who laid
with his eyes shut
waiting patiently
for the mines to be
opened. I know the man
who knows the artist
and changes his color
at will, touched
and found between
blue and brown.
I know the man

whose fingers bleed
tearing up through
earth; I know the man
who built his strength
bringing turquoise
to the sky. He told me
stones are like this:
bones wrapped in heat
and hardness, rasping
the seasons around
on a gourd and
holding the planet
in place.

The parts of a poet

for Terry Garey

Loving

the pottery goodness
of my body

> settled down on flowers
> pulling pollen in great
> handfuls; full & ready
>
> parts of me are pinned
> to earth, parts of me
> undermine song, parts
> of me spread on the water,
> parts of me form a rainbow
> bridge, parts of me follow
> the sandfish, parts of me
> are a woman who judges.

Mount Saint Helens/Loowit: An Indian woman's song
March 30, 1980

Having unbuckled themselves
from their airline seats
the passengers found each
a tiny window on the left side
of the jet and stared like voyeurs
into the bellows of her throat,
watched the convulsions shaking her
till she raged
and waved her round hands
in the sky.

Some gave up easily,
said "She looks just like
any mountain covered with snow
as winter eases
into spring." Others
closed their eyes,
and waited for supper.
I applauded,
called for an encore,
and wished to soar
around her in an honoring dance
because in her labor
she holds
the planet in place.

In five minutes
we had flown completely by,
leaving her eastern slope blackened
and eyelids fluttering
as one slowly waking.

Southeast
Mazama nods
and waits.

Poet Woman's mitosis: Dividing all the cells apart

> It is a little unfair to the Indian that we
> expect him to make a permanent
> transition from a primitive to an ultra-
> modern citizen overnight—a feat which
> took us thousands of years to
> accomplish . . .
> —J. Poncel, Tucson Indian
> School, 1950

Urban Halfbreed, burro-faced
no more nor less than the number
of remembered songs and the learning
to sing them a new way.
The Singers are of another generation;
throats ready with the bell and beat of the sky
while mine can do no more than mimic
the sound heard while my hand danced on paper
looking for the rattle of old words.
Here I am now: body and heart and soul Hopi,
details, pinpoints, tongue something else,
foreign and familiar at once
like sores that grow and burst
no matter what.

Entering the desert: Big circles running

Mojave Desert, California

Mounting the Tehachapis
where my magic is mapped
in desert pulse: Hopi-style,
I wrap the wind about my legs
and cuff my wrists in cactus flowers.
Just over the mountain, then east
through blowing sand, then a leap
over the river, and almost home.

All this is a part of my soul's fossil strata:
where the shock of English fog
tornados with the mammoth bones
in my blood.
Skin within the setting sun,
the sun itself
setting into Hopi clay;
the clay at my feet
that was a butte or mountain
or something that
approached the sky.
Using my eyes to see distance
not words in print.
The strength is of earth
not the being on earth.

Arthur and I like aliens
like space dust, like
San Francisco Bay Area beach debris.
We are unseen explorers
reaching for a morning to which
we are tied.
We'll roll to the river,
to the slope of the world's rim
where California gives up and
Arizona begins. This traveling
is the wait between dimensions;
someone
is
expecting
us.

> Earth airborne, dust
> in the wind: ourselves
> carried into the sky
> on the backs of bees
> pollinating with poems.

Builder Kachina: Home-going

Third Mesa, Hopi Reservation, Arizona

Thirty years ago
a shred of brown cotton blew
from the cottonwoods
of Hotevilla; the sky lightened
to give it a passing to the west.
I remember: one lone Hopi
made it to the sea. It was 1947
but the scars are fresh
in me. They speak in my flesh,
they rasp and shake in my bones,
they circle like buzzards
in my soul.

Must I explain why
the songs are stiff and shy?
Like this: too much voice
about me already
to shuffle in with
my tuneless noise.
California moves my pen
but Hotevilla dashes through my blood
like a great and
crazy dragonfly.

Carefully
the way we plant the corn
in single places, each place
a hole just one finger around.
We'll build your roots
that way. He said this
as badgers marked their
parallel lines on his skin,
each one a clan mark,
as Builder Kachina
hooted beside him, invisible
yet touching me all over
with his sound.
What we can't find
we'll build but
slowly,
slowly.

Epilog (to *Lost Copper*)

Drop a kernel of corn on a rock
and say a prayer. It will shoot up
proud and green, tassel out,
pull the next crop from the thunderheads
That's the Hopi way.
If the corn doesn't grow
you eat the rocks,
drink the clouds
on the distant plains.

Silko and Allen and Harjo and me:
our teeth are hard
from the rocks we eat.

Halfbreed Chronicles: Isamu

> Rocks . . . anywhere in the universe
> all you find is rocks.
> —Isamu Gilmour Noguchi,
> stonecarver/fountain-maker, when
> asked why he carves

Your American mother
swims in the rocks
          and may not return
          to make you native.
          nor pluck the stone flakes
          from your teeth.
Yet she has counted
each rock four times
and told you "These
are your faces, the feet
you will know when
you come home for summer."
          Still among her rocks, bravely
          she gives you granite organs
          to push blood and bile between you
          and your Japanese father, that fading image

who glimmers and vanishes
and looks at you only when
no one is looking at him.

Isamu: boy with brown curls,
boy wearing marble chips
instead of merit badges,
boy whose father
will not touch him
and hungrily snatched
back his name, boy left
waving his arms alone
on the outward-bound boat,
boy who from
the intolerant stillness
of the fishing village
fished for himself
a destiny, stripped
immortality from
the island marble and
into his divided world.

    Isamu, your mother loses count
    in the strokes of her orbit.
    for you launch every day
    your comets behind her.
        From moons you have stirred
        eruptions of water and canyons
        twice-circled by tomorrow;
you tell us now you are free
from the bonds of betrayal,
friend to no one, continual crossing
back and forth of the sea.

The Pueblo Women I Watched Get Down in Brooklyn

> The Hopi people are built like little
> brown bricks.
>   —1977 travel guide

Fat women full of water
rain poetry and prayers
from their navels made
of brown brick dried

in the sun, crevices filled
with pebbles, white quartz
and ochre sandstone.
They sit straight-backed
against the air, paint thunder
on the sky in minute squares.
Their feet are dancing
on the moon, pulling hornets
out hissing and scraping
to carry the honey
away in their legs.
Their eyes open
to the ache of words,
their throats catch
on song weaving webs
that cover earth
as tarantulas cover earth
bush to bush, stone
to stone, prey to prey.
They are locked into rock,
abstracted into gravel,
ground into sand.
They will be forests,
or beaches or mountains;
they will be cut
or silenced or raped.

Punk Party [They Told Me It Was Literary . . .]

Their chains are
polished,
carefully arranged.
Like monks
their heads are shaven.
The host wore tight leather pants
as hosts often do
but my southwest eyes were not prepared
to see the leather
painted silver-blue and tucked
into Brooklyn cowboy boots.

They came to pick up each other
and here I am one of three women
and with me two up-home Mohawks
one of whom knew the score.
So this is what that punk thing
is about; some of us old enough
to remember those fifties punks
who neither polished their chains
nor arranged them and who
smelled like urine.

Like any party
they barged into each other
and would have crashed
but for the metal of
their motorcycle helmets. Bikers
with helmets . . . that's not right.
With brass knuckles made of putty
they touch each other too light,
do not let the trembles and desires
go beyond the candy-flavored forcefield.
Like any party
they photograph each other but forget
to develop the film.

Julia

Julia Pastrana, 1832–60, was a singer
and dancer billed in the circus as "The
Ugliest Woman in the World" or "Lion
Lady." She was a Mexican Indian, born
with a deformed bone structure of the
face and hair growing from her entire
body. Her manager, in an attempt to
maintain control over her professional
life, married her. She believed in him
and was heard to say on the morning of
her wedding, "I know he loves me for
my own sake." When she gave birth to
her son, she saw that he had inherited
her own deformities plus some lethal
gene that killed him at the age of six

hours. In less than a week, Julia also
died. Her husband, unwilling to
abandon his financial investment, had
Julia and her infant son stuffed and
mounted in a wood and glass case. As
recently as 1975 they were exhibited at
locations in the United States and
Europe.

Tell me it was just a dream,
my husband, a clever trick
made by some tin-faced village god
or ghost-coyote pretending
to frighten me with his claim
that our marriage is made
of malice and money. Oh tell me again
how you admire my hands, how
my jasmine tea is rich and strong,
my singing sweet, my eyes so dark
you would lose yourself swimming,
man into flesh, as you mapped the pond
you would own. That was not all.
The room grew cold
as if to joke with these
warm days; the curtains blew out
and fell back against
the moon-painted sill.
I rose from my bed like a spirit
and, not a spirit at all, floated
slowly to my great glass oval
to see myself reflected
as the burnished bronze woman,
skin smooth and tender,
I know myself to be in the dark
above the confusion
of French perfumes and
I was there in the mirror
and I was not.
I had become hard
as the temple stones of Otomi,
hair grown over my ancient face
like black moss, gray
as jungle fog soaking green
the tallest tree tops.

I was frail as
the breaking dry branches
of my winter wand canyons
standing so still as if
to stand forever. Oh
such a small room—
no bigger than my elbows outstretched
and just as tall as my head.
A small room from which
to sing open the doors
with my cold graceful mouth,
my rigid lips, silences
dead as yesterday, cruel as what
the children say, cold
as the coins that glitter
in your pink fist.
And another terrifying magic
in the cold of that tall box: in my arms
or standing next to me
on a tall table by my right shoulder
a tiny doll that
looked like me . . . oh my husband
tell me again
this is only a dream
I wake from warm
and today is still today,
summer sun and quick rain;
tell me, husband, how you love me
for my self one more time.
It scares me so
to be with child
lioness
with cub.

Evening Ceremony: Dream for G.V.

We are turned to the sun
looking west, the petals
of our eyes wrinkled into slits
sidewise. We imagine antelope feet

make bashful drum beats—they
approach and spin, become fawns again
and we leap in the circle and out,
running hard to our childhood
to later emerge, dancers masked
and painted priests, women
encircling the full baskets,
grandmothers bent
under blankets and squash.
The blue smoke lays low
and chokecherries gossip;
the song rumbles up
from underground men.
Shoulder to shoulder
we are the mesa edge,
tipping into space or
tumbling through the stones,
turning to ruins
among rabbits and bones.

The man walks across
those ancient voices, peeling
one by one the masks
and the shields.
We have tightened the dust
for him to stir; his feet
flex the ground whirling
clay into mud, flesh
into water. He says "I've been tricked"
his cheeks gold with fever,
death flowering
in his bowels. "It is you"
he mumbles "who came dancing
like a mosquito to my hand.
You are the bile
of my afternoon sleep,
the convulsions of
my pale morning. You
are the wall I am forgetting
to climb, the witch
I forgot to reckon with."
And then I knew who he was,
could name every bone
in his blue-black feathers.

Look how the people
push down the sun,
pull the stars out
with their teeth.

The Indian Women are Listening: to the Nuke Devils

Your death, she said, is covered
like a bride might be covered
at a distance from her husband.
That is what the whiteman brought—
brides covered, things to hide,
and burning stones where each of us
must burn in blue Nevada canyons
words we cannot read.

I am your mother
and I tremble
            up from my blankets, shake and howl
            at you with hands outstretched in front
            to shield you or to push you ahead.
I come to take you
to the only place safe,
the only path going
to old age;
            pulling at the stakes I am angry still
            at the cross and nails, the hair they harvest
            from my hungry head. And if you push me
I will deny that you
are my daughter, you
who burst into this world
with the song of my belly,
my sisters' hands pulling;
            you who beat your arms about you
            chasing the heat futilely away.
            This is my cry, my vision,
            that you do not see me though
            like fog I rise on all sides
            about you, like rain
            I feed your corn.

I am hungry enough
to eat myself and you
for my blood runs from the river mouth,
from my bony banks flashfloods
bubble. I breathe on you again
to freeze you in one place, to catch you up
as you melt like grease and as I tumble and whirl
with arrows in my side, antelope eyes open
and wind blowing high in fir and tamarack,
I topple the machinery
that rolls in the buffalo mounds,
break from electric trees
their tops, fall completely and forever
into star dust.

The Poet Haunted

Ghosts are attacking me, crowding up from
my childhood like coyotes or priests
rosaries rattling between claws and teeth.
I want my infancy back, another chance
for things to be different, for the ghosts
to return gravebound in the summer.
In these yellow dunes stretching
like butts through galaxies of
remembered pain
are golden ages given
to the drunk and crazy
but never to the haunted or
the remembering.

Ghosts these fathers
Ghosts these children
Ghosts these clans
Ghosts these pictures
Ghosts these afternoons
Ghosts these pills
Ghosts these kittens
Ghosts these hospitals
Ghosts these fires

Ghosts these bullets
Ghosts these horses
          Captured bits of thunder
          pushing in from the Pacific
Ghost winds, sliding
          the warmth of myself through it all
          like a red unicorn weeping, fooled again
          by an ancient virgin;
Ghosts of myself fooled
Ghosts these virgins
Ghosts these brothers
Ghosts these mountains
Ghosts these buffalo
Ghosts these lovers
Ghosts these stars
          Understand now
          how ghosts are made
Ghosts these thirty years;
          I sleep, they
          stride by.
Ghosts these walkers
          I am left
          to bandage the marks
          from their incessant
          mouths
Ghost among ghosts
Ghosts left alive
Ghosts these mirrors
Ghost of my self

Naming Power

They think
I am stronger than I am.
          I would tell this like a story
          but where a story should begin
          I am left standing in the beat
          of my silences.
There has to be someone to name you.

There must be hands
to raise you sun-high, old voices
to sing you in,
> warm fingers to touch you and give
> the ancient words that bind you to
> yourself, ogres with yucca stalks
> your uncles in disguise waiting
> as you learn to walk.
There has to be someone to name you.

These words have thundered in my body
for thirty years; like amnesia this way
of being a fragment,
> unfired pottery with poster paint
> splashed on dayglo pink, banana yellow,
> to hide the crumbling cracking commonness
> of porous insides, left in the storeroom
> for a quick tourist sale (they will make
> their buck or two from me but I will never
> be among them)
There has to be someone to name you.

I will choose the tongue
for my songs. I am
a young woman still
> joining hands with the moon, a creature
> of blood and it's the singing of the blood
> that matters, the singing of songs
> to keep thunder around us, to hollow out
> the sage-spotted hills, to starve
> not for rabbit stew but
> for being remembered.
There has to be someone to name you.

Aging with the rock
of this ancient land
I give myself to the earth,
merge
> my red feet on the mesa like rust, root
> in this place with my mothers before me,
> balance end by end like a rainbow
> between the two points of my birth, dance
> into shapes that search the sky for clouds
> filled with fertile water.

Across asphalt canyons, bridging river
after river, a thirty year old woman
is waiting for her name.

Hanabi-ko [Koko]

A visitor recently stopped by to see
Koko. On greeting the 180-pound
gorilla, the visitor pointed to her and
then made a small circle with her open
hand in the air in front of her own face,
signing *You're pretty*. Koko digested
this comment for a moment and then
stroked her finger across her nose; her
reply meant *false* or *fake*.
—FRANCINE PATTERSON,
Koko's instructor in
American Sign Language, from
The Education of Koko (1981)

With her voice
she grooms me   sounds
          like falling rain, like wind
          like something I don't remember
          not quite
touch me here
and here, on the underside
of my thigh, the back of
my hand, all over
the top of my head.   I remember
          I remember the little
          sounds of suckling
          the struggle to walk,
the taste of hair flesh salt
mother   This one went away
          and this one returned.
          Is this my mother
this rain wind touch of sound?

Carol Lee Sanchez

Prologue

Message-Bringer-Woman
came I, into this dimension
this mattered reality
filtered through
many layered substance
to sing
these Rainbow songs

Two Cubero men climb down
and begin swinging 300 lb.
bags onto the truck bed.
A couple of Indian men
climb on the back to help.

> 'Bueno . . . *amigo* . . . the *Patron* says
> to tell you we weigh it *mañana* . . .
> about 10 o'clock.'
> '*Sta Bien* . . . *amigo* . . . we be there.
> 10 o'clock.

A year's work . . . measured in
several thousand lbs. of
wool . . . rolls slowly back down
a rutted dirt road to be
stored in a barn til there's
a carload full.
Then . . . it will be shipped by
rail to Woolen Mills on the
East Coast. A year's worth
of food and clothing for
one family . . .
on account . . .
at the 'Old Cubero Store.'

> '*Ga-wa-sti* . . .'
> '*Dow-wah-eh* . . .'
> 'Is that you? . . . my goodness . . .
> you're such a big girl now . . .
> how's your mama? . . . we haven't
> seen her in a long time . . .'

Deep red . . . flowered shawl. Silk fringed . . .
the special one . . . for outings. Hugged close
in winter and draped behind the shoulders
in summer . . . always hiding rich black hair.

> 'We used to keep you with us . . .
> do you remember? . . . you were so
> small and always running away
> from your mama.'

And there was always some cellophane wrapped
rock candy in the pocket of your checked
gingham apron. The checks were cross stitched
in bright colored thread and the smell of
fresh baked bread and wood smoke clung to
the edges of it.

> 'How much . . . *Hah-stu-nah-stah*?
> don't you understand Laguna?'
> 'No . . . Aunt Marie . . . only a few words . . .'
> 'Shame on you . . . you should get
> your grandma to teach you . . .'
> 'I will Aunt Marie . . . it's good
> to see you . . .'
> '*Shro-oh* . . .'
> '*Ha-ah* . . .'
> 'Well . . . we must go now . . . tell your
> folks hello for us . . . you come to
> Paguate sometimes and visit us . . .'

Tribal Chant

yo soy india
pero no soy

nacio mi abuela
on the reservation, a
Laguna Indian—but her daddy
was a Scotsman.

un gringo, tambien, un anglo y
yo soy anglo
    pero no soy

yo soy arabe
    pero no soy
nacio mi papa
en un land grant town
se llama Seboyeta
en un canyon de los
ceboletta mountains on the
east slope of mt taylor
en Nuevo Mexico
su papa
nacio en Lebanon
across an ocean
in another continent
embraced by those *gentes coloniales*
de mejico
spoke spanish, arabic and
finally english
pero sin facilidad
mi papa is a *seboyetano*
heir to the grant
raised with mexican/spanish customs
y yo soy chicana
    pero no soy

Este llanto plays in my head
weaves in and out
through the fabric
of my days.

        yo soy india
        pero no soy
        yo soy anglo
        pero no soy
        yo soy arabe
        pero no soy
        yo soy chicana
        pero no soy

The Way I Was . . .

summer nights
august hot
rio grande valley
alfalfa blooms
thick in the air . . .
belen fiestas & post war
good times—the dances
at tabot's hall after
bumping & sweating in
the *carpa* in the plaza
—*un nikle* a dance—
tres dias the *corrida*
of the day—*y linda*
mujer la cancion
everybody sang at the
drop of another nickel
in the jukebox right
next to hank's lovesick
blues & buddy gallegos
was golden gloves
that year & steve
guttierez was going
to college—pre-med
& ted montoya was
going to georgetown
& our dreams were
large & ducktails
high fashion with
pompadors and '*Chukes*'
y mi prima wanted to
change her name from
baca to baker because
she was a *guera* &
neither side would let
her in & parking
along the rio on those
sticky nights in ronnie's
convertible 'making-out'
& me or my *prima* dolly
who was really *dorotea*

would break everyone up
with our favorite *chiste*
right in the middle
of a 'french kiss':
jou don't kees me
cuzyou love me—
jou kees me cuzyou
wanna do me sometheeng.

later at the sweep shop
drinkin gallons of cherry cokes
& smoking luckies riding up
& down main street in belen
hollering out of the car
windows at the guys:
how come you kees me by
the reever, & on the strit
jou don told me hallo?
—those *fiestas*—
puro fiestas
hermanos, hermanas felices,
talk bad—talk mad—
mira como eres y jou betchu
que si . . .

mama yo quiero—
mama yo quiero
ma—ma—yo quiero a
aprender . . .

later in september—
fiestas in santa fe
pit roasting a *cabra*
in the ground *y*
tengo que buscar
una linda mujer.
we were all *linda mujers*
& all the guys were
johnny *chiarasquiados*
& i miss those
easy days of:
echa otra nikle en
en el nicalodian . . .
& affection *y costumbre*

—mira como andas mujer
por tu querer—
growing up in
qualquier pueblo
in new mexico *o tejas*
or colorado *o arizona*
y otras partes . . .
tengo sentimientos
for those long gone
days—easy—lazy—
days. *y:*

tengo que buscar
una linda mujer.

Open Dream Sequence

1.

We come to dream this reality
sus
   pended
        between the arcs of
space & time
unable as yet to measure
duration
or even the barest meaning
       of bones cracking
beneath us: with the best
possible choice in any candy store
or ice cream parlor
   always waiting
   to be chosen
      with care.

2.

he carries a whisper of dew drops
from berry bushes

with the kindest caress he can
man
    age
and replaces them with his
own tears
when they melt
        into re
            cognized
                mounds.
they will serve some future
historian: holding keepsake memorials
until then—
while; until now/still holds
the ache of his passing.

3.

my language is defunct:
deflected just this side of
mountain passes,
no clear trail ahead
only the one I hack out
           alone.
private notes mislead the many—
entice the few
to file boulders in the closet
for later talleys: added to
           the pile.

4.

i cannot show you the road
        to Damascus—
i can only tell you it is there
and begin the long wait
for you
to find it.

5.

preside over this moment
        if you will

and cradle pine boughs in
frozen breaths of winters
                laced with snow.

that image
you carved on a window pane
                did not escape
the light of yesterday's glance—

encrusted as it was/with
                tomorrow waiting.

6.

in this dream;
i grasp the symbol of your
                earthly essence

fleshy phallus
rigid muscle : pulsating :
placed between my thighs
pushing :
demand entrance into—
pushes forward
invades my warm interior
between us/a pleasure palace
                main/tained
push & shove
through release/
                of us united : the dream
changes tone
shifts planes
encloses new measures
                of being
in this sleep.

7.

i pause to reflect on spider/webs
sparrows' nests &
                apple cores :
beside this schooled memory

entertained in disconcerting jumps : like
                hop-scotch in the park—

this tense translucence
welded to the constancy of
                    a kiss

in a dream:
i did not make-up
this time.

                    Quotes from a review of a woman's
                    conference of writers on the silence of
                    marriage: 'you put your best self into it
                    you put your best self asleep, that
                    silence, like stones pressing down, the
                    way one can't share one's subjective
                    life, which is our real life, with the man
                    one lives with.'

love longs to touch the ordinary places—
momentary what-nots scattered through the years
from dresser drawer
to china closet
and way up high on the linen
closet shelf.

(she sd.: 'you put your best self
into it, you put your best self asleep')

I remember youngly doing that:
my adolescent . . . 'playing house'
a man a stranger in my bed
curled up against
the little girl in me
fighting innocence
fighting woman—
gave way to lustful boredom
lots of sex and finally none.

a dusty what-not that
late teen-age flower—
early marriage: silent stones
pressing out, now 'down'

the child was more important
than the cubicle form
of Master and Slave
we lived inside and called a home.

we danced well together: 'a handsome couple,
well matched' they sd.
and they never knew
we hated more fiercely

Yesterday

I can't go there
             where
you would have me go
             anymore.
It's an unfriendly place
people with unguarded thoughts
and released anger
             and
I feel uncomfortably un
civilized
             somehow.
Call, you will
call to remind
and remember those
lost days spent
in wine, to conjure
up nothing, to claim
             we are
whatever it is
we were then—
hoping none of us
really remembers the
absence of everything
we worked so hard
             to pretend
we didn't want.

Some of us
            are still there
pretending.
            Some of us
have gone away
            accepting.

1.

My God Garrity!
this amusement park has
gotten out of hand!
I can't stop the cannibals
from going at it—but I do
think we can slow the pace.
            mime the rhyme
            in frequent spaces
            conjure up
            the boney ash—
            the brain WILL will
            what has been
            put upon it.

Stand up I say!
and speak your moment:
this monumental effervescence
complains the gnashes in my ear.
trip easy to the vortex
hold steady in the eye
then cast the whale
from Lochinvar
window jumping clever cleavers
in my mind.
            quote by rote
            the assignation—
            some simple
            commentary
            of the hour

2.

mildew edges
bricked walks
on faces bobbing
light ahead

typewriter clacking monster
knocks up the words
swollen, fattened
on the page—
won't rot in warmer weather
crawling back
to bed the lights,
the faces molding
in the sea.

3.

Calamity Jane & Two Gun Lil
see-saw the daw
up and down the count
to ten and up again
the bloody West
is gone—the Gun
guns here guns here—

crackerjack prizes
and tin badges conduct all
the parades in the squares and
I salute you
I salute you.

4.

Come back
the morning of mourning
and count the notches on
the hanging trees swinging there
machine gun tattooed—
roses on the markers:
broken teeth and dented skull
to tell us who we are.
Headline Photographs Daily News
poignant etching count down the moon
to tell us who we are.
museums bulging fatted
for the feast
we've come to town
we're on display
come! tell us who we are!

5.

misa de los angeles
mixed meditations of the saints
litanies of language
tumble from my tongue
cantos—encanto
enchanted mysteries
misteriosos lugares
disappear into folklore
myths and theologies
come back to haunt
the dead and
here we are:
resurrecting all we were.

6.

Cayuga falls
sky blue sequin splattered
coats of arms
BIA Numbers richly
embroidered or beaded on
Tribal Crests—
Clan Symbols and Mottoes
reverently displayed
proof of lineage
AND Ancestry—
you see, it all depends on
the point you pick
to squint across, he sd.

that's where you start out,
then you just
follow it right into this adventure
and pretty soon
you can ride the valley
on that owl's hoot
and slide hollow logs uphill
all day,
like I sd.
earlier.

7.

—Grandfather's comin back
one of these days—
　　　　　　he sd.
and tears sprang to my eyes
I couldn't stop
—but in the meantime
we just have to be ordinary
trapped humans and I resent that!—

third planet from the sun
moving in
Grandfather's comin back
to check us out
see if we made it
and how
and I sd:
they don't even understand
the meaning of Coyote—

all things are only symbols.
that Eagle feather represents:
did you hear what I sd?
is a connecting point
a synapse jump
to that other place we
have forgotten about.

this place is In-between
a backwards way of going home
like Coyote playing tricks again
and hiding in the Drum.

they—understand their Jung—
and long to hold their dreams awake
but cannot see relationships of:
　　　　　　bone to feather
　　　　　　breath to wind
　　　　　　sun to spirit
　　　　　　earth to mother
　　　　　　rock to sand
Coyote laughing all the time
disappearing in the desert
to consult the Badger Twins

Old Spider Woman nodding wise—
                    These reminders
                    all around us
that Grandfather's comin back one day
to tell us another dream
to call the wind
and lift the sun
and shift the morning star
while Old Coyote laughs the moon away
and maybe—if we remember those
                    long ago dreams—
                    He'll tell us
                    Why
                    we are.

Conversations from the Nightmare

intend the impossible, he sd.
and never mind the aftermath;
the consequence of any action
will compromise you in the end.

whatever motion is begun, will
continue—planked as it were—
on the edge of anything.

of course, none of this is clear
to you—and may never be—
but any form of communication
has a way of connecting something
for somebody—somewhere.

it doesn't matter when or why.
nothing really does on the largest
scale of things proposed and
left undone.

it never matters who or what
either; the odds are always stacked,
the house wins most of the time,

the time is always now: anywhere
and a name for glory is as arbitrary
as anything else.

luck and chance belong to the same
game, he sd.—and the winner
always loses the other tournament.

this deliberate language warp
is intended to jangle.
these juxtapositions—
to recoil against your
civilized, robotized sensibilities
and you must react!
get pissed!
reactivate your gut response
and hurl a "slummer" or two—

ever watch
the quiet ripples
of moonlight
etch deep telepathic shadows
on mountain walls.
this everlasting bigness
rises out of movements
tenders time into
trinities of beginnings;
          let it slide
          let it slide slowly by.

the cross unfolds segments
of cruel ecstasies,
inquisitional
witch hunts,
hellfire sulphurs—
smoke obscured invasions
of the mind.
untrue! untrue!
those garbled interpretations;
dogmatic tyrannies left over
from another history
          let it slide
          let it slide slowly by:

be alive! or be lived.

relive—relie—
make note of lives
JOT it DOWN!
we will all be REwritten
whether we like it or not.

(The Syl La Ble Speaks En Erg y/Sound)

mort
alentity in
tertwined
fathom
less   beingun
derstood   for
everas   a
nyverb
almess
age
less   thanno
thing.
thatit   be
comesmo
tion   mov
ingdis
creet
lyon   wavesof
sound con
nect your
heart pure
lyto thisen
ergyre
leased   on
to   youfr
om   here.
movimiento,
            to move
move over to

clutch the grab
for this mass

my message stamp
infused   to   be
to want to

        into
the move of

      now
locate the place
        to fall the
verb and
        leave it there,
will it.

it will stay to
stabilize my heart
in sound   out   this sacred
tonal   phonemic
phenomenon of   speak.

we speak
in waves and wait
     to echo
     off   ourselves

each other,

       hear in mirror
fashion
reflections of
      the grab
this mass of en
       ergy moved back
     and forth re
        leased as al
ways
always
outward over

there: outside those
      mirrored echos

moved,

we speak in
     Now.

Mary TallMountain

Indian Blood

On the stage I stumbled,
my fur boot caught
on a slivered board.
Rustle on stealthy giggles.

Beendaaga' made of velvet
crusted with crystal beads
hung from brilliant tassels of wool,
wet with my sweat.

Children's faces stared.
I felt their flowing force.
Did I crouch like *goh*
in the curious quiet?

They butted to the stage,
darting questions; pointing.
                Do you live in an igloo?
                Hah! You eat blubber!

Hemmed in by ringlets of brass,
grass-pale eyes,
the fur of *daghooda-aak*
trembled.

Late in the night
I bit my hand until it was
pierced
with moons of dark
Indian blood.

The Last Wolf

the last wolf hurried toward me
through the ruined city
and I heard his baying echoes
down the steep smashed warrens

of Montgomery Street and past
the few ruby-crowned highrises
left standing
their lighted elevators useless

passing the flicking red and green
of traffic signals
baying his way eastward
in the mystery of his wild loping gait
closer the sounds in the deadly night
through clutter and rubble of quiet blocks

I heard his voice ascending the hill
and at last his low whine as he came
floor by empty floor to the room
where I sat
in my narrow bed looking west, waiting
I heard him snuffle at the door and
I watched
he trotted across the floor

he laid his long gray muzzle
on the spare white spread
and his eyes burned yellow
his small dotted eyebrows quivered

Yes, I said.
I know what they have done.

Crazy Dogholkoda

Wind from the river warm on our backs,
birds bustling blue from nowhere.
What time was it? We did not care.
In Nulato there is no time
in the summer of midnight sun.

Why are they here? These caches,
huddled in rows like sad old men,
their faces silver grey.
What do they hold that the robber hours
did not filch from them yesterday?

The logs were rich with years of salmon
kept safe since the walls were new.
Heavy snows had slanted them west.
Winter would topple them
in the end.

Niguudzaagha moved. Always he moved
like a drifting log.
"You think we should pull them down?"
His look was ebony.
I shook my head.

"Oh, sure, we got new ones.
But we keep these. This bunch I built
when I was just young."
Shrugging lazy, he shot
a jet of chew
brown to a hummock of grass.
"That one," he rumbled, "one time
we put in biggest bunch of *k'odimaaya*
anybody ever trapped.
Those ones over there. We stayed in there
that winter our *yah* burn down.
This one, *eeta bitoa'* die in here.

We sat and watched a while.
When it was time to go, he got up.
"*Onee'*," he said, face warm as the sky.
"Crazy *dogholkoda*, hah?" he growled,
looking over his shoulder.

Matmiya

for my Grandmother

I see you sitting
Implanted by roots
Coiled deep from your thighs.
Roots, flesh red, centuries pale.
Hairsprings wound tight
Through fertile earthscapes
Where each layer feeds the next
Into depths immutable.

Though you must rise, must
Move large and slow
When it is time, O my
Gnarled mother-vine, ancient
As vanished ages,
Your spirit remains
Nourished,
Nourishing me.

I see your figure wrapped in skins
Curved into a mound of earth
Holding your rich dark roots.
Matmiya,
I see you sitting.

The Ivory Dog for My Sister

oh sister
how those Nulato sled dogs howl
at sunset it

haunted me a lifetime
by river's edge they mourn
passing the hours
of summer

all day
they lie chained
bury their noses under
fluffy Malemute tail plumes
grey-blue eyes watch the People
getting ready the nets and
fishwheels

under strong skulls they
remember winter
the rushing freedom how they
leap and bark and when the
harness tangles
how the whip whistles down to nudge
their furry backs

Clem says fifty years ago he
and a half wolf husky named Moose
worked the team how
icy the air
how white
the flowing breaths
of men and dogs

the ivory dog
from Nulato a piece of my life
I thought he could tell you
about the moving of time and
what it is to wait
he's done it so long now
sister
the ivory dog is true

Now watching you in lamplight,
I see scarlet berries
Ripened,
Your sunburned fingers plucking them.
With hesitant words,
With silence,
From inmost space
I call you
Out of the clay.

It is time at last,
This dawn.
Stir. Wake. Rise.
Glide gentle between my bones,
Grasp my heart. Now
Walk beside me. Feel
How these winds move, the way
These mornings breathe.
Let me see you new
In this light.

You—
Wrapped in brown,
Myself repeated
Out of dark and different time.

Good Grease

The hunters went out with guns
at dawn.
We had no meat in the village,
no food for the tribe and the dogs.
No caribou in the caches.

All day we waited.
At last!
As darkness hung at the river
we children saw them far away.
Yes! They were carrying caribou!
We jumped and shouted!

By the fires that night
we feasted.
The old ones clucked,
sucking and smacking,
sopping the juices with sourdough bread.
The grease would warm us
when hungry winter howled.

Grease was beautiful
oozing,
dripping and running down our chins,
brown hands shining with grease.
We talk of it
when we see each other
far from home.

Remember the marrow
sweet in the bones?
We grabbed for them like candy.
Good.
Gooooood.

Good grease.

Once the Striped Quagga

Look upon my face.
Its like shall soon be gone:
Flotsam of yet another race
Jettisoned, this trace.
While time still is,
I write. Someone may hear
Below the roar of cities
My unstressed Athabaskan tones.

Hung on my wall, their faces
Framed in silver; I can see
That my twin great-nieces
Resemble me, although
Slant black eyes are subtly tamed,
Cheekbones flattened.
Their blood carries tiny banners
To reinstruct the genes.

Like Ihalmiut, Khmer, Hohokam,
Like the Hanged Man, suspended—
We pass through mortal change:
Our features subside,
Bleach, soften, dissolve . . .
Just as when film runs backward
Almost forgotten landscapes
Thread away to nothing.

Once the striped quagga lived,
And the tender hyrax
Populous as Bengal Tiger,
Princely golden cat whose destiny
Hangs in the scales with ours:
Trees, beasts,
Other life-things who will
Inescapably surrender.

Sever the flesh from my bones.
Hang them above a fireplace,
Frame the mounted head
In arctic fur
Or exotic plumage
Such as is seen only in zoos or
Left captive in rapidly dwindling
Rainforests.

Ts'eekkaayah

In the month of Beaver
I watch the night sky,
Thinking this was the time of year
We made *ts'eekkaayah*.
Memories stretch and pull around me—
Bark drying on a new canoe.

Hunters sprawl by the fire,
Outcamp-bread bubbles in grease,
Duck soup gurgles
In the old black dutch oven.
'Way off, drifting through *kk'eeyh*
Fat smells drown our mouths.

Mom calls, "*Onee!*"
Yelling we race to camp,
Tumbling brown bear cubs.
Uncle and Papa grumble at us
In gruff voices
I have heard for a lifetime.

Listen. My brothers are singing.
Bernie squeaks a high note,
Makes Billy start giggling.
They wrestle awhile.
After supper they make caribou song,
Honking on a tin harmonica.

Echoing cloud voices call
Over Nulato, over *Kkaayah*,
High over Denali, over Chugach,
Over miles of islands,
Years of dancing, mourning,
Loving, dying.

Crowfeather shadows crawl
Along thin blue edges of *tsagha*.
Great horned owl sails low,
Winter-grey wings fan the river,
Her yellow eyes blazing
Threaten bad luck *yeega'*.

We yawn into our beds
Inside a ring of sleeping dogs.

Papa says they keep away *nak'aghon*.
We snug down furry,
Billy and me, wrapped in
Dark music of spruce trees.

Miyeets flows through our spirits
From forest, flames, owl's wings.
Our breath is one
Under the high shining eye
Of *Doltol*
Walking through the sky.

Naaholooyah

Nobody's hands were quite like Mamma's. They were narrow with long thin fingers, and thumbs that bent out at the ends. The nails were scarred with nicks from the cutting of Salmon. In fish time they had rims of black, which had faded by winter till they were their usual pink-brown color. The hands acted as if they knew just what they were doing. When Mamma rested they folded, one on top of the other, and it seemed as if they were sleeping, but they were always ready to jump up. When they did, the turned-out thumbs gave them a busy air. The skin of her hands was both soft and rough. She thought about Mamma's hands coming toward her and Michael, usually holding things. It made her drowsy and comfortable.

At fish camp she had spent hours watching those hands work.

The right hand sailed clear up over the mother Salmon's big grey and pink body to her head, where it made two short strong chops with the sharp *toeeaamaas* that made Salmon's head slide away on the slippery table. From then on, how fast it moved! Every move was important. First, the two upper fins were flipped away and the lower one was sheared off low on the pearly breast over the sweeping fan of the tail. Next, Mamma's hand lifted and *toeeaamaas* drew a long red stroke that opened Salmon's belly. There in her silver lining were the perfect little jelly-red eggs. Ever so slowly, the right hand pried out the clump of eggs. Not much else was there, because Salmon ate hardly anything when she was going home with her eggs, which Mamma said were baby Salmon. Now the right hand ran *toeeaamaas* in another quick red line along the ivory-colored backbone. Both hands pressed the two halves out flat. They picked up *toeeaamaas* again and made slanting slices out from the thick inner body almost to the thin outer edges. These cuts were so fine that the skin was still all whole and was one skin, and its inside was red velvet. There was the fresh smell of new fish, the smell that Lidwynne thought she had always remembered from some dark place inside. It was a good smell and made her saliva bubble up. She thought she would like to taste a piece of that beautiful red velvet, right now.

When Mamma cut Salmon, the hands acted more careful than they ever did. It took both of them to dip Salmon into the tub of water and hoist the two halves up to hang over the drying rack. Lidwynne kept thinking now about the full racks of red king salmon, and the taste buds puckered more strongly. She could almost taste the sweet, smoky fish, the oil that was being heated out by the sun. How heavy *toeeaamaas* was, how Salmon's body pushed back at the sharp blade, but always gave and divided under it. Someday, she intended to cut Salmon herself. By the time she got to be ten, maybe even nine, Mamma would let her do it. Her hands would be big enough then, but now they were too small. Most Salmon were as big as she was. Much bigger than Michael, she thought.

He was grinning at her, with one tooth missing. It made him look wild and cockeyed. A blue sweater peeked out under his wadded and patched overalls that had once belonged to Lidwynne. "Where *eenaa*?" he asked. The wind gently rumpled his curls.

"In the house, Michael." She looked up at the window. Nobody was there. She had been upset, these days. Mamma and Daddy Clem had talked a lot, secretly. She was sleepy and lazy now because she'd lain awake so long trying to hear what they said. Mamma was very tired, too. Scary things had happened yesterday: first the soldiers fighting here in the yard, then Sister coming to see Mamma, her heavy black veil over her face that frowned. It seemed that all over the village, people were mad.

Mamma came outdoors. It was the first time since lunch that she had been out to see what was going on. Lidwynne was kneeling by *naaholooyah* now. There was a row of three, each with its little skin roof. The clay dirt had got dry, and the flaked mounds of the walls were pale brown, the color of pancakes. She pointed. "Look at *naaholooyah!*"

"*Snaa'*, you make dandy winter houses." Mamma sat down with her on the hard-packed ground.

"Maybe we go to Kaiyuh this winter and live in *naaholooyah*," Lidwynne said, excited inside at the thought. She had never been to Kaiyuh to winter camp. Sometimes Mamma and Grandpa and uncle and aunt and their children went out there to the old hunting grounds. It was supposed to be a wonderful place.

"Mmm-hmm." Mamma's face had gotten serious.

"But you said we could!" Lidwynne cried.

"I said maybe, you little dickens!" Mamma grabbed her and carried her over to the boardwalk. Michael was rolling around on it, giggling. Suddenly he tumbled off into the soft grass. Mamma gave a big laugh and picked him up so he wouldn't get scared, but he squirmed and squealed, unusually cross.

Lidwynne complained, "Why didn't you come see *naaholooyah*? I called but you didn't listen."

Mamma's lips moved against her cheek. "There's no time. Too much visiting." She yawned.

"Why do they all come here and visit?" Lidwynne frowned.

"It's just one of those times." Mamma carried them into the cabin and put them down. When she poured milk into a pan to heat, Michael wrinkled up to cry. She laid him slanty on her lap and pried open his mouth. "There's a new tooth coming," she said. Lidwynne craned her neck. "*Baghoo'*," Mamma said, showing her the new tooth poking up.

"*Baghoo'*," Lidwynne repeated. "When I was four did I have those growing too?"

"Sure, and you were cranky too, like he is right now."

"I was?"

"Oh, you're a cranky little girl." Mamma grinned into her eyes. "You're just like Grandpa. Look there."

Lidwynne stared at herself in the looking glass. She didn't think she looked at all like Grandpa. She was so short and he was so tall.

"See? Short and wide, like him. And you sure have got his temper." Mamma's dimple showed.

Michael sucked loudly at his bottle. "He's not mad any more. Look at that. He was plenty mad today, though. He bawled a lot." Lidwynne patted his warm little forehead. Now that he's four, she thought, he ought to eat regular food like I do. Not just that milk. Doctor Harry got mad when she wouldn't drink milk. She didn't like it at all. Maybe if she ever went Outside, she would get to drink real cow's milk. Now they just drank canned Carnation milk, mixed with water. Mamma and Nellie had to talk real hard to get her to drink it at all, but Michael never got tired of it. His face smoothed out now, and his eyelids kept shutting. His arms dropped back and his mouth slipped off the bottle. Mamma laid him in *ts'ibi*. "You can cover him up," she said.

Ts'ibi was a shallow pouch of heavy, well-worn canvas a yard square, hung from the ceiling by four solidly braided ropes passed through a fat gray coil spring and made into a ball-shaped knot, from which they splayed out to the corners of the frame and looped under the hard wide lip of wood over the edge of which the canvas curved up tightly; precisely spaced, the ropes wrapped around and under the lip and were nailed with the edge of the canvas to the smooth bottom. It was a sturdy smooth bowl deep enough to hold Michael safely. A nudge of the hand set the spring dancing lightly to put him to sleep; a harder one set it bouncing fast enough to awaken him without frightening him. Uncle Obal had made it. Lidwynne was going to have one too, when she had babies herself. She never missed a chance to watch Michael sleeping. Then she gently rocked him in *ts'ibi*. But she was too excited to sit still today. She pulled up the marten fur blanket and tucked it solidly around him.

Mamma sat down in her rocking chair by the window. "Hand me my thimble," she said. It was a regular thing they did, and Lidwynne gave her the thimble, which was a piece of caribou horn, shaved thin and curled to fit Mamma's thumb. Mamma threaded a needle with the papery thin *tl'aah* made of reindeer sinew she used for sewing hides. The *tl'aah* was tough, all right. Those hides were strong. Lidwynne watched her mother intently. Piles of *yoo'yoo'*, pink, silver, and blood-colored, gleamed in the fat sunbeam that dangled across the room. Those long fingers picked up a pink bead on the very end of the needle and stitched it to the piece of moosehide in her lap.

"Some day Lidwynne's going to do that." She leaned on the arm of the rocker. "That's going to be mittens," she announced. "Mittens for Lidwynne this winter."

"Yes," Mamma sighed. That thinking look was in her face again. "For Lidwynne this winter."

"What's the matter?" Lidwynne looked into Mamma's face that was bent over the beads, so bright in her brown hands.

Mamma looked at her. "*Snaa'*," she said, lingering over the word. There was something different in the tone of her voice today. "I have to take you and Michael to stay with Doctor and Nellie."

"What for?" Lidwynne thought: Again? it must be a joke.

"I'm going to be too busy to keep you this week."

"What you have to do?"

"I have to be ready if Grandpa calls me to council meeting."

Lidwynne's face brightened. She wasn't going away this time.

"Council meetings are about you and Michael."

"Why? What did we do?"

"Nellie and Doctor asked me if they could adopt you. You know that."

Oh, that crazy adoption stuff, again. "That what Grandpa was so mad about yesterday?"

"Mm-hmm."

"You mean you want to give Michael and me to them?"

Mamma looked out the window. The wind had started to blow in the grass, and the river was all rough. "Yes," she said.

Lidwynne's eyes got hot and trembly. "Why do you want to do that, Mamma?"

"Oh, *snaa'*, I don't want to." The last two words sounded heavy through her nose. But she went on talking in that funny sounding voice. "It's because I'm sick. That's the reason I have to let them keep you kids so much. They can take care of you better."

It wasn't a joke at all, then. Suddenly Lidwynne remembered Mamma coughing this summer, even when it was hot weather. And how when she laid her cheek on Mamma's chest she heard little whispers in there. She had thought before that it was just the way she breathed. Was that part of this sickness she was talking about? "They want to keep us all the time? At night and everything?"

"Yes, that's right." Mamma kept her face down looking at *yoo'yoo'*. Why won't she look at me? Lidwynne thought, putting her hands on

Mamma's face. She turned around then to look out of the window, and it felt like she'd gone a long way off.

Real fast, Lidwynne hugged her. "You love me?"

Mamma made a deep chest sound and began to cough. Lidwynne got one of her big white handkerchiefs and Mamma blew her nose. She stared into Lidwynne's eyes, and now she was back from wherever she'd gone. "Of course I love you, foolish little one. I don't want you to go away. But if you do, I know you'll have a nice life, the way Doctor and Nellie do."

"Grandpa won't let them have us."

"He hasn't got anything to say about it. He just makes sure council does everything right. They have to decide. He stays with them till they do." Mamma snipped off a little thread close to the knot she'd made in back of the mitten. She put the skins away and closed the box. Everything in the room got clear and sharp like Lidwynne's reflection in the mirror. She would never forget *yoo'yoo'* burning like fire in the sunbeam.

She flung her arms around Mamma. She wanted to hold her so hard that she couldn't get away from her, ever. "I don't want to go any place, not even with Michael. I want to stay here."

"Ah," Mamma said to herself. She nuzzled her face into Lidwynne's neck. Her breath was warm on Lidwynne's skin, and her words made puffs of damp air, tight against the little wrinkles of fat under her chin. "I want you to stay, too."

"But why do we have to leave you? Can't we just visit them like we visit Auntie Madeline?" Lidwynne moved away and stared into Mamma's huge eyes, the color of shining blackberries.

"Now, I told you I'm sick. We can't help that. It's just lucky the Merricks are here. You've already told me you like them. If you don't, why do you want to go there visiting all the time?" Mamma's words sounded like echoes of themselves in a big dark cave.

Lidwynne knew her lower lip was beginning to stick out. It was getting colder in here. It must be the wind. She kept silent.

"They're good to you. They love you, Lidwynne. Don't you see, after a while I'll get sicker." Her rough hands came up and held Lidwynne's cheeks tight, and she saw her own reflections like dark still twins in Mamma's eyes.

"You're never going to get well?" Tears jumped out of her own eyes. Mamma wiped them. Then her face was buried in Mamma's apron and the hands were on her hair, patting, patting.

"Lidwynne, remember this word. Consumption. Your mamma has consumption, and she can't get well."

"It's terrible, to hurt you," Lidwynne sobbed, throwing her arms around Mamma's legs, hugging. The hands kept patting. Mamma rocked gently, and it was quiet in the room except for the little squeak of the rocker.

"Hey, *snaa'*, remember how mad Grandpa was yesterday, jumping all around?" Mamma was shaking a little. She must be laughing. Lidwynne peeked. Mamma was all dimpled up and her eyes were squeezed shut. She hollered, "Hoh, hoh! that funny Grandpa!" Lidwynne started to think of Grandpa and how he had looked. His face was red, his eyebrows were squeezed down into a white fringe so you couldn't see his pupils, and oh how mad he was, just yelling and yelling. Pretty soon she was laughing too, and they laughed till they were so tired they couldn't laugh anymore, and they were hugging and kissing, and Mamma wiped their faces and rocked her a while. Squeak, squeak, that's all that you could hear, and the two of them there warm and cozy in the quiet place.

Suddenly Lidwynne sat straight up. "Why can't we live at the barracks with Daddy?"

"He works for Uncle Sam, and he's got to go to Fort Gibbon pretty soon because Uncle Sam needs him there."

"Oh, that Uncle Sam!" Lidwynne filled the granite dipper at the water pail. She gulped the fresh river water, trying to swallow something that seemed to have gotten stuck in her throat.

She stared out the window. The wind had grown so strong it roared around the trees, stirring them up as if it had a spoon as big as a cloud. It whined over the roof and down the stovepipe and teased the fire so it flickered fast as red devils back of the little flower-shaped vents in the firebox of the stove. Its voice was like lots of people singing, far away.

It had blown *naaholooyah* away. There were only three small brown circles left on the ground.

Judith Mountain Leaf Volborth

Vihio Images

Coyote,
pineneedles
braided into his fur
mimics Porcupine.

Almost transparent
abandoned lizard skin glows.
Fall moon fills the void.

Lunar snow bones clink,
stark maple shadows emerge
ghost forest landscape.

Self-Portrait

Crooked Old Woman
sits, composes shadows,
weaves tapestries
of dust and cobwebs,
sings to the lines
in her face.

A Time of Turquoise

for Paula

We have traveled
among Thunder—
between chaos
and creation.
From a dark wanting
we enter now into
a time of turquoise.

It is a time to drum,
a time to pray
and a time to heal.

Three sisters—
our songs will be many
as we mend our tears
with strands of light
Our pain and our visions
will become the tales of old women,
of three sisters
born from a dark void
where Thunder sleeps.

Three Songs to Mark the Night

I

On the Moon's rim
abalone horses
circling,
circling.
And here I stand
with an empty bridle.

II

On the green leaf
they are sleeping,
the beetles,
they are sleeping;
below them
a wet-nosed Coyote
about to sneeze

III

Mist-filled Moon
rising,
rising.

The odor of sea-foam
meets the fog.
And Coyote out collecting
dream chips along the shore.

Dusk Chant

I

Old Shadow Woman, old thing,
Lift your painted breasts,
Let the Spirits speak to us.
The only sound now is you
Stirring within our hearts.
Old Shadow Woman, old thing,
Lift your painted breasts.

II

"You Know," Black-Coat went on,
"Our Shepherd loves all lambs."
"Yes, but does he love Coyotes?"
"Why of course, Our Shepherd loves all,"
Black-Coat explained,
"Why Our Shepherd can even save you."
"Save me," Coyote laughed,
"Save me from what,
a flock of sheep?"

Vihio Images

I

In the buffalo's skull
the drone of fat-bellied flies
makes a lean Coyote impatient.

II

Night turned and paled,
Coyote was heard
directing the vast dome
overhead.

III

Three pausing Blackbirds
become invisible
as it begins to snow.

IV

Foaming at the mouth
growling, pausing,
the mad dog
faces the shotgun.

V

Coyote beneath the Cottonwood
watching the evening's shadows dance
to the pulsating rhythm of crickets.

VI

Confiscated twigs, straw
suspended by brown fingers:
grass isle of the crow.

VII

Enameled eyes stare
between the crevice of rock.
A rattle sounds.

VIII

The palm of Autumn
amber and red blistered leaves;
fire in the eye.

IX

Blown from bending branch,
spiders leave their strings behind;
music of the mouth-bow.

X

Old Woman bent by heavy snow,
in the weight of her breath
a Sky-Loom appears.

XI

On the lake lunar rings
flow and ebb
about the Loon's cry.

XII

Glazed, mucus yellow eyes
watch
spotted clay hands tremble in lap.
Pueblo ghost appears.

XIII

Black obsidian eyes,
crescent-moon fangs,
polished desert turquoise
parts the colored sand,
winding, winding.

XIV

Sewn inside a seal-skin boot,
an amulet of power
walrus scrotum.

XV

Bold body arched,
split fur,
froth beneath the Peacock's tongue.

Goat-Woman Dares

Into the fire
she flings the tongues
of toads,
spits at the Moon,
waits for crickets
to answer.

Corn-Woman Remembered

Beneath salt beaked birds
in sandscript we spoke.
Your delicate scent of split fur,
taut and frothy
caused me to climb
with moist tongue and eyeflesh.
The moon . . . almost touched
now festers my side.
Among flowers that enclose us
I sing now with candor,
I sing now with regret.

Beneath your sky blue eyes
in your sleeping arms (I hid),
while you still mute
on your mesa of shell.
A pause of recognition—
we become strangers to ourselves.
I cannot sever the bud
for I tremble in its strength.
In flight I grieve,
my fur matted by desire.

How Came She to Such Poppy-Breath?

On the tongue of smoke
her song ascended to the
bellysky,
curled plumed lips
about the fruited nipples
to find milk
sweeter than hummingbird's breath.

Iron-Door-Woman

Iron-Door-woman,
behind downy plumed clouds.
Crows await your eyes.

Annette Arkeketa West

Coyote Brother Song

for Geron

As if passages of stone
could turn your thoughts
to the conventional
I worry and question your wit

you are a coyote among men

I saw you once
on my way to the city
you were turning away from the road
dull yellow eyes sharp against the sun
you ran beneath a barbed-wire fence
lost in the fields

a year later
I saw you again
among your brothers

imagining the safety you shared
and laughter you felt
when your shadows touched
in the warmth of the night

far from the fist
of your mother's
flesh

Naming the Rain

within the damp wind
our fingers will sift the rain
for the breath of morning

I hear night whistle
singing through eaglebone
while braided sweetgrass
filters this antelope home

like the stone
we remain in darkness
waiting
for mountain echoes
to swell the rivers
freeing tired arms and tongue
of Wise Spirit

who sweats his sweet medicine
for you

tangled tumbleweed torso
bent like cracked nerves
tufted in dead waves of
cold

only had you not dropped
from the ceiling
I would not have smashed you
into the glitterless tile

yet there you lay
all balled up
I can only roll you under
the carpet now

Child Poem

I.

eyes like
small field mice
waken

the dawn slips
between manila
venetian blinds

we accept the day

II.

dressing and feeding
birdsongs
far from the bare trees

little one
you rise from
the ashes of
our dreams

with a voice
soft against
these rooms

making it good
to feel you
among us

Poem for My Father

for Benjamin Arkeketa

I watched you grow old
beneath your own light
and saw brightness
retire from your eyes

you look up to yourself
taking your dreams with you
in magazines with beautiful
anxious pictures

touching stone,
tree,
finding water in a rhyme

because we could not
share the same words
my uncertainty remains

like the times
I have been reminded
by the tiny print
of newspaper faces
and the proud hunger
of eyes
I will never know

Blackbird Winter

blackbirds fat with winter
you would do better in my yard
looking for stale cracker dust
and burnt toast
than you would hiding
behind the forgotten
buffalo grass
which offers only
the cold

Calumet Early Evening

Your name grows across
fields of cotton and alfalfa
against boards
which saturate voices
of ghost wind
settling over river trees

The chant of an old woman
in evening shadow
unwrapping thin black braids
calling you home
calling you home

glenpool

for jay

night approaches
we clear the misted windows
with our songs

in another room
across the fields
our sons
hold a jar full of letters
poking to find the words
they can save

beneath the sighs of darkness
we catch their warmth
and hold them

asking ourselves
to "remember the grandfathers"

we are not
alone

salt man

rain licking the
parched pavement
saturating
the menace of
my daughter's
confusion

she flees the books
laid before her
the telling of words
a teacher takes for
granted at the jr. high

and she will fail
because in our home
we speak
the color
of the
heart

Roberta Hill Whiteman

Beginning the Year at Rosebud, S.D.

No pavement chalks the plain with memories,
rows of curb crumbling to dirt each twilight.
Raw bones bend from an amber flood of gravel,
used clothing, whiskey. We walked, and a dead dog
seemed to leap from an iced shore, barks swelling her belly.
Three days I've waited, eyes frosted shut
to illusions of scrap and promising wind.

I'm untrapped here, in another place where the banister
interned my smile and glued my soul to the lion's mane,
walls nibble this new year. While cedar cradles
its medicine in ironing, I see my father's red eyes lock
thunder in the living room. Someone's brain cries in the basket,
watches steam and church bells fade. My empty hands ache
from stains and cigarette smoke. I am a renegade,
name frozen at birth, entrails layered with scorpions.

Hay fields have poisoned my ears by now.
The fourth day grows heavy and fat like an orchid.
A withered grandmother's face trickles wisdom
of buffalo wallows and graveyards marked
with clumps of sage. Here, stars are ringed
by bitter wind and silence. I know of a lodestone in the prairie,
where children are unconsoled by wishes,
where tears salt bread.

Midnight on Front Street

"Peacock colored tears and rotten oranges,"
said the fire. "You swim in salt and think
it is the sea." Thief, webs like crowns keep us
near this door. You laugh. One hundred voices answer,
"No migration." You act the warrior, wind thief,
yet watchers from shade declare your sky stormless.
By whose right do you court exhausting thunder
bound in leaves?

Whose night rocks do you drown like mossy turtles?
I shelter with claws one final whisper.
Ashes for a tired moon.

Once *Mosquito* sang in swamps
on the far moon rim. Green flanks bridged the silence
with music. A thief hidden in the clouds,
hacked his tail, a sea sound thundered,
hacked his wings, rustling trees broke,
smashed the flanks. The silent dust boiled
into mountain, forest. Birds flooded from his head.
Animals ran from mouth or ear. The legs
jumped stiffly on the grass. Shells cracked.
Each one a man. Granite. Each a nation.
The fire steams and spits. Look skyward,
my fingers curl.

The eaglebone cries. My lair mushrooms.
Seven echoes fell the walls. Across glaring fields,
light sweeps in a rush of stars. Notes burn
on an empty rise. In Wyoming,
she howled and dark plains drank up rainbows.
I rub my arms with magic stones.
Call nets down, down into mud,
hunt for other thieves. My rooms fill with frost
and snarled roots. Haze around a streetlight grows.
I must wait. In the mirror a woman
is answering sleep. Elms bend against the night.

Lines for Marking Time

Women know how to wait here.
They smell dust on wind and know you haven't come.
I've grown lean walking along dirt roads,
under a glassy sun, whispering to steps.
Twenty years I've lived on ruin. When I escaped
they buried you. All that's left is a radio
with a golden band. It smells of heat,
old baseball games, a shimmering city inside.
The front door has stopped banging and the apple tree
holds an old tire strange children swing in.

This house with broken light has lost me.
Now when the sweetgrass dries, its scent lingers
in the living room among sewing and worn-out shoes.
In your silence, I grew visions for myself, and received
a name no one could live up to. Blood rises
on hot summer wind, rose petals trickle
past rough solemn wood. Hear the distant sobbing?
An Indian who's afraid of tears. She charms her eyes
to smiling, waits for the new blue star. Answers
never come late.

Look west long enough, the moon will grow
inside you. Coyote hears her song, he'll teach you now.
Mirrors follow trails of blood and lightning.
Mother needs the strength of one like you. Let blood
dry, but seize the lightning. Hold it like your mother
rocks the trees. In your fear, watch the road, breathe deeply.
Indians know how to wait.

Star Quilt

These are notes to lightning in my bedroom.
A star forged from linen thread and patches.
Purple, yellow, red like diamond suckers, children

of the star gleam on sweaty nights. The quilt unfolds
against sheets, moving, warm clouds of Chinook.
It covers my cuts, my red birch clusters under pine.

Under it your mouth begins a legend,
and wide as the plain, I hope Wisconsin marshes
promise your caress. The candle locks

us in forest smells, your cheek tattered
by shadow. Sweetened by wings, my mothlike heart
flies nightly among geraniums.

We know of land that looks lonely,
but isn't, of beef with hides of velveteen,
of sorrow, an eddy in blood.

Star quilt, sewn from dawn light by fingers
of flint, take away those touches
meant for noisier skins,

anoint us with grass and twilight air,
so we may embrace, two bitter roots
pushing back into the dust.

Dream of Rebirth

We stand on the edge of wounds, hugging canned meat,
waiting for owls to come grind
nightsmell in our ears. Over fields,
darkness has been rumbling. Crows gather.
Our luxuries are hatred. Grief. Worn-out hands
carry the pale remains of forgotten murders.
If I could only lull or change this slow hunger,
this midnight swollen four hundred years.

Groping within us are cries yet unheard
We are born with cobwebs in our mouths
bleeding with prophecies.
Yet within this interior, a spirit kindles
moonlight glittering deep into the sea.
These seeds take root in the hush
of dusk. Songs, a thin echo, heal the salted marsh,
and yield visions untrembling in our grip.

I dreamed an absolute silence birds had fled.
The sun, a meagre hope, again was sacred.
We need to be purified by fury.
Once more eagles will restore our prayers.
We'll forget the strangeness of your pity.
Some will anoint the graves with pollen.
Some of us may wake unashamed.
Some will rise that clear morning like the swallows.

The Long Parenthesis

For my students at the Wisconsin
State Reformatory, Fall 1977

I didn't want to walk through remote control doors,
the bars, peeling paint, a fifties beige. I didn't hope to save you,
just to teach dashes, colons, the verb you need
for better days outside. My card: "Education."
The Lieutenant warned: "You smile, it's rape
and all your fault. I've filed each armed and dangerous.
Never shut the door." The scar across his left eye
burned brighter than his shirt.

I've been here before. My father wore his heart out on you cons,
Twenty-nine years of math, gum on the ass of his second suit,
he served his time. Imprisoned by an ache, he couldn't return,
kept seeing the spoon pierce his student's throat,
the death rattle fill the hall, blood dry on his palm.
The library door was open; the guards were hours away.
He kept saying one of you had drowned.
This mold for a society could make the seas decay.

You live the long parenthesis; each of you a man
who listens to the water drip, sees dust hang in each tier,
whose dash and strut and rebel glare,
ah, rebel that I am, had made you seed for anarchy
or harbingers of war. I'm glad I found you
flesh, sweat, excuses. For weeks your number dropped:
one went home, collared the next day on another warrant,
one anxious in his learning found morning in the hole.

Seven of you were left: three races in one room, four billboards
peppered with holes, six windows faced concrete.
What records can they keep of inappropriate looks?
At first you thought, "a woman." I memorized restraint.
When others peered inside, I began to shut the door.
Our classroom needed thunder, a forest lit with moths, the smell
of blooming sweet flag and faces clean of such arrogant despair.
I see you, each writing his escape:

one locked up more inside than bars will ever do;
one sharpened foreign rhetoric like an unforgiving blade;
one puffed up for flight, a comic-loving sparrow;
one craved a mean piano and almost didn't pass;

one smiled at me for weeks and must have worked in secret;
one walked in like a leopard, practiced in his moves;
one, with sleight of hand, planned to reraise himself.
I dragged those early lessons like a red ant does her sand.

Pile one wall there, a peephole here, so each can see the other,
human and alive. My passion's equally vain.
We're out of place in this tyranny of routine,
the suave American Dream where one of every six
guards the thick or dead. Scraping all at once like winter weeds,
we hassled with a future that strongarmed us back to now.
We con ourselves: just one chance to snatch a generous pitfall.
Your eyes need time to heal, and healing's hard in there.

We live by more than breath. Behind the all pervading air,
creation quickened seed, flower, fruit and pith. Love's always
changing form. A self that stays divided finds an early grave
or mirrors still more misery in parentheses again. Draw miracles
from yourself. Stumbling in the dark, I'm too vulnerable for answers,
but that delicious morning when you're free, I hope good deeds
take shape behind you, like scarves drawn from a magic hat
one after the other shimmer boldly in the wind.

Fire Dragon, Fall Near Me Again

"You're never gonna find it, Allen." The older boy sneered, stretching his long jean-clad legs over the rumpled blanket on Allen's bed. Allen threw tee shirts and underwear to one side of the banged-up maple drawer while the mirror attached to the top shivered. As he grubbed around, slamming the top drawer and yanking open another, the sun buried itself in a summer cloud. Lyle watched his brother's anxious rummaging, then rolled on his back to stare with cool conviction at the ceiling. Every now and then, Allen saw his brother's face in the mirror gleaming with a well-balanced beauty: two prominent eyes emphasized by a wide sweep of cheek, the long nose and slightly up-turned mouth, reflecting a mild, but permanent jeer. The younger boy, a scrawny seven-year-old, reached under a second pile of jeans and grabbed a nub of granite.

"I found you at last," he cried, stroking the bumpy black and white rock. He hopped past his brother to the window ledge and set it down, waiting for sunlight to catch hold and make it glitter.

"That's not gonna help." Lyle said, sliding over to the window for a peek. "You think rocks are alive? Listen, mental, another comet isn't gonna fall just because you set up a rock tower. All those tales grandpa told you are superstitions. Not little, but super. You think something's gonna happen just for you? Comets and meteors burn up. Fizst. Little cinders no bigger'n an ant. You hear me? Fizst. Fizst." With each sound, Lyle popped open both fists into Allen's weasel face. Allen knew what was next—a slam on the arm. Scooping up the rock, he plunked it in his pocket, ran down the dark hall past Lyle's bedroom and into the living room.

Following him, Lyle caught up before he reached the couch and gripped one thin arm above the elbow until the strands of muscle shifted under his pressure.

"Gimme it, fool," said Lyle.

"No. Leave me alone," shouted Allen, squirming to reach the couch. From the living room, both boys heard their mother washing dishes around the corner.

"Lyle," she called out. "You want me to call Uncle Junior again?" The dishes clanged against the sink.

"This one time I'll forget it," Lyle said as his brother swung beneath him and thudded on the floor. "I don't want to hear anymore about Fire Dragons and old stories. Some of my friends think you're too weird to be my brother."

Without a glance behind him, Lyle walked down the narrow hallway past the kitchen and out the back door. Allen got up and sat at the table. He watched his mother washing dishes and looking out the window over the sink. A small woman with large waves in her greying hair, she cared for him and Lyle, who had already gotten a head taller than she was. Last year Uncle Martin, her youngest brother, had gone to jail for a long time, they said. After that, they all moved back to Oneida. Then last winter, Dad went to Chicago to look for work. It seemed so long since he had written them. His mother slammed a pan into the drying rack and Allen said a prayer, hoping his dad would come back soon.

"Ya know what, mom? I'm gonna get something really great, something Grandpa Emory said to get for all the people."

His mother glanced back at him past the corner cupboards. "I doubt if you understand how senile Grandpa was before he died. He would have come to stay with us now, but he was eighty-six and very hard to talk to."

"I'm gonna do it like he said, and get a Fire Dragon to come save the people," Allen said, walking past her to the back door.

"Honey," answered his mother, "The only thing that's gonna save the people is hard work. Did you clean your room?" But Allen was out the door and running through the trees with the nub of granite in his pocket.

"*Onʌ·ya*," he whispered as he trudged through the trees behind the house. "Help me. I carried you from the quarry and I'm taking you to the ridge to join the others. I don't know if this will work because Green Bay is so close." He remembered how Grandpa Emory shook his head when he spoke of *kanata·ke*, as he called it in Indian. Allen needed a few plants, the right stones, and the right August night. A white stone guided the people through long periods of war, so they called themselves *One yote a·a gah*, People of the Standing Stone.

He could hear Grandpa Emory's soft lisp as the words, English and Indian, wafted on the summer wind. Allen could see the stone moving, turtle-like, through the hardwoods. Those woods weren't like they are now, Grandpa had said. Now people see three or four stubby trees and call it woods. Then the woods crowded millions of lives around the people. The stone gleamed in the middle and told the people how all the lives were related. As he walked he tried to remember the names of the plants. Bloodroot grew deep along the creek; its pale flowers snuggled in shadows and moisture. Everlasting rose up along ridges with a garland of small white flowers and stems soft as a winter sheet. What were their names? His mind swelled up with the answer. *Tewatnikwʌhtalyaks*. Now the other. He pulled out the granite and put it close to his ear, hoping to hear its soft, high-pitched voice. Maybe the lost words would come to him more easily after the Fire Dragon came.

Grateful the alarm didn't wake anyone else, Allen rose fully dressed and shoved a small mirror, a pouch of tobacco, and a rattle in his pockets. With leaves stirring above him, he loped past the playground, the community building, and elderly housing, out to the road. Moonlight rippled into each woods and along the meadows, where a startled lark cried out in dark weeds. Chirring crickets lightened his gait, while, warm and heavy with the scent of roses and mallow, the wind affirmed a cherished hunger in his lungs.

He climbed the hill and passed horses sleeping in the fields of their new white owner. What were horses and solid frame houses compared to the power of a Fire Dragon, a child of that everlasting being, *ladnʌʔalúdyéda*, He Who Bumps His Head? Ears mossy from the silence, Allen slowed for the first time to look up at sweeping bands of stars. Amazed and drained, he flapped feet downhill and felt a mystery close to insanity or love. He broke his stride in wistful pauses and rubbed the sack of tobacco with a sweaty thumb.

"I'm gonna do it like you said," he whispered to himself. "Get a charm to help my kind." He thought about the trouble such charms could cause, yet Grandpa had said we needed them as much today as ever, at least as much as cars, cash registers, and atom bombs.

Mosquitoes landed on his neck and forehead first. Teasing him in clusters, they were the remains, he told them, with long pauses between each phrase like his Grandpa, only the remains of a giant killer hacked to pieces long ago.

After he offered tobacco to the water, crossed the bridge, and began to climb the hill, something on the fringe of his senses made his neck tingle. A metallic scraping keened through the moist night air. A grizzled white and brown dog hopped over the grass, coming his way. He heard it snort in the wind behind him, its chain jingling in the grass. It followed him steadily along the ditch.

Along the ridge, the lights of the reservation were scattered blobs of red, blue, and white, while to the northeast, the glow of Green Bay lit up a few clouds and dissolved the stars. Allen loved the moonlit night, the soft colors of the trees, and the perfume of the roses. That August thirteenth, he lay in the grass and thought how Lyle had changed. It wasn't the distance of years. Secret hurts and resentments built slowly after Dad left. Lyle, whom he had once loved so fiercely and who had chased him, tickled him until he peed, now refused to share anything. Lyle had gotten lost somewhere inside the house while Dad had gotten lost somewhere in Chicago.

Not one star let go a chip of light. Perhaps he missed the meteors. He peered into the darkness toward the path in the oaks and saw the dog scratching itself twenty feet in front of him. Every now and then, its tail thrumped into the grass and its ears twisted back and forth as if to catch an echo of distant voices.

"Here boy, come on." Allen called hesitantly, wanting someone to meet with, other than the wide sky and shadowed earth. "Maybe you're a mad dog and that's why you won't come." The dog whined, wagged its fluffy tail, and skirted away. As it passed, Allen saw its intelligent eyes and heard its sniffing. Next he waded through thistles and Queen Anne's lace to reach his favorite tree, a massive burl oak growing in a meadow, gradually being overtaken by scrub.

If he were strong and believed the songs, Grandpa Emory said a Fire Dragon just might come. At first Allen thought "strong" meant physical strength, but leaning against the tree, he thought it might be closer to patience or hope. From his position, Allen saw the tower in the clearing to his right, yet in the moonlight, it often merged with grasses and changed places with red willow or hawthorn. It wasn't large. He walked toward it and sat down, rubbing the twelve stones piled in a rough pyramid with everlasting flowers sticking out around the bottom and wilted bloodroot petals, appearing like white luminescent paint, scattered across the top. He had counted on all those everlasting beings like the Fire Dragon for help. *Yowelu·tu*, the wind, the water and the rattle, the thick night and the star. He tried to remember the other plants and animals, but sorrow clutched his lungs and he felt the obstinate night wind run through the grasses nearby.

"Oh, Grandpa, I thought surely you were right, being so old." A great sob shook him and he curled around the tower, head down in the grass, drawing in his thin knees and letting the great wheel go spinning its way sunward.

A beetle darted out from under his rocks. Something landed—thwip—in the grass. A gold-green cinder went out. He sat up as fireflies dazzled the border between oak and meadow. Beginning high in the treetops, they blinked in fits and fell lower and lower among the brush and grass. He rose and tried to catch one, but they confused him. Appearing closer than he thought, then suddenly flashing above his hand, they taught him the meaning of space. He went to sit under the oak, turning his back on the tower. They can have the meadow, he thought, taking out the rattle and shaking it as he sang softly.

From the tree's shadow, he felt the edge of moonlight miss his face. Was it that dog's whine, or a tear in the moonlight that made him look up through the dark leaves? One meteor slipped from the dark, plunging into the lights near *kanata·ke*. Another meteor burst above him, careening fuller and faster toward his tree until it was snuffed out directly overhead.

He took out the mirror and focused it toward the tower behind him. He sucked in the air, hoping he wouldn't die from the Dragon's poisonous breath. He saw a zig-zag flash, like a will-o'-the-wisp, spurt along the ridge through the oaks. Fireflies? A small chameleon scampered over the rocks. From its throat, a rattling submerged the woods and brought down the stars' soft colors.

Singing like blackbirds at dawn, then again like wind in the oak, the Fire Dragon spoke to Allen's heart. It didn't look lizard-like anymore. Big as a dog with a snout, it lay on the earth, curved around the tower, its body streaming rainbows through the air. He wasn't certain how it spoke, but songs came from deep in his mind, songs he never knew before. It spoke of how it had known grandfathers before grandfathers way back in the beginning. It sang of the universe and of love. It taught him how to sense the future in the rocks. It sang of famine and disease, as it sank like lake water into the rocks of the tower to become his shadow and guide.

When he woke, his hand was thick with goose bumps. Toward the east, a trace of white tinged half the sky and the warm and brilliant stars hung suspended from webs in the deep blue. Hearing a dog's whine, Allen watched the flop-eared dog come bouncing toward him from the scrub. Frightened, he shoved his things in his pockets, straightened his numb legs, and hobbled to the tower. The dog peered through the grass as Allen sifted through the gravel remains of his tower until he found it—no larger than his palm and perfectly round—a small moon dropped earthward for him. He dropped it in his tobacco pouch and walked back up the dirt road through the trees, listening for that dog's ching, ching, ching along with the wind's familiar flutter in the grass. Meadowlarks sprang up singing in the early dawn, redwinged blackbirds called to him, "*kaskali'saks*," and every blade in meadow and field sparkled deep green, silvery with dew, as Allen headed home.

Allen spent two days caring for the rock. He straightened up his toy men, his collection of beat-up stuffed animals, and his cars. He made a cave for the rock out of a small cardboard box covered with tee shirts in his drawer. When he slept, he put it under his pillow. One afternoon he brought it down the hall, through the living room, circling through the dining room, the kitchen, and out the back door, explaining how he felt and how it was on earth.

He explained how he loved his bedroom, even if the window sill had teethmarks from a child who lived there before. He could jump on the green vinyl sofa in the living room because a spring had already shot through. The plastic-topped table had enough chairs for all of them when his Dad returned. Another day Allen left the rock in his drawer and spoke to it in his heart. He offered it his first bite of food and felt its presence like a small bellyache in his chest.

That bright afternoon he came into the living room as his mother shook out the towels and folded them. Careful not to sit on the broken spring, he said, "I did it, Mom. We've got a Fire Dragon to help us now."

"Allen," she answered, picking up another towel and snapping it in the air. "You're hanging onto something that's gone. I know Grandpa meant a great deal to you and with your father gone, I know it's hard. Now, go help your brother dig potatoes out back."

"But ma, you don't understand. I saw a fire out of the sky colored like a rainbow."

His mother smiled and ruffled his hair. "Yes, Allen, I'm sure you did. Now go on," she said, giving him a light shove toward the back door.

He slammed the back door and walked down the path toward the garden on the opposite side of the house. Grasshoppers flipped out of his way as he stomped toward Lyle, whose hair stuck up as he jumped on the pitchfork and pulled up a plant. He scooped up four potatoes and tossed them into one of the boxes at the end of the row.

"It's about time, wiener dreamer," he said. "You only took four hours to clean your room. Grab the pitchfork or pull out the potatoes from the turned-over plants."

Allen flopped down in the dirt and plowed his hands through the clods.

"Over here, thimble brain," Lyle called, pointing to a plant. "Look in here. The potatoes are bigger 'n rocks and so fun to dig up. You might find some little guy in there."

"Lyle," Allen said, shoving the cool earth up to his elbows. "Lyle, you gonna run away if Dad comes back?"

"Prob'ly."

"Lyle, I did see it. The Fire Dragon." Allen leaned toward his brother as Lyle dropped down to dig out a few more potatoes. Allen heard Lyle's breathing and caught his cynical eyes.

"It was all blue and red and green. It floated into the white rock I got hid in my dresser." Allen waved his arms, showing how it could float. "It's got the future inside, just like those rocks you crack open for fossils. I know it'll guide us now."

"I pounded it to bits this morning, Mental," Lyle said, more to the buried potato than to anyone else. Lyle glanced at his dwarf of a brother, as if getting ready to make a joke. "It didn't scream. You gotta learn or other kids'll beat that shit outa you. This is America. Magic is for babies. Nothing happens just for you. Not for anyone else either."

"But Lyle," Allen started, making fists with his hands in the dirt. Lyle continued, raising his voice. "See that dumb brown dog sniffing around the shed at Cornelius's? He's as close to a Fire Dragon as you're gonna get. Go talk to dogs. At least other kids'll think you're ok."

Allen wanted to shovel himself into the earth. He saw blood and faces flying apart from bombs. He heard a thunder in his ears he couldn't squelch as he threw potatoes, pebbles, dirt, stems, and leaves at Lyle. As he jerked off his shoes and hurled them with fury, he screamed, "We're doomed. Doomed. You don't care about anybody or anything."

Lyle covered his face as a large potato hit him above the temple. He tried to rise again, but a shoe struck his ear and he winced in pain, collapsing, his eyes narrowing into slits. As Allen saw Lyle's mouth begin to form words, Allen grabbed the pitchfork and smashed the handle against Lyle's mouth. The dog bounded toward the fighting boys. Blood dripped down Lyle's chin. He twisted and gouged at his back and buttocks, arching his back against an overturned potato plant. Allen pounded him on the ribs and hips, shrieking, "No heart. No heart. We'll all die cause of you. You threw everything away. Lakes and trees, flowers and people. We're doomed forever."

Lyle writhed on his belly, softly gasping for Allen to take something out of his back pocket. The dog yipped and pranced around them both. Allen saw the bulge and dug out the white rock. With spit in the corners of his mouth, Lyle choked to regain his breath.

"Liar," Allen said bitterly. "The Fire Dragon told me his father's coming back here. A great comet who'll make everyone hungry. He'll change the wind's direction and the earth'll wrinkle up under everything like it's all on a rug." He sighed, lowering his voice as he continued. "The fields will burn because people like you don't care about anything. The Fire Dragon inside this rock is the great comet's child. He said he'd guide us through the awful time if only we'd take care, but how can I, Lyle?" Allen's narrow face darkened. "Grandpa knew, really he did." Allen brought the rock closer to Lyle so he could see it. The dog whined at them as it lay, watching at the end of the row, its chin down in the dirt.

Allen looked up at the great expense above, the bright sun pulsing through the sky, and the shadows darkening under ash and beech trees. When the wind rose in a long purling blast, he saw a long sweep of green-yellow light curve beyond the garden, then roll, rising into blue green above him. Below him, his brother spit out his blood. It trickled down his forearm into the dirt. Between them both, nestled in Allen's palm, the round white rock sparkled with blue and green reflections from the sun, while Allen, still uncertain, tried to remember words that meant "forgive us" in his own lost tongue.

Shirley Hill Witt

Seboyeta Chapel

1.

Shy midwinter sun
Pierces clothes and souls
Better than armies
Of soldiered padres.

Never has this cult
Of Spain been more benign
On steps, in sun,
At Seboyeta.

The chapel slumbers
Dreams fitfully
Of chances lost
To chain the world.

No more in anger
She sheaths her sword
And waits her end
At Seboyeta.

2.

Old guardian dog
With soft ears folded
Limps to our sun
At Seboyeta.

Your right hand, my left
Open together
In tune, no plan
As sign to him.

The ancient code he
Reads then salaams then
Yawns, lounging out
At Seboyeta.

I smile to you.
Your dangerous face,
Yet wary, breaks
To dazzling smile.

3.

You son of monsters,
Spanish thieves,
In the morning sun
You shine like gold.

I see the affinity
Between gold and you
And blood drenched quests
For each other.

I know as well
How sad Malinche
Cringed fearful of
That cobra charm.

Then laid her head
On the armored lap
To await in sun
His sweet slaughter.

4.

Those rank days long past
When you killed me
And I slew you
At Seboyeta.

Yet today we share
Midwinter sun
With aged dog
And dormant church.

And I, Malinche,
Lay cheek to steel
And think of gold
At Seboyeta.

Punto Final

You Spaniards. You evil ones
Of the golden tongues and
Miraculous dreamweaving!

Once again a believing Malinche
Finds herself with amputated
Hands, feet, heart,—like Acoma.

You never have enough, do you?
There are always the Seven Cities
Of adventure beckoning
For you to plunder, loot and rape
Always upon the horizon
Awaiting for your deflowering.

And Malinches like me,
We always surrender, don't we?
No matter how proud we be
Always we capitulate
In the darkest night
To your cobra persuasion.

This Malinche yet stands
While the joy that had grown
Inside her bronzen body
Melts away searing her limbs
With molten streams of shame,
Of humiliation.

Someday soon I will be
Old and ugly and wear a wig
And live in a foreign hotel
Eating my meals alone.
And I too will mouth my thoughts,
No one to hear me.

It must be the daiquiri
But they all look like Navajos
And I keep dropping my bread.
I want to weep for La Vieja
Two booths away,
But I can't: she is me.

La Mujer de Valor

Ah. Well, it has been a generation since I came into this valley, this slope between two rivers, high in the mountains. And that was only a few months after Finca Taioga became a reality, although of course, he had communed here many times before, in his dreaming time.

The campesinos tend to smooth out the wrinkled places of legend for the better telling and also for their own better understanding. In this way, they discharge those questions left unanswered in their time as so much uselessness: the tale weaves better the more simply told, anyway.

And so they squint out upon verdant cascading mountains and say, "Sí, La Mujer de Valor came here to our parts even before the birth of my Pepe who is a grown man now and has his own ranchita only a little arriba de aqui," or ". . . just a chichitico time after the year we had no frijoles, after which the new president gave everyone who wished to plant new fields free seeds. It surprised us very much—not the arrival of La Mujer, no—but the frijol programa, porque the new president was like the one before, hand in pocket and pocket in hand of the Norteamericanos. What did he know of frijoles?" How came I, why came I, with whom came I, have long since been flattened out in the fabric of the recounting: all that remains is that I came.

At the end of that dry season, just as it drew to a close with the first warm rains, we climbed the mountain. Then at that time, we were the curious people from the outside, distinguishable as a group but not as individuals. "Ai, what strange people these must be to live in such chichiticas casas made of cloth set down here on the ground." They passed by or stood close up to discuss not the tents but the owners of such things.

But he was distinguishable even then, not for his own reputation but because he was the young friend of Porfirio Mora, a man much esteemed in the region. It was one link in his chain of dreams that took us up the mountain.

The infiltration of campesinos into each next valley in casual pioneering threatened the remaining retreats of the wildlife. When the family group became too large or when an especially strong new couple felt the push to colonize the next ridge over, the hiving off meant less space for the intimidated quetzals and pacas, tepezquintles and monkeys.

And although he, too, would soon tame a mountainside, there was for him the balancing deed to set aside zones where the animals would remain free of humans. Our ascent of the mountain was for this purpose: to demark the boundaries for a new national park. This would be, after convoluted paper machinations in the capital city, an area set aside as wilderness lands.

This is not to say that hunters would stay away. Indeed, they would not. But the hunters would be more the local campesinos and less the weekend killers of the high-powered rifles from the city, whose lethal works accomplished more in days than could the campesinos in years. (Ah, but even so, the campesinos dearly coveted those rifles!)

We went as far and as high as the horses could take us approaching the mountain. The trails sucked the hooves when ascending and caused the little ponies to slither down on red clay slides when descending. There was enough rain to render the trails hazardous but not bad enough for us to abandon them. In another week or two, they would be passable only for the most desperate, determined traveller. Often the horses crashed back down the slick red ribbons, tails first, finally coming to rest against a tree trunk. Then much threatening was necessary to inveigle them to attempt the climb once more. Or, on a downslope, straining legs and sharp hooves were not enough to halt the careening. More than once he spun off his horse, landing like a dancer or an acrobat, just as all control collapsed, the horse turning a slow tumble down the trail.

To ascend these mountains, one also goes down, tracing the fall lines to find the next practicable upward slope to assault. So, climbing and falling, we left our footprints on the sides of the grandfather mountain, footprints washed away seconds later by rivulets enamelling the clay.

With all the rain and water, we still reached the last pinnacle of human habitation with sore throats. A small spur of the mountain appeared like a fantasy, emerald green grass, rose bushes and hibiscus flowers in hedges surrounding a thatched choza. The spur was narrow with barely enough room for the horses to make the circuit around three sides of the house, so that they were again facing into the mountain. But even here—or perhaps it was because of being here—we needed to duck our heads lest we run into the radio aerial.

From the dark doorways female faces regarded us. It was Porfirio's sister-in-law, an Indian woman, and her daughters. Leishmaniasis had dug out great pockets of skin from the cheeks of the two girls but had since healed over, leaving a moonscape in its wake.

The men were in the milpas arriba y abajo. The "oopay" announcement—some say a last remnant of Indian culture—forewarned them of our approach. They would arrive soon to see the curious creatures brought by Porfirio.

Drizzle and streams of fog lifted the emerald spur onto a sea of cloud. Even sound was cut off: only the birds in the red blooming hibiscus hedges and our own voices filtered around this island.

But the respite was short. Now, without horses, without trails, we climbed straight up behind the little house, sometimes crab-like, hoisting our weight with handfuls of grasses and plants, hoping they would not give way. When they broke loose, we slid in churned greens and red mud until a stronger handful was caught. So intimate were the hands, eyes, glassy mud, and plants that each new stronghold had a character of its own. This was all the more accentuated when remembering the soft words of one of the daughters below; that she would not come here because there were so many serpientes.

I must tell you that hot tears of anger and frustration pushed out of my eyes again and again, and I wondered at my own madness which had brought me to this, and I wondered at the madness of Porfirio, in whom I no longer held confidence. It seemed to me any Indian could make a better trail simply by following animal paths. But he surely had some plan, else how could we be approaching the mountaintop?

Through the great strain of the climb, the dreamer never ceased being lighthearted. I became briefly angry at him for not appreciating my suffering, for not validating my bruises and cuts. Many times flashes of anger toward him would come and as rapidly fade away. He would smile. He would wink. He would reach out his hand to help me avoid a crevasse. And then I would again be alone in my struggle, the anger building, the aches mounting.

At some juncture our group split into two, unplanned. "Oopay" calls from time to time kept us in contact but seemingly no closer. The sky was no longer blue or the white of clouds to me, it was a wash of slick greens, up and ever. The singing machetes were of little use. To swing it one lost the purchase of a handhold. The machetes stayed sheathed.

Time was only lush ooze sleeking our bellies when we slid upwards, sidewards, and backwards. There was no temperature. There was only wetness. A long green wetness, shiny and streaked with red, remains as my only gauge of the time it took us to reach the pinnacle.

The sheer joy of being able to stand upright engulfed me. I have often wondered about the human penchant for equating health and well-being with standing up on two legs. Think now of some accident you may have seen: was there not an immediate attempt to help the victim stand upright to walk? It is more than it seems: it is our assertion of our species' uniqueness.

The two little groups approached each other on the flattened but thickly covered dome. When we entered a small clear area, Porfirio was already intent on cutting down two palmito trees, to carry back down lengths of heart-of-palms for eating. "Muy sabrosa," all agreed. But to carry anything at all on such a mean descent blanked out my mind, least of all tree trunks.

But the reward was there. The machete music opened up a hole in the verdant wall. Stepping through, above the clouds, above the mist, we were fused in gleaming sunshine, in an azure bowl of sky. And beyond, the Pacific Ocean lay dormant, gleaming. Even a rainbow arched from lesser mountain to vale. We were not the first to make this odyssey, but we felt we were.

Well, I will not tell you about our way back down, although I recall that it was even more difficult than the way up. This seemed inexplicable to me, but it was true. So often I knew Porfirio was lost and that any-one—maybe even I—could find a better line for descending. Maybe he was not lost. I continued to be convinced he was, more to satisfy my needs than the needs of what was really true. The hundreds of watching waiting poised serpientes no longer claimed my concern. If I should be confronted now, annoyance would be my transcending emotion. I would boot her out of my way. But even so, I had second thoughts sometimes when I reached out blindly to fortuitous fame.

He and I rode on horse the rest of the way down the mountains and foothills to the flat oil palm acres and then to the beach. Most of the way we were escorted and the news of the conquest of the nameless mountain and especially by una mujer carried along with us.

Yes, that was a generation ago, more than a generation ago. He bought the land from the hacienda owner, paying the bank back bit by bit, but ever faithfully. He was meticulous in all his dealings. He reported the cow killed by snakebite, for example; bad news the bank did not need to know about. Thousands of trees were brought in on human back, horse-back, ox cart, and then later by tractor and jeep. It was over a year later before the tractor made its way to the house just then being constructed.

The trees were the first concern, the prime reason for the Finca. He brought in many varieties though concentrating on walnut, cypress, and cedar among the wood trees, and citrus and macadamia among the other types. He went on seed-collecting expeditions and sometimes I went along with him to help. There was an old German immigrant who had come here before 1900 who let us collect eucalyptus seeds. The dreamer believed in the healing properties of eucalyptus and intended to build a sauna where its leaves, along with cedar and cypress, would heal the most city-filled lungs.

He let me plant the four royal palms below the house site and then other kinds of palms elsewhere. The pejibaye were put in later, along the roadcut.

My contribution of labor was miniscule, but even so I feel that I had a hand in the creation of Finca Taioga. Of course the name sprang from out of my heritage, meaning the place where two rivers come together. But I think the bees were my best contribution; that is, the idea for the bees and arranging for the meeting of him with the bee expert at the university. He felt about honey more or less the way he felt about eucalyptus; healers both. Where the citrus orchard was put in, the beehives were set up that second year. When they swarmed, they clung to the lemon dulce branches where Pepe could retrieve them.

Although Porfirio continued to be his sponsor and advisor, Pepe and Cecelia became the hands and hearts of the Finca. Always the dreamer would be the soul and mind, but Pepe tied all that down to earth. From Cecelia sprang a succession of babies of apparently two species: those who talked ceaselessly like herself and those who uttered few soft moth-like words like Pepe.

But I am digressing. Those first years saw the birth of his first dream-links. A giant cedar, the strongest of the forest, became the wood for the entire house. Its red trunk dove down into the creek where Porfirio saw to its being sliced into board lengths. The great cedar was blessed and new young cedars were planted around his bole to grow in his place. We began forming the pond at this time, a simple matter of piling a few more stones at the time of each bathing in the breath-catching sweet water.

The house was much larger than expected once its construction got under way. He had chosen the site before I had ever been there, but I do believe I influenced him to extend it out from the hill rather than keeping it back on the flat top. When the smoke swirled one moonlit night, it was decided that this house site must surely have been used by the Native Americans in centuries gone by. Its view enclosed the ring of mountains and arroyos, the sun came in late in the morning but stayed late in the evening. Two creeks and two rivers laced the slopes. In the late afternoon great moist clouds rolled in from the Pacific and swallows dived through them looking for their insect meals. A prismatic effect of the sun through the clouds strengthened all the hillside colors, plucking out white cows or a red roof to be seen miles distant. And then, seconds later, all was obscured in a purple mist, except that now the mountain top was visible above the advancing cloud. A thin string of trees marched along the far ridge, in token respect for the law requiring that all ridges be left uncut to combat erosion.

La Mujer de Valor visited and toiled on the Finca time after time as the years passed. I was torn between the need for preparing the campesino children for the things to come and wanting to throw myself into matters of health and disease. And so I did both, and probably neither was done well. I taught them cultural relativism rather than economics and I was a curandera, not a surgeon: I healed more with the strength of will than by sleight of hand.

He gave me a room in the house, La Casa Grande now, and though it was a few years before I could stay on without attending to outside business, I knew my room would always be there, ready for me.

The house, the orchards, the milpas grew and flourished under his strong but gentle hands, hands small but square in shape, broad for sculpting and small for painting. For these things he would do, also. Though always busy, somehow there was time enough to paint that hillside, to carve Porfirio's wrinkled face, to play the harmonica at dusk. When Grandmother Moon shone down and received her greetings, there was time enough for talk of love and beauty.

The time inexorably came when he could no longer put off taking a wife. An investment of soul and toil wants future generations to receive the fruits.

And so he went to the university to seek a wife. In truth it did not take long. He had many friends eager to help him out of one problem into another!

And so one day she came to visit. I was in the high reaches of the mountains sitting with a laboring woman when she came. I never learned how my presence in the house was explained to her. But upon my return, Cecelia washed me with torrents of words about this female visitor. In all, she must have done well, for Cecelia would be highly critical under such a circumstance. She would come to be his wife. But, much more crucial than that, she would be the mother of his children.

It was before the wedding and before I saw her for the first time that the accident occurred. Rocksadne had always been a poor trail horse. In fact, she did little that a good horse does. Coming down a steep trail after twilight in the Pacific rainy season, she slid off the trail, I on her back. In slow motion we rolled over and over together, dreamlike, and then I stopped while she churned down and down below me. I did not seem to be hurt; nothing hurt me. But I could not move. I was wedged in some tree roots which let me fall no farther. I could hear nothing of Rocksadne. I learned later that her neck had been broken. Poor sad red pony, never to bear foals and to feel the pull of firm mouths on the teats.

The night passed, long or short, I do not know. I did not feel cold or wet or hurt. Only my mind seemed alive and it was serene, without anxiety.

Some of Porfirio's children found me the next day. It took another two days to get me to the hospital in the capital.

So now you see me, what is left of me. If I could speak, we might talk of these things. I have told you all this silently in my mind, because I become alive in remembering those days of creation. And because I love you, child of the dreamer, one of his many creations, but the essential one which validates all the others. You and your sisters and brothers justify struggle and pain if you would but receive in grace this Finca Taigo, a man's dream, a woman's treasure. Without you, without the hope of you, this clearing in the mountains would never have come to be.

And now Cecelia tells you that I was once a great beauty! Ah, that

Cecelia, that talker. But all you see is the ruin of a torn face, a patch covering an empty socket, a paralyzed body. She takes good care of me, Cecelia, but more and more it is her Marianita who struggles with my bones. She, the round-faced two-year-old when the casa was built, who was born into the species of talkers.

But answer your mother's supper call, you there looking at me with such great questioning in your eyes. Only my brain can respond to you and it has no vehicle by which to carry itself. All else is dead. I so often wish all of me were dead. I cannot even stop my own existence and as long as he guides life here, I cannot expect him to let me go faster than he would abandon any other living thing, a calf, a teak seedling.

In the evenings sometimes he will bring me hot agua dulce and will talk of how things prosper or need more encouragement. Or he plays for me the Guaria Morada and the Blue Danube on the harmonica.

And then I understand why I persist in this dead body behind this ruined face: when I die, he will have lost the sole witness to a decade's dreams materialized. His children are all the reward he sought, but when he comes to me with my glass of an evening, we share a world gone by, yet alive, because there are still the two of us. A streak of light touches his beard, which I see is fast becoming silvery among the red. I can feel his smile in the dark and his hand touches my dead one.

"Well, good woman, how go our little plans, eh?" And then he tells me of the most recent events and progressions.

And I stay alive, bathed in more love than a barren woman has a right to expect, even La Mujer de Valor.

GLOSSARY

Terms defined by authors for previously published works have been incorporated, with the authors' permission, into this glossary, and these definitions, along with others supplied specifically for this work, are indicated by the author's name in parentheses. Unidentified definitions have been supplied by the editor, who takes full responsibility for any inaccuracies or misinterpretations of these often complex concepts. Obviously, this glossary cannot form a complete dictionary of materials unfamiliar to readers; it will serve, rather, as a rudimentary tool for understanding some ideas, concepts, and usages common to the authors included herein.

Adair County. One of the five traditional Cherokee county strongholds in Northeastern Oklahoma, where many people still speak Cherokee and maintain religious traditions (*see also* Stomp Dance).

Agua dulce. A sweet, mildly alcoholic drink, usually served warm. Literally, "sweet water."

AIM. The American Indian Movement, an outgrowth of various militant ethnic/nationalist movements of the mid-twentieth century (such as Black Power, the Brown Shirts, and the Farm Workers). Begun by Ponca, Navajo, Mohawk, and Sioux activists in urban centers like Minneapolis, the movement soon came to be associated with specific Sioux men like Dennis Banks, Leonard Peltier, and Russell Means and with specific events like Wounded Knee II and the take-over of the B.I.A. in Washington.

Anadarko. Site of the annual Anadarko Fair, one of the largest seasonal Indian gatherings in the country, this Southwestern Oklahoma town serves as the center for several Indian governments, the Cheyenne-Arapaho, Kiowa, and Comanche.

Anishinabe. The Anishinabishag, Ashinaabeeg, Shinnabbee (or Ojibwa and Chippewa) people who live in Canada and the Northern plains and woods of the United States. So-called Woodland people, they call themselves Anishinabe—The People, of course.

Arriba de aqui. "A little way from here."

Ata'ya. "Principal tree" or "oak" in Cherokee. (Cardiff)

Athabaskan. Peoples of the North, from a large language-family that includes Navajo. They occupy parts of the Alaskan coast and interior, having mixed heavily with Russian settlers in the nineteenth century.

Badger Twins. The equivalent of Coyote in some Southwestern Indian peoples' legends.

Baghoo'. "His teeth" in Athabaskan. (TallMountain and Jones)

Band cards. "Indian I.D.'s" or pieces of paper identifying someone as registered or enrolled in a status band in Canada—sometimes used by border Ojibwa and Mohawk groups. In the United States, Indians from federally recognized tribes carry CDIB's, Certificates of Degree of Indian Blood, or enrollment cards.

Beendaaga. "Mittens" in Athabaskan. (TallMountain and Jones)

Bélen fiestas, etc. A poem in Spanglish or Tex-Mex, as it is called on the other side of the border from New Mexico. Belen (or Bethlehem) is a New Mexican town where teenagers hung out, just after World War II, listening and dancing to such local hits as "Tres Dias" (Three days) and "Linda Mujer" (Beautiful woman) and national hits such as "put another nickle in the nickelodeon." The refrains are all from songs or popular street sayings of the day. "I want to kiss a beautiful woman" and "mama, I want to know" underline nostalgia for the goat roasts and good times of small-town life before friends separated, never to return.

Belle Starr. The famous lady cowboy-outlaw who lived in the Oklahoma territories. Married to a Cherokee from a well-known family, she and her outlaw gang often hid out in Cherokee country.

BIA. The Bureau of Indian Affairs, part of the U.S. Department of the Interior, developed out of the old War Department. It was specifically mandated to maintain the trust relationship, specified by treaties, between the United States government and federally recognized Indian tribes (that is, tribes who negotiated treaties with the government). Generally the subject of jokes and the object of ridicule by many Indian people, the Bureau remains the major agency within which the government-to-government relationships between the United States and the Tribes are maintained.

Black-Coats or Black-Robes. Catholic priests. In spite of the acceptance of Christianity by many Native people, the presence of the Black-Coats always symbolized the changes in cultures brought by the European way of life.

Black drink. *Ilex vomitoria*, or yaupon leaves, gave the Southeastern Indians their traditional daily social and ceremonial drink. Consumed only by males, it was drunk in large quantities in the eighteenth and nineteenth centuries.

Black Hills Survival Gathering. A protest staged in South Dakota in 1981 by a coalition of Indians, ranchers, and environmentalists. Taking place over a period of several weeks, the gathering's purpose was to call attention to damaging minerals development in the sacred Black Hills.

Bonnie and Clyde. Bonnie Parker and Clyde Barrow, bank outlaws of the early twentieth century. Based in Dallas, they became cult heroes, dying in a famous shoot-out with FBI men that was later memorialized in song, book, and film.

Brush arbors. Structures made of small branches with leaves, put up by many Southeastern Indian peoples for the purposes of worship, shelter, ceremony, and escape from the heat. Like the Seminole "chickee," it keeps people cool with its open sides and loosely thatched roof. Choctaws, among others, make them in the twentieth century for singing songs, often Christian hymns in Choctaw.

Builder Kachina. Wendy Rose's personal kachina (Rose). Kachinas, in their many forms and variations, are the spirits of the Hopi and Puebloan peoples, often coming to earth in semihuman form for ceremonies and represented for ceremonial purposes as carved and dressed dolls.

Bullheads. Also called sculpin, bullheads are fish common to Alaskan Pacific waters. Bottom fish with a large head and spine, they have a small body and tail. (Dauenhauer)

Calley. William Calley, the U.S. Army lieutenant who commanded troops in My Lai, Vietnam, when they participated in a massacre of Vietnamese women and children. He came to stand for the horror that was Vietnam.

Campesinos. "Mexican peasants or farmers" in Spanish.

Cantos-encanto. "Songs," usually religious, in Spanish.

Carnegie. The seat of government for the Kiowa people, located in Southwestern Oklahoma.

Cayuga. A tribe once part of the seven tribes of the Iroquois Confederacy, the so-called League of the Iroquois. Parts of the tribes were removed from their New York valley home and now form, with the removed Seneca, a confederated tribe in Oklahoma.

Chemehuevi. The Numic-speaking folk of the great Southwest desert in Arizona and California, part of the larger Paiute tribal people.

Chicharrones. Fried pork skins, called *cuchifritos* by Puertorriqueños and cracklins' by Southern whites and blacks. Crisp and greasy, they are favorite foods of Latino, Southeastern, and Southwestern peoples.

Chichitico. "Tiny or insignificant" in Spanish.

Chickasaw. One of the Southeastern tribes, part of the Five Civilized Tribes of Oklahoma, removed to Oklahoma from their Southern home. A small group now, they were once successful and well-known traders.

Chicle. Spanish for chewing gum. Sold all over the streets of Latin America by children, who rarely have other goods or other income.

Chindis. "Devils" in the Navajo language; dust devils or whirlwinds to Anglos in the Southwest.

Chinle. An outpost of the Navajo Nation in the Chuska Mountains of Arizona.

'Chota. Echota, the Cherokee spiritual homeland, one of the ten capitals of the Nation before Removal. It is representative of the Cherokee notions of independence, empire, and freedom, and was the ancient peace capital of The People. Now covered by the Tennessee-Tombigbee dam.

Choza. "Hut" or "cabin" in Spanish.

Clans. All people belong to clans, some determined through the male, others through the female, line. Usually smaller than a tribe, the clans are related by blood and by some ceremonial relationship to spirits and the natural universe. One ordinarily marries outside one's own clan, no matter what the tribe, and inter- and intra-clan relationships impose specific rules of individual behavior.

Coosaponakeesa. Mary Mathews Musgrove Bosomworth, the titular leader of a major band of Creeks in the eighteenth century, when English colonists came into the Creek territory that would become Georgia and Alabama. Controversial both in her own time and in historical recollection, she married several Englishmen, served as a broker between the Creeks and James Oglethorpe, the leader of the colonists, and fought bitterly to retain Creek lands against all odds. She is virtually a forgotten figure now.

Corn pollen. A physical expresson of prayer, used like holy water by Hopi and Puebloan peoples in ceremonial rites (Rose). It represents the spirit of corn and Corn Mother, and is spinkled on entranceways, pathways, and ceremonial objects.

Corn Woman or Corn Mother. Corn Mother gave the people life in some tribes' emergence tales. She is part of the first stories because she taught the people how to grow corn, how to domesticate it in many varieties, how to preserve life. She is the essential female symbol.

Council Tree. On the ancient Law Ground of the Eastern Cherokee in Georgia, the tree marked a rendezvous place for tribes and a place for scalp-taking. (Cardiff)

Coup counting. A Plains warrior's way of gaining battlefield honor. Instead of killing an enemy, a warrior merely rode close enough to strike him with a decorated coup stick, thus humiliating him. A practice forever removed by the prominence and necessity of rifles in Western-style battle.

Coydogs. Animals that result from the mating of coyotes and domestic or feral dogs. Unafraid of humans, they roam the hills in the Southwest and North-east, howling out in the mesas, stealing chickens from the edges of towns, and giving real coyotes a worse reputation among sheepherders, farmers, and ranchers.

Coyote. The Trickster and Transformer, the crazy one. He figures out ways to get around the rules, to defy behavioral norms. He is always around, telling lies, boasting and getting himself and everyone else in trouble. He likes women too much maybe, and he always causes trouble for them, but plenty of them outwit him. People tell many stories about him, even blaming him for things he didn't do.

Creek. One of the so-called Five Civilized Tribes of Oklahoma. First residing in what is now Georgia, the Creeks were dispossessed and removed to Indian Territory along with other tribes. They still retain many of the cultural habits (see Stomp Dance) that distinguished them in the old Indian South.

Cubero. One of the many Spanish land-grant towns in New Mexico, established by Don Cubero. It is home to Paula Gunn Allen and Carol Lee Sanchez.

Cuchillo. "Knife" in Spanish; also a mountain range in the Spanish Southwest.

Daghooda-aak. "Caribou parka" in Athabaskan. (TallMountain)

De-horning. A rare occurrence that came about only when the Iroquoian Clan Mothers or Beloved Women deposed a chief they had chosen and put in office. In such an action, they literally removed the horns of office placed on his head in the ceremony of installation. The metaphoric and symbolic meaning of de-horning may well be universally understood, but may also be left to the reader's fertile imagination.

Denali. Mount McKinley, in Athabaskan. (TallMountain)

Dentalia. Small, white horn-shaped shells commonly found in Pacific waters, used widely for jewelry and for exchange among coastal tribes.

Dine or Dineh. The People, in this case, the Athabaskan-speaking Navajo name for themselves. Most Native peoples have some name for themselves that means The People or Human Beings.

Dino and Gary Butler. Siletz Indians who were members of the American Indian Movement (*see* A.I.M.), imprisoned at Kent Institution, British Columbia, for activism in the fishing rights movements of Northwest coastal peoples. (deClue)

Dogholkoda. Winter caches, little storehouses made above ground to keep meat and other stores safe. (TallMountain and Jones)

Dog Soldiers. Members of the Dog Warrior societies of the Cheyenne; also one of the ten Cheyenne bands, though not based on kinship like the other bands. Dog warriors were particularly noted for their bravery and zeal in warring activity and were counted on for their good advice to chiefs.

Doltol. Athabaskan for "moon." (TallMountain)

Dow-wah-eh. "Fine, thank you," in response to the question "how are you?" in Laguna Keresan. (Sanchez)

Eenaa. "Mother" or "my mother." (TallMountain and Jones)

Eeta bitoa. "Grandfather" in Athabaskan. (TallMountain)

Ela. "The earth" in Cherokee. (Cardiff)

Ellsberg. Daniel Ellsberg, a psychiatrist who protested the war in Vietnam and was deemed anti-American by the president and F.B.I. He was spied on illegally by President Nixon's functionaries and later won a Supreme Court case challenging the government's right to spy on him.

Eskimo Whaling Commission. Established in the late seventies in response to political and environmentalist attacks on whaling throughout the world, the Commission lobbied successfully for a law that exempted traditional Native whaling from the restrictions laid on Japanese and Russian commercial fishermen, who were reducing whale populations and threatening Native subsistence.

Flower Mountain. A small, high mountain outside Cubero, west of Laguna. (Allen)

Forty-nine. The '49 or 'Nine, a contemporary Indian dance now done mostly by younger people, starting after midnight and continuing all night until dawn. No one really knows where the term came from, though there are various speculations, most of which trace the dance and its mixed vocable and English lyrics to Oklahoma around the turn of the century. With tunes and forms taken from Kiowa, Comanche, and Ponca war songs, the lyrics joke and tease, as in "hey, honey, I don't care if you're married, I'll love you anyway, heya hey, heya hey."

Four. The sacred number for most Native people (as opposed to three for European and Mediterranean people), though seven, nine, two, and three also have some currency. Four is the four directions, the four colors (red, black, yellow, and blue—or green), the four winds, the number of times that episodes in stories or lines in chants might be repeated.

Gallup. A New Mexico town resting on the border of New Mexico and Arizona, at the edge of the Navajo reservation. Notorious for its large number of Indian bars, derelicts, murders, accidents, and stores that charge high prices for minimal goods and services, Gallup has come to be synonymous with the deterioration of Indian life.

Ga-wa-sti. "How are you?" in Laguna Keresan. (Sanchez)

Give-away. A form of wealth redistribution practiced largely by Plains peoples, but adopted for pan-Indian purposes in the powwow by many people. The give-away is held to honor someone—in today's version it might be a returning veteran or a recent college graduate. The honoree's family gives away goods of all kinds—blankets, shawls, yard goods, beaded vests or other clothes—to friends, relations, and special guests. While it does not have the aspects of status competition associated with the Northwest Coast potlatch, the give-away honors the pan-Indian notion that truly "good" persons share what they have with others of the community.

Goh. "Rabbit" in Athabaskan. (TallMountain)

Grandfather. Grandfather Sun or just Grandpa, sometimes a distinguished and

honored older man. Although lacking the enormous religious and mythic
significance of "Grandmother," the term still evokes reverence and respect.
He too raises children, teaches them good judgment, and gives tribal people
good advice.

Grandmother. Grandmother Turtle, Grandmother Spider, or just Grandma. She
brought the people to earth and gave them the rules and knowledge they
needed to live. Indian peoples have many grandmothers, real and mythic.
Some are biological relatives, some adopted ones. Grandmothers raise children; they tell stories in the winter and teach children the skills they need for
survival. Grandmothers are the central characters in the daily and symbolic
lives of Native women—indeed, of Native people.

Grandmother Turtle. In the Iroquoian world view, the world sits on her back.
Many believe she brought the world into existence, and her representation,
quite common to many tribes, reminds people of her persistence and support.

Green Corn Ceremony. For many Southeastern peoples, the major world renewal
ceremony of the seasonal calendar. Meant to insure the fruitfulness of crops
and the people's survival.

Hah-stu-nah-stah. "How much?" in Laguna Keresan. (Sanchez)

Hilahi'yu. "Long ago" in Cherokee. (Cardiff)

Hiwassee. A river of some importance to the Eastern Cherokees in their com-
merce and travel. (Cardiff)

Hohokam. Prehistoric predecessors of the Pima and Yuman peoples of the ar-
boreal desert, who built extraordinary canals that the Salt River canals now
follow.

Hopi. Probably descended from the ancient Anasazi and Hohokam peoples of the
Southwestern desert, they have occupied Northern Arizona mesa land for
over 6,000 years. Confined to three mesas in the middle of the Navajo reservation, they remain among the most culturally conservative of Indian
peoples.

Hotevilla. One of the traditional Hopi villages located on Third Mesa.

Humma ho. The phrase Laguna people use to signal the beginning of stories, particularly so-called Culture Hero tales. It is the equivalent of "long-ago" or
"once upon a time" or "in the old days."

Ihalmiut. Eskimo for "The People." (TallMountain)

Ijajee. "Uncle" in Osage (deClue). To most Indian peoples, uncles and aunties are
important in some of the same ways as grandmothers and grandfathers.
Mother's brothers or father's brothers, depending on the kinship configura-
tions of the tribe, raise children and teach them how to live. But any respected person, in some tribes, may be called Auntie or Uncle in an implied
relationship between older and younger people or between those who have
different statuses based on their knowledge and level of respect in the kinship
group or tribe.

Iyetiko. The Mother of the Pueblo people. Her home lies in the Underworld,
reached through the shipapu, where The People used to live.

Jacklight. In the South, the will-o'-the-wisp or swamp gas, the unexpected and
haunting flash of light in the dark and deserted place. In the North woods,
the word is a verb. People jacklight deer or rabbits, flashing a blinding light
in the eyes of the hunted animal.

Kanata·ke. "Green Bay" in Oneida. (Whiteman)

Kaskali'saks. Red-winged blackbirds. The name comes from what the Oneida think the bird says. (Whiteman)

Ka-waik. The Pueblo Lake Village, or "beautiful village by the lake." (Allen)

Khmer. Traditional agricultural folk from Cambodia, who were among those hill tribes dispossessed by wars in Cambodia, Laos, and Vietnam. Many have resettled in the United States and elsewhere.

Kkaayah. Ancient Kaiyuh country, in Athabaskan. (TallMountain and Jones)

Kk'eeyh. "Birches" in Athabaskan. (TallMountain and Jones)

K'odimaaya. "Muskrat" in Athabaskan. (TallMountain)

Konce. The Osage name for the Kansas River. Of no special historical note, it is a geographical marker for the region. (deClue)

Kopistaya. The collectivity of spirits for Puebloans, the joining of spirit forces for good. (Allen)

Kushkutret. The first home of the Pueblo people, the White Village. (Allen)

Ladn?alúdyéda. Oneida for a periodic comet possibly sighted long ago and during 1833, 1868, 1898, and 1901. In the 1949 recordings of the WPA Project, Nelson Cornelius, an Oneida, spoke as if the coming of the comet had been foretold. He described it as a big flame coming from the earth, visible for an instant, and then heading west. People were not allowed out because of the comet's "strong-smelling body." It was said to have rattled as it passed and finally to have bumped into the ocean. (Whiteman)

Laguna. San José de Laguna, a pueblo. The home of some Keresan-speaking peoples, it was a distant part of the Spanish colonial empire in what became New Mexico. Composed of the central pueblo along with a number of small land-grant communities (*see* Cubero), it thrives today in South Central New Mexico.

Los hombres de las sombras. In Spanish, men of shadows, shadow men, men of sorrows.

Low-riders. Mexican-American hot-rodders of the West and Southwest, who drive cars with hydraulic lifts so that they can bounce them up and down at intersections and elsewhere on the "drag." Defiant of law and mainstream social convention, they are part of a vital ethnic youth culture.

Lugarou or loup garou. A creature that appears to humans as a wolf or wolf-like human. A wolf-man who will steal blood, body, and spirit from humans, he is the great hairy man who signals the destruction of the people to many Indians. Both Anglo-French and French-Indians of North America believe in the Lugarou.

Magama. The huge volcano in Oregon that created Crater Lake. From an airplane at 35,000 feet, Mount Saint Helens and Crater Lake can be seen at the same time. (Rose)

Maheo. The Cheyenne All-father Creator. With the Sacred Powers who give everything supernatural existence and the Sacred Persons who guard the universe, he gave the Sacred Arrows to the great Prophet of The People. Thus the Cheyenne are the "singled-out" people, Maheo's people, and they follow his sacred laws.

Making tobacco. Making or remaking tobacco is a Cherokee way of talking about a kind of magic. The People use the tobacco spirit to cast a spell, get someone to love them, or ward off something bad.

Malinche. Malinaali Tepenal or Doña Marina, the Mexican Indian woman who served as diplomat and interpreter to Hernan Cortes, the "Conqueror" or "Invader" of Mexico. She bore him a son and became the maligned symbol of her country's fall to the Spanish, in spite of evidence that she tried to lessen the negative impacts of colonization on her people.

Medicine bundles. Special collections of individual, spiritually important objects in some sort of container. Used by political and spiritual leaders as symbols of knowledge and authority or by medicine men and women in healing, these items are sacred, powerful, and private, to be opened and used by no one to whom they have not been given in proper ceremony. In recent years, they have become the objects of controversy, as Native people and museums have engaged in dispute over their acquisition and display.

Milpas arriba y abajo. "Irrigated fields here and there" in Spanish.

Misa de los ángeles. "Mass of the Angels"; also mass for the city, Los Angeles, in Spanish.

Misteriosos lugares. "Mysterious places" in Spanish.

Miwok. A group that once occupied part of the Northern California coast but was decimated by the 1849 Gold Rush. Few Miwok now live in their homeland. The branch Wendy Rose's mother descended from lived in Bear Valley, Mariposa County, thirty miles from Yosemite, but no one lives there now. (Rose)

Miyeets. Breath of life. (TallMountain and Jones)

Mohawk. Part of the Iroquois Confederacy, living in both Canada and the United States. Known to both British and American troops as some of the most formidable Indian opponents, they finally cemented their historic alliances with the British. Like other Iroquoian peoples, they divide their religious life between Christianity and the so-called Longhouse religion, and their politics between progressives and conservatives.

Monahsetah or Me-o-tzi. Said by Cheyenne women to have borne a child by George Armstrong Custer; others claim she was raped by Custer. (deClue)

Muy sabrosa. "Very tasty" in Spanish.

Naaholooyah. "Old-style underground winter house" for Alaskan Athabaskan peoples. (TallMountain and Jones)

Nak'aghon. "Wolves" in Athabaskan. (TallMountain and Jones)

Naming. Names give power to people and to those who know the names of others, animal or human. If we call spirits' names, they have to listen or come— good reason for many Indian peoples not to say a spirit's name out loud. Animals and humans may have many names and may change them according to the events or visions in their lives. Names may be mocking, given for silly or foolish behavior, but in general, they represent a kind of special power reserved for the person having the name.

Nanapush or Nanabush. The Ojibwa term for the great rabbit Trickster hero, much like Coyote to other tribes. He is the religious Culture Hero to Algonquian peoples, a transformer, more sacred than Coyote in many respects, but a jokester still.

Nanye'hi. Nancy Ward was the last Beloved Woman (or Clan Mother) of the Cherokee people before Removal. She was a major decision-maker for the people, operating under the old matriarchal system so disrupted by the encroachment of European governmental forms and social values. She introduced commercial cattle-raising and banking to North Carolina and helped develop the valuable resources that unfortunately made the tribe the envy of all around. On her death, she became a kind of folk heroine to the Cherokee people, remembered even in the Oklahoma Cherokee tribal symbol taken from a sculpture carved by the Cherokee artist, Willard Stone.

Niki nonk'on. "Hear the words of these People" in Osage. An injunction used to signal the beginning of ceremonials or songs. (deClue)

Niki wathon. "The songs of the people, the Osage." An injunction used in the beginnings of songs. (deClue)

Noni Daylight. Lives in New Mexico, but is originally from Oklahoma. Joy Harjo met her in an Indian bar at Fourth and Central in Albuquerque while she was trying to snag some Sioux pool-player fresh from Pine Ridge. Her other name is Trouble. She looks a lot like my sister.

Nulato. An Alaskan coastal town where Mary TallMountain was born. Nulato served as a port for the many Russian and Japanese trawlers that did business with Alaska. (TallMountain)

Oconoluftee. The pre-Removal mountain home of the Cherokee people, in North Carolina.

Oglethorpe. James Oglethorpe, the general given the Crown's task of colonizing the Southeastern coast in the eighteenth century. He worked with various Creek bands to organize trade and arranged the infamous treaty of Coweta, which, while recognizing ancient Creek dominion, gave the settlers a foot in the door. Mary Musgrove's relationship with Oglethorpe was important to the Creeks and to the English, but the nature of that relationship was the subject of unsubstantiated gossip.

Ohlone. The Costanoan peoples who, like the Miwok, occupied the Northern California coast. Reduced to a few mixed-blood peoples now, they are almost extinct. (Rose)

Okies. The derogatory California term for Depression-era migrants from the Oklahoma and Kansas Dust Bowl. The term also applies to Indian Oklahomans, known to be the best singers and drummers for powwows and the Forty-Nine dances following.

Onee. "Come here!" or "come on!" in Athabaskan. (TallMountain and Jones)

One-eyed Ford. Literally, a car with one headlight. Metaphorically, it is an "Indian car," a broken-down, undependable, too costly automobile gotten from the white car dealer near the Rez. At home, on the Rez, people live in the cars, keep them in the yard, and cannibalize them for parts for other broken-down Indian cars. In the '49, one verse says, "hey, honey, I'll take you home in my one-eyed Ford."

Oneida. One of the seven members of the League of the Iroquois, removed to Wisconsin from New York.

Oneida Community and Amana Villages. Idealistic and utopian communities of the nineteenth century, formed in the Midwest agricultural heartland.

One yote a·a gah. "People of the Standing Stone," one of the names for the Oneida people. May also be translated as "there is a rock set up." There are various stories of how the stone came to be, just as there are various stories of what happened to it and where it is now. (Whiteman)

On·ya. "Stone" or rock in Oneida. (Whiteman)

Osiyo Club. A real bar, in the tribally owned hotel in Tahlequah, Oklahoma. "Hello" in Cherokee.

O wononk'onieh. "We hear them," a phrase used by the Osage people to signal recognition of the initiation of a traditional narrative. (deClue)

Paitamo. "Son of the son." (Allen)

PHS. Public Health Service, better known as Indian Health Service. It is often thought of by older Indians as the place to go to die and by younger generations of women as the place to be sterilized. The PHS services, guaranteed by treaty, are often the only health care available to reservation Indians.

Pole-benders. Female competitors in a rodeo-like event, much like the ski slalom, in which horses are run in between and around poles stuck in the ground. Usually this event takes place outside the formal rodeo competition; the only formal event in which females can run is the barrel race.

Pomo. A tribe of people from California noted for their exquisite traditions of basketry and for their female shamans or dream healers. They have faced virtual extinction of their people and traditional culture in modern times, yet they survive with appreciable strength.

Prayersticks. Wooden painted sticks used by the Hopi in ceremonial contexts, either planted in shrines, put in the ground for ceremonials, or held out to invoke certain spirits and feelings. (Rose)

Pretty Shield. A medicine woman of the Crows, Pretty Shield lived around the turn of the century. Her classic story of traditional life was written down by Frank Lindermann in 1932.

Quetzals, pacas, pejibayes, tepezquintles. Jungle animals in tropical Central America.

Rancheria. Literally, "settlement" in Spanish, a mini-reservation in California. The rancherias are state-trust, rather than federal-trust, lands, and constitute home to the many small California tribes and bands. Some of them, like the pueblos, were derived from Spanish land-grants.

Ranchita. "Small ranch" in Spanish.

Rebozo. A shawl, traditionally worn by Latina women on the shoulders or around the head and shoulders. Plain or gaily embroidered, crudely or finely woven, it is the symbol of adult women in Mexican or American Indian communities.

Relocation. A policy of the United States government enacted in the forties to remove Indians from reservations to cities. Chicago, Los Angeles, Dallas, Minneapolis and other cities came to be Indian ghettoes where the promise of jobs and a better life was rarely fulfilled for those people taken from reserves.

Rez. The reservation is Indian homeland for the thousands of federally and state-recognized treaty Indians who live on reserved lands. But the Rez, as younger Indians call it, is more. It represents poverty, joblessness, booze and trouble, but it also represents freedom, no whites, Indian ways, Home, the center of identity.

Ribbon shirts. Made like a modern cowboy shirt out of calico, cotton, or satin, but with a smocklike body and elaborate ribbon-work on sleeves, back, and yoke, the shirt is contemporary pan-Indian dress. Derived from a combination of older, traditional hide shirts with hair decorations and European common trade shirts, these were adopted and adapted by Indians in the Great Lakes and Central Plains in the late nineteenth century. Now new-wave Indians wear designer versions.

Scholder. Fritz Scholder, a Luiseño artist, paints in bright acrylic colors. Noted for his translation of new and old Indian themes into modern artistic statements, he represents the vanguard of contemporary Indian art.

Seboyeta or Cebolleta. A Spanish land-grant town in New Mexico, near Mount Taylor.

Sherman. A BIA school near Riverside, California, to which many Hopi and other children were forcibly sent; now closed. (Rose)

ShinKu KuGe. "The robin" in Osage. (deClue)

Shipap. Shipapu or Sipapu, the place where The People—in this case, the Pueblos—emerged from the Underworld, the Second World, into the world as we now know it. To make The People remember where they came from and where Iyetiko dwells (*see* Iyetiko), the shipapu is a hole in the floor of the ceremonial room, the kiva.

Shiwanna. Persons, in Pueblo belief, who have been struck by lightning; also applied to spirits of the dead who became cloud beings. Those struck by lightning could use their power to heal if they so chose. (Allen)

Shro-oh and Ha-ah. Part of the responses in saying goodbye in Laguna-Keresan. (Sanchez)

Sioux. The generic name for the Lakotan and Dakotan peoples, spread throughout the plains and woods of the north and central United States. A nomadic, hunting people, they were noted for their skills in battle and for their traditions of charismatic leadership. They were among the primary victims of the land grabs, wars, treaties, and reservation movements of the nineteenth century.

Snaa. "Child" or "my child" in Athabaskan. (TallMountain and Jones)

Sokoya. "Aunt" (mother's sister) in Athabaskan. (TallMountain and Jones)

Star quilts. Developed by Native women from sewing methods and forms brought by Europeans, the Texas or Bethlehem star quickly became uniquely Indian in the Northern Plains. Major ceremonial items in give-aways, these quilts feature one bright-colored central star with six points. They are often used as blankets by men undergoing vision quests (see Give-away and Vision Quest).

Stomp Dance. Creek and Cherokee people participate in these old tribal religious dances during the spring and summer. They gather at the ritual stomp grounds late at night, to sing and dance until dawn. Creek singers are thought to be the best, and many of the songs—sung in a call-and-response form—are Creek songs. The songs are accompanied by the sounds of turtle-shell rattles, which the women wear on their legs and shake as they dance.

Sweetgrass. *Savastana odorata*, always used by a wide number of Native people from East to West in their basketry and ceremonials. Burned for ceremonial purposes, it is believed to summon good spirits and feelings, to induce a holy presence, to bring the sacred into play.

Talihina. Center of the Choctaw Nation of Oklahoma—literally "red (*okla*) people (*humma*)" in Choctaw.

Tattoos. Often given to young women among the California tribes when they reached the age of puberty. (Rose)

Tecumseh. The Shawnee "Patriot Chief," the "panther lying in wait," who battled whites to prevent land cessions and Indian defeats in the early nineteenth century. He tried to unite many tribes in the Territories against the U.S. Army, joining the British in a last desperate attempt to save his land and people.

Tehachapis. A horseshoe-shaped mountain range in Southern California, running east to west. The fertile San Joaquin Valley rests on one side and the arid Mojave on the other. (Rose)

Tewatnikwʌhtalyaks. Bloodroot, a small plant used by Oneidas for healing. (Whiteman)

Thunder. Protects and nourishes the Cherokee people, having assumed guardianship over them long years ago when they established a relationship of faith together.

Tl'aah. "Sinew" or thread in Athabaskan. (TallMountain and Jones)

Tlingit. A subgroup of Athabaskan people who live on the Northwest coast of the U.S. and the southeastern part of Alaska. They remain coastal fisherfolk, much like their Haida and other Northwest coast neighbors.

Toeeaamaas. In Athabaskan, a woman's fish knife. (TallMountain and Jones)

Trail of Tears. The route of Removal for the Cherokee people, leading from the Southeast to Oklahoma, Arkansas, and Texas, where thousands died. Forced to abandon their rich plantation lands by Andrew Jackson, the people fell into poverty, illiteracy, and political anonymity, from which they have never fully emerged.

Tsagha. "Darkness" in Athabaskan. (TallMountain and Jones)

Tsa'lagi. The Cherokee people, one of the predominant Southeastern tribes, who now reside in both Oklahoma and North Carolina. Agrarian Iroquoian speakers, the Cherokees developed the first American Indian language syllabary and universal education. Before Removal on the Trail of Tears, the Cherokee population was universally biliterate and bilingual.

Tsa'nadiska. "They say" in Cherokee. (Cardiff)

Ts'eekkaayah. "Spring cap" or lake, in Athabaskan. (TallMountain and Jones)

Tseg'sin. Jack the Devil, the European trickster, or, to the Cherokee, the Trickster perhaps transformed into Andrew Jackson. Whatever his origins, he is stupid, unlovable, tricky only by low cunning and default, victorious only because everyone else is so stupid. The Cherokees talk about him the way Germans talk about Baron Munchausen, but with little of their fondness.

Ts'ibi. "Baby swing" or swinging cradle, in Athabaskan. (TallMountain and Jones)

Turtle Mountain Chippewa. A Métis or mixed-blood Ojibwa group from the North Dakotan–Canadian border (*see also* Anishinabe).

Ushuaka. "The Self" in Osage. (deClue)

U'tanu. "Fully developed" or "great" in Cherokee. (Cardiff)

Vieja. Simply, the female old one, in Spanish, frequently said affectionately, but just as often used pejoratively.

Vision quest. A Plains term for a practice of many Native peoples, in which a person, usually male, fasts and prays, either in isolation or as part of a ritual ceremony, with the goal of attaining a dream or vision that will give spiritual guidance.

Washinga. The Osage word for "bird." (deClue)

Wein . . . thonba . . . thabathin. "One, two, three" in Osage. (deClue)

Winslow. A town near the Hopi reservation in Arizona.

Wounded Knee. A descriptor that really covers two battles, both involving the Sioux people against United States officials—the Cavalry in the nineteenth century and the FBI in the twentieth century. Both battles were defenses of Sioux land and law against encroachment of the United States government, and both rallied sympathetic support for the still volatile legal claims of the Sioux Nation.

Yah. "House" in Athabaskan. (TallMountain)

Yeega'. "Spirits" in Athabaskan. (TallMountain and Jones)

Yoo'yoo'. "Beads." (TallMountain and Jones)

Yo soy indio, pero no soy, etc. "I'm Indian, but I'm not. My grandfather was born on the reservation, but my daddy was Anglo, but I'm not. I'm Arab, but I'm not. My daddy is from the land grant and his Papa was born in Lebanon, and he is Mexican and Spanish. I'm Chicana, but I'm not, etc." A poem about the confusions of being mixed-blood.

Yowelu·tu. "The wind" in Oneida. The final sounds of the word are always whispered, which makes it a beautiful word to the people. (Whiteman)

BIBLIOGRAPHY

Works by and about Native American Women Writers

Most of the works included in this section are novels or volumes of poetry (the latter, unless otherwise noted). Short stories unique in the corpus, such as those by Gertrude Bonnin, are also listed. The editor has included biographies, critical works, or multiple-author collections that seem particularly substantial and useful. For the purpose of historical record, individual authors included in collections as well as authors whose works do not appear in this collection are mentioned.

Allen, Minerva (Assiniboine). *Like Spirits of the Past Trying to Break Out and Walk West*. Big Timber, Mont.: Seven Buffaloes Press, 1974.

Allen, Paula Gunn (Laguna Pueblo/Sioux). *The Blind Lion*. Berkeley: Thorp Springs Press, 1975.

——. *A Cannon between My Knees*. Brooklyn: Strawberry Press, 1981.

——. *Coyote's Daylight Trip*. Albuquerque: La Confluencia, 1978.

——. *Shadow Country*. Los Angeles: American Indian Studies Center Series, 1982.

——. *Star Child*. Marvin, S.Dak.: Blue Cloud Press, 1981.

——. *The Woman Who Owned the Shadows*. New York: Spinsters Ink., 1983. A novel, some sections of which have been previously published in *Shantih* and in this volume.

——. "Poems." In *Four Indian Poets*, edited by John R. Milton. Vermillion, S.Dak.: University of South Dakota Press, 1974.

——. "The Grace That Remains: American Indian Women Writers." *Book Forum: Special Issue on American Indian Writers* 3, no. 1 (1981), edited by Elaine Jahner.

Allen, T. D., ed. *Arrows IV: Creative Writing Project of the Bureau of Indian Affairs*. Washington, D.C.: Government Printing Office, 1972. Many poems by writers of high-school age.

——, ed. *The Whispering Wind*. Garden City, N.Y.: Doubleday, 1972. Poems by six young writers—Liz Sohappy, Janet Campbell, Ramona Carden, Donna Whitewing, Patricia Irving, Agnes Pratt.

Benedict, Nana. "The Dress." In *The Only Good Indian: Essays By Canadian Indians*, edited by Waubageshig. Toronto: New Press, 1970. A short drama.

Blicksilver, Edith. "Traditionalism versus Modernity: Leslie Silko on American Indian Women." *Southwest Review* 64, no. 2 (1979): 149–60.

Bonnin, Gertrude Simmons (Sioux). "Soft-Hearted Sioux." *Harper's* 102 (March 1901): 505–508. A short story, quite romanticized, like all Bonnin's work.

——. "Trial Path: An Indian Romance." *Harper's* 103 (October 1901): 741–44.

——. "Warrior's Daughter." *Everybody's* 6 (April 1902): 346.

Brigham, Besmilr (Choctaw). *Heaved from the Earth*. New York: Alfred A. Knopf, 1971.

Burns, Diane (Ojibwa/Chemehuevi). *Riding the One-Eyed Ford*. Brooklyn: Strawberry Press, 1982.

Callahan, Sophia Alice (Creek). *Wynema: A Child of the Forest*. Chicago: H. J. Smith and Co., 1891. Probably the first novel by a Native woman, the well-educated daughter of a prominent Oklahoma Creek family.

Cardiff, Gladys (Cherokee). *To Frighten a Storm*. Tacoma, Wash.: Copper Canyon Press, 1976.

Contact II: Special Issue on Women Poets 15, no. 27 (Fall/Winter, 1982/83). Reviews of volumes by Wendy Rose, Linda Hogan, Mary TallMountain; reviews by Joy Harjo, Diane Burns, Paula Gunn Allen; poem by Elizabeth Woody.

Cook-Lynn, Elizabeth (Sioux). *Seek the House of Relatives*. Blue Cloud Quarterly 29, no. 4 (1983).

————. *Then Badger Said This*. New York: Vantage Press, 1977.

Erdrich, Louise. *Jacklight*. New York: Holt, Rinehart and Winston, 1984.

Erikson, Sheila (Blood). *Notice: This Is an Indian Reserve*. Toronto: Griffin House Publishers, 1972.

Evers, Lawrence, and Dennis Carr. "A Conversation With Leslie Marmon Silko." *Sun Tracks* 3 (Fall 1976): 28–33.

Faderman, Lillian, and Barbara Bradshaw, eds. *Speaking For Ourselves: American Ethnic Writing*. Glenview, Ill.: Scott Foresman, 1969 and 1975. Works by Juanita Platero, Wendy Rose, Liz Sohappy.

Fisher, Alice Poindexter. "The Transportation of Tradition: The Works of Zitkala-sa and Mourning Dove, Two Transitional American Indian Writers." Ph.D. diss., City University of New York, 1979. A good critical piece on two early and important writers.

————, ed. *The Third Woman: Minority Women Writers of the United States*. Boston: Houghton Mifflin, 1980. Poems and prose by contemporary and historic women writers, Bonnin and Mourning Dove, Wendy Rose, Joy Harjo, Paula Gunn Allen, Roberta Hill, Anita Endrezze Probst.

Fry, Maggie Culver (Cherokee). *The Umbilical Cord*. Tulsa, Okla.: Windfall Press, 1953.

————. *The Witch Deer: Poems of the Oklahoma Indian*. Claremont, Ohio, 1954.

Gorme-Zano, Keth (Mesquakie/Apache). *The Man Who Turned into a Woman*. Iowa City: LeBeacon Presse, 1981.

Green, Rayna (Cherokee). *Native American Women: A Contextual Bibliography*. Bloomington, Ind.: Indiana University Press, 1983. Comprehensive bibliography covering every aspect of Native women's political, social, cultural, and biological life; includes many Native women authors. Introduction evaluates trends, themes, issues.

————. Review of *Co-ge-wea*. *Tulsa Studies in Women's Literature* 1, no. 2 (1982): 217–21.

Greenfield Review. Special Issue On Native American Writers. (Fall 1981). Writings by and reviews of the work of several women writers—Wendy Rose, Joy Harjo, Paula Gunn Allen, Linda Hogan, Charlotte de Clue, Marilou Bonham-Thompson, Diane Burns.

Hale, Janet Campbell (Sioux). *Custer Lives in Humboldt County*. Greenfield Center, N.Y.: Greenfield Review Press, 1978.

————. *The Owl's Song*. New York: Avon, 1974.

Harjo, Joy (Creek). *The Last Song*. Las Cruces, N.Mex.: Puerta del Sol, 1975.

————. *She Had Some Horses*. New York and Chicago: Thunder's Mouth Press, 1982.

———. *What Moon Drove Me to This?* Berkeley: Reed and Canvas, 1978.

Hobson, Geary (Cherokee). *The Remembered Earth: An Anthology of Contemporary Native American Literature.* Albuquerque: University of New Mexico Press, 1979 and 1981. Poems by Native women poets, some not yet represented by their own book-length works (Sandie Nelson, Genevieve Yazzie), but most now recognized writers.

Hogan, Linda (Chickasaw). *Calling Myself Home.* Greenfield Center, N.Y.: Greenfield Review Press, 1979.

———. *Daughters, I Love You.* Denver: Loretto Heights College, 1981.

———. *Eclipse.* Los Angeles: UCLA American Indian Studies Center Series, 1983.

———, ed. *Frontiers: A Special Issue on Native American Women* 6, no. 3 (1981). Poems and stories by Louise Erdrich, Wendy Rose, Joy Harjo, Rayna Green, Sandra LeBeau, Paula Gunn Allen, Anna Walters.

Isom, Joan Shaddox (Cherokee). *Fox Grapes: Cherokee Verse.* Palmer Lake, Colo.: The Filter Press, 1978.

———. *The Moon in Five Disguises.* Tulsa, Okla.: Foxmoor Press, 1981.

Jahner, Elaine. "A Laddered Rain-Bearing Rug: The Poetry of Paula Gunn Allen." In *Women and Western American Literature*, edited by Susan Rosowski and Helen Stauffer. Troy, N.Y.: Whitson Press, 1982.

Johnson, Emily Pauline (Mohawk). *Canadian Born.* Toronto: Moranz, 1903.

———. *Flint and Feather: The Complete Poems of Pauline Johnson.* Don Mills, Ontario: 1912 and 1972.

———. *The White Wampum.* Toronto: Coy Clark, 1895.

Josie, Edith (Cree). *Here Are the News.* Toronto: Charles Irwin, 1966. Very entertaining news columns from a grassroots woman.

Lincoln, Kenneth. *Native American Renaissance.* Los Angeles: University of California Press, 1983. A critical work that deals with Paula Gunn Allen, Leslie Silko, and Wendy Rose, among others.

Littlefield, Daniel F., Jr., and James W. Parins. *A Bio-bibliography of Native American Writers, 1772–1924.* Metuchen, N.J.: Scarecrow Press, 1981. Volume 2 in a general Native American bibliography series, this work includes extensive documentation of Native writers—many whose works have appeared in Native newspapers and journals.

Lowenfels, Walter, ed. *From the Belly of the Shark.* New York: Vintage Books, 1973. Poems by a number of Native Women—Juanita Bill, Dolly Bird, Betty Oliva, Niki Paulzine, Sandie Johnson, Gladys Cardiff.

Mirikatani, Janice, et al., eds. *Time to Greez! Incantations from the Third World.* San Francisco: Glide Publishers, 1975. Poems by Wendy Rose, Janet Campbell (Hale).

Mourning Dove (Humi-she-ma). *Cogewea, the Half-Blood.* Lincoln, Nebr.: University of Nebraska Press, 1927 and 1981.

New America: A Journal of American and Southwestern Culture. "Women Artists and Writers of the Southwest: A Special Issue" 4, no. 3 (1982).

Niatum, Duane (Klallam). *Carriers of the Dream Wheel: Contemporary Native American Poetry.* New York: Harper and Row, 1975. Poems by Anita Probst, Liz Sohappy Bahe, Wendy Rose, Roberta Hill, Leslie Silko.

Northsun, Nila (Paiute). *Diet Pepsi and Nacho Cheese.* Fallon, Nev.: Duck Down Press, 1977.

———, and Kirk Robertson. *Coffee, Dust Devils and Old Rodeo Bulls.* N.p. 1979.

"The Poetry of Gloria Emerson." *Indian Historian* 4, no. 2 (1971):8–9.
Rose, Wendy (Hopi/Miwok). *Academic Squaw: Reports to the World from the Ivory Tower.* Marvin, S.Dak.: Blue Cloud Press, 1977.
———. *Hopi Roadrunner Dancing.* Greenfield Center, N.Y.: Greenfield Review Press, 1973.
———. *Long Division, A Tribal History.* Brooklyn: Strawberry Press, 1976 and 1982.
———. *Lost Copper.* Morongo Indian Reservation: Malki Museum Press, 1980.
———. *What Happened when That Hopi Hit New York.* New York: Contact II Publications, 1983.
Rosen, Kenneth, ed. *The Man to Send Rain Clouds: Contemporary Stories from American Indians.* New York: Vintage Books, 1975.
———, ed. *Voices of the Rainbow: Contemporary Poetry by American Indians.* New York: The Viking Press, 1975.
Ruppert, James. "Paula Gunn Allen and Joy Harjo: Closing the Distance between Personal and Mythic Space." *American Indian Quarterly* 7, no. 1 (1983): 27–40.
Sanchez, Carol Lee (Laguna Pueblo/Sioux). *Conversations from the Nightmare.* San Francisco: Casa Editorial, 1975.
———. *Coyote's Journal.* Berkeley: Wingbow Press, 1981.
———. *Message Bringer Woman.* San Francisco: Taurean Horn Press, 1977.
———. *Morning Prayer.* Brooklyn: Strawberry Press, 1977.
———. *Time Warps.* San Francisco: Taurean Horn Press, 1976.
Sands, Kathleen M., ed. "Special Symposium Issue on Leslie Marmon Silko's *Ceremony.*" *American Indian Quarterly* 5, no. 1 (1979).
Silko, Leslie Marmon. *Ceremony.* New York: Viking Press, 1977. A novel, her best-known and most distinguished work.
———. *Laguna Woman.* Greenfield Center, N.Y.: Greenfield Review Press, 1974.
———. *Storyteller.* New York: Seaver Books, 1981. A collage of traditional tales, retold, other stories, poemlike sequences, family history.
Sneve, Virginia Driving Hawk (Sioux). *Betrayed.* New York: Holiday House, 1974. Children's fiction.
———. *High Elk's Treasure.* New York: Holiday House, 1972. Children's fiction.
———. *Jimmy Yellow Hawk.* New York: Holiday House, 1972. Children's fiction.
———. *When Thunder Spoke.* New York: Holiday House, 1973. Children's fiction.
Swann, Brian, ed. *Shantih: A Special Issue on Native American Literature* 4, no. 2 (1979). Works by Paula Gunn Allen, Mary TallMountain, Judith Volborth, Linda Hogan, Wendy Rose, Roberta Hill.
TallMountain, Mary. *There Is No Word for Goodbye.* Marvin, S.Dak.: Blue Cloud Press, 1982.
Tapahonso, Luci (Navajo). *Seasonal Woman.* Santa Fe, N.Mex.: Tooth of Time Press, 1982.
Volborth, Judith Mountain Leaf. *Thunder Root: Traditional and Contemporary Native American Verse.* Los Angeles: UCLA American Indian Studies Center Series, 1978.
Whiteman, Roberta Hill. *Star Quilt.* Minneapolis: Holy Cow! Press (forthcoming, 1984).

Audiotapes and Videotapes Featuring Native American Women Authors

Healie, Elouise (producer). *Paula Gunn Allen: Interview, Paper, and Discussion.* Video production. Los Angeles: KPFA, 1982.

Lange, Geri (hostess). "On Common Ground" and "In Her Own Write." Readings by Carol Lee Sanchez. Video series. San Francisco: KQED. 15- and 6-minute segments aired in 1978 and 1979.

Poetry of the American Indian Series: Wendy Rose. Video series. American Visual Communication Bank, 1978.

Thorington, Helen (producer). *The Key Is Remembering: Poetry and Interviews by Native American Women (Linda Hogan, Mary TallMountain, Wendy Rose, Paula Gunn Allen, Joy Harjo, Diane Burns).* Tapes for radio production. New York: Art, Inc., 1982.

Wiget, Andrew (producer). *Readings and Interviews with Wendy Rose and Joy Harjo: Dartmouth College Native American Poets Series.* ½-inch color video, one hour. Hanover, N.H.: Dartmouth College, 1980 and 1981.

Presses and Journals That Regularly Publish Works by and about Native American Women

American Indian Culture and Research Journal. Kenneth Lincoln, Editor. American Indian Studies Center, UCLA, Los Angeles, CA 90024.

American Indian Quarterly. Wendy Rose, Editor. American Indian Studies Department, University of California, Berkeley, CA 94127.

Association for Studies in American Indian Literature. Karl Kroeber, Editor. 602 Philosophy Hall, Columbia University, New York, NY 10027.

Blue Cloud Press. Brother Beñet Tvetdten, Editor. Marvin, SD.

Contact II. Maurice Kenny, Editor. PO Box 451, Bowling Green Station, NY.

Greenfield Review Press. Joseph Bruchac, Jr., Editor. Greenfield Center, NY 12833.

Spawning the Medicine River. Philip Foss, Editor. Institute of American Indian Arts, Santa Fe, NM.

Strawberry Press. Maurice Kenny, Editor. PO Box 451, Bowling Green Station, NY.

Suntracks, Lawrence Evers, Editor. English Dept., University of Arizona, Tucson, AZ 85721.

CONTRIBUTORS

In order to avoid redundancy, these biographies refer only to information and works that appear neither in the credits nor in the bibliography.

Paula Gunn Allen (Laguna/Sioux/Lebanese) was born on the Cubero land grant in New Mexico. A poet, writer, and critic of some note, she has taught at the universities of New Mexico and California at Berkeley and Los Angeles. Best known for such critical efforts as "The Sacred Hoop: A Contemporary Indian Perspective on American Indian Literature" and for her editing of the collection *Studies in American Indian Literature*, her works, critical and artistic, have appeared widely in journals and anthologies. As a poet, she has received an appreciable amount of critical attention herself, and she has held a number of fellowships for writing and research, including a National Endowment for the Arts Creative Writing Fellowship in 1977. A political activist, she has been involved through the years in the antiwar, antinuclear, and American feminist movements, concerns that are very much reflected in her work.

Diane Burns (Chemehuevi/Ojibwa) was educated at the Institute of American Indian Arts, where she was awarded the Congressional Medal of Merit. She later attended Barnard College of Columbia University. A member of the Third World Writers' Association, the Feminist Writers' Guild and the Poets' Overland Expeditionary Troupe—which brings poetry to life in theatrical settings—she has read her work throughout the country. Her work has appeared in *Greenfield Review*, *Blue Cloud Quarterly*, *White Pine Journal*, and *Hard Press*, and her first chapbook appeared through *Contact II*. She lives in New York City, currently working on a new collection of poems and a "perverse science fiction novel."

Gladys Cardiff (Eastern Cherokee) was born in Montana but is related to the North Carolina Owl family. Educated at the University of Washington, she studied with Theodore Roethke, among others. She has lived in Washington state with her family for years. Active in the Poets in the Schools programs as well as other community activities, she has been a recipient of a National Endowment for the Arts Fellowship and held a Centrum residency.

Charlotte de Clue (Osage) lives in Lawrence, Kansas, but was born in Enid, Oklahoma. A young and emerging poet, her work is beginning to appear in journals across the country. Her interest in Osage history and culture, much reflected in her work, is scholarly as well as artistic. After fleeing to Lawrence from urban Kansas City, where she attended the University of Missouri, she writes while raising a garden and one teenager.

Nora Dauenhauer (Tlingit), a Native Alaskan, lives in Anchorage but was born and raised in Juneau. Coming from a family of noted carvers and beadwork artists, Nora is one of Alaska's best known Native linguists and cultural preservationists. Respected for her development of many instructional materials in the Tlingit language (*Beginning Tlingit*) and for her translations of traditional texts and performances by Tlingit elders (*Because We Cherish You*), she is also a committed teacher, scholar, and traditional dancer. As a poet, she has established a growing reputation in Alaska, where she and her husband, the poet laureate of

Alaska, actively work to develop publications and media presentations for traditional Native performance and oral arts. They were named Humanists of the Year by the Alaska Humanities Commission in 1981. Her soon-to-be-published manuscript of poetry, *The Droning Shaman*—from which selections are taken in this volume—will join her other work on Glacier Bay history, Tlingit spruce root basketry, and Tlingit ethnopoetics.

Louise Erdrich (Turtle Mountain Chippewa) grew up in Wahpeton, North Dakota, and attended Dartmouth College. She has taught poetry in the schools, worked on road construction, and edited the Boston Indian Council's newsletter. Her short story "The World's Greatest Fisherman" won the first Nelson Algren award in 1982, a prestigious prize for American writers. "Scales" will be included in Houghton Mifflin's *Best Short Stories* for 1983 and won a special mention for the *North American Review* in the National Magazine Awards. Quickly gaining a national reputation for short fiction, with publication in the best-known magazines of the country (*The Atlantic Monthly, Ms., Redbook, The North American Review*), she has completed one novel and has another in progress. Her poetry has appeared in a number of journals, and her first volume of poetry has recently been published.

Rayna Green (Cherokee) holds joint citizenship in Texas and Oklahoma but has lived in exile in Washington, D.C., and New England since 1970. With a Ph.D. in Folklore and American Studies from Indiana University, she writes on folklore, applied anthropology, and ethics in the field. Best known for her work on Native American traditional science and women, which has appeared in *Science, Ms., The Massachusetts Review*, and *Signs: A Journal of Women in Culture and Society*, and her articles on traditional obscenity, which have appeared in *Pissing in the Snow and Other Ozark Folktales, The Handbook of American Folklore*, and *Southern Exposure*, she is a contributing editor to *Corona* and *Sweetgrass*. Green has also been involved in production and script work in film, television, and museums. She has carried on her primary work, in Native scientific and technical development, as the director of American Indian projects for the American Association for the Advancement of Science and Dartmouth College. She is at work on a novel, *Give-Away*, about Ramona Sixkiller, an Indian detective, as well as other poetry and short fiction.

Joy Harjo (Creek), originally from Oklahoma, has lived in Arizona and New Mexico and currently resides in Santa Fe. She is a filmmaker and artist, as well as a widely known and increasingly recognized poet, whose three volumes of poetry have been well received by critics and readers. She is very much involved in community service, Poets in the Schools, and national public service, as a contributing editor of *Contact II* and as an advisory panelist for the National Endowment for the Arts Policy Panel. She is also one of the most requested readers and lecturers among the younger Indian writers. Increasingly known for her work as a scriptwriter for television, Joy translates her intensely visual imagination into film at the Anthropology Film Center in Santa Fe and is working on several scripts for television and film.

Linda Hogan (Chickasaw), originally from Oklahoma, now makes her home in Colorado, where, as a teacher, poet, playwright, and writer of fiction, she resides in the hills outside Boulder. Her chapbooks and a new play, produced in Oklahoma in 1981, as well as her efforts on behalf of Native women's literature, have brought her increasing attention as a writer and scholar. Her facility in several genres is demonstrated by her experimentation with drama and with the novel (*A Crate of Wooden Birds*) and by her sustained effort in an unpublished collection of poems, "The Diary of Amanda McFadden." She held a Yaddo Colony fellowship in 1982. A Newberry Library Fellowship in 1980 enabled her to continue her research into the history of the Chickasaw people, and she is active in the antinuclear movement and the American Indian Movement, commitments reflected in her poetry.

Wendy Rose (Hopi/Miwok) is an artist of some note as well as a writer, editor, and anthropologist. Educated in California, she is currently on the faculty of Native American Studies at the University of California at Berkeley and serves as editor of the *American Indian Quarterly*, one of the best-established journals of Native literature, policy, and history. Her major work, *Lost Copper*, was nominated for the American Book Award in 1981, and her numerous other works of poetry, published in chapbooks, magazines, journals, and anthologies—as well as many lectures and readings—have brought her a well-deserved reputation as a younger poet. She has also written some short fiction, and her book on *Aboriginal Tattooing in California*, as well as themes in her poetry, reflects her continuing interests in Native American anthropology. Her newest work, *Halfbreed Chronicles*, will appear in 1984.

Carol Lee Sanchez (Laguna Pueblo/Sioux) is a poet, painter, and educator. She teaches at San Francisco State University in the School of Ethnic Studies, primarily in American Indian Studies. Born in New Mexico, she came to the Bay Area in 1964. Her three books of poetry and her contributions to many journals and anthologies, along with her paintings, have made her a well-known figure in the Bay Area and elsewhere in the country. Deeply involved in community arts activities, she has also been very active in the women's movement, teaching feminist literature and lecturing. Her work *Conversations from the Nightmare* was nominated for the Edgar Allan Poe award, given by the American Academy of Poets, in 1975, and her reputation for arts administration has increased with her recent coordination of the final segments of the First Western States Biennial Exhibition.

Jaune Quick-to-See-Smith (Salish-Kootenai) lives in New Mexico, with her history in the Bitterroot country of Montana. One of the best-known younger artists in the country, her paintings, pastels, drawings, and collages have received increasingly positive critical attention. She has exhibited in a large number of one-artist and group shows in some of the most prestigious galleries and museums in the country, and critical notice of her work in interviews and articles has escalated steadily. She often writes works to accompany her moving political abstracts, which treat of Indian history and culture, and she is very much involved in community projects in Montana, New Mexico, and elsewhere to serve the advancement of Indian art and artists.

Mary TallMountain (Athabaskan), resident of San Francisco but born on the Yukon River, is an expatriate of the Alaska bush. Part Russian and Scots-Irish as well as Indian, Mary returns to Alaska frequently to teach in the bush schools and to restore the sense of culture and art that she reflects in her writing. She began writing in 1970, working first under Paula Gunn Allen, and eventually publishing a well-received chapbook, *There Is No Word for Goodbye*, which won a Pushcart Prize in 1981. TallMountain is finishing a novel, *Doyon*, set in Alaska in the early 1900s.

Judith Mountain Leaf Volborth (Apache/Comanche) was born in New York City. She studied at UCLA and currently lives in Santa Monica. A younger writer, her first collected work was well received, and her work has appeared in several periodicals and poetry collections. Her interest in performance poetry and haiku is reflected in her readings.

Annette Arkeketa West (Otoe-Creek) grew up around Tulsa, Oklahoma, and is currently an undergraduate student in Chickasha, Oklahoma. Married to another Oklahoma poet, Jon West (Southern Cheyenne), Annie is very involved in public education and combines her interest in poetry and the arts with her interests in community service. Her work has appeared in several anthologies, and she has one chapbook published. She gives readings throughout the state of Oklahoma.

Roberta Hill Whiteman (Oneida) grew up around Green Bay and now lives in Eau Claire with her husband and children. She attended the University of Wisconsin and the University of Montana, where she earned a Master of Fine Arts Degree in 1973. She taught at Rosebud, South Dakota, and Oneida, Wisconsin, before taking her current position at the University of Wisconsin–Eau Claire. She has participated in the Poets in the Schools programs in Arizona, Minnesota, South Dakota, Wyoming, Oklahoma, Montana, and Wisconsin. Her poems have appeared in anthologies and magazines, including *The Nation, A Book of Women Poets from Antiquity to Now, North American Review*, and *Carriers of the Dream Wheel*. Her first book of poems, *Star Quilt*, will be published in 1984 by Holy Cow! Press of Minneapolis and will be illustrated by her husband, an Arapaho artist.

Shirley Hill Witt (Akwesasne Mohawk) is currently the director of the Department of Natural Resources for the state of New Mexico and was formerly the director of the Rocky Mountain Regional Office of the US Commission on Civil Rights. Holding a Ph.D. in anthropology from the University of New Mexico, Dr. Witt has devoted her career to tribal, civil, and human rights. Active in the Native American women's movement as well, she is known for her essays on Native women (see Green, 1983) and for her books, *The Tuscaroras* and *The Way: An Anthology of American Indian Life and Literature* (with Stan Steiner). Her lifelong interest in Hispanic peoples is reflected in her poems and stories appearing in this volume.

CREDITS

The editor gratefully acknowledges the authors and the following presses and publications for their kind permission to reprint the copyrighted works noted below.

Blue Cloud Quarterly Press for Mary TallMountain's "Indian Blood," "The Last Wolf," "Crazy Dogholkoda," "Matmiya," "The Ivory Dog for My Sister," "Good Grease," from *There Is No Word for Goodbye*, 1982; Annette Arkeketa West's "Coyote Brother Song," "Naming the Rain," "Child Poem," "Poem for My Father," "Blackbird Winter," "Calumet Early Evening," "Salt Man," from *Prairie*, 1978.

Contact II Publications for Wendy Rose's "Punk Party" and "The Pueblo Woman I Watched Get Down in Brooklyn," from *What Happened When That Hopi Hit New York*, 1983.

Corona, a publication of Montana State University, for Rayna Green's "High Cotton."

Frontiers: A Journal of Women Studies for Rayna Green's "Naneye'hi," "Coosaponakeesa," "Another Dying Chieftain."

Greenfield Review for Nora Dauenhauer's "Jessy"; Charlotte de Clue's "Morning Song," "Place-of-Many-Swans," "In Memory of the Moon. (A Killing)," "Ijajee's Story"; Rayna Green's "Old Indian Trick," "Road Hazard," "Palace Dancer, Dancing at Last"; Mary TallMountain's "Ts'eekkaayah."

Greenfield Review Press for Linda Hogan's "red clay," "calling myself home," "Leaving," "Song for My Name," "Going to Town," "Nativity," "Heritage," from *Calling Myself Home*, 1979.

I. Reed Books for Joy Harjo's "Early Morning Woman," "The Blanket Around Her," "Conversations between Here and Home," "I Am a Dangerous Woman," "There Was a Dance, Sweetheart," "Someone Talking," "There Are Oceans," "Fire," "Obscene Phone Call #2," "She Was a Pretty Horse," "A Scholder Indian Poem," "It's the same at Four A.M.," "The Last Song," "Morning Once More," from *What Moon Drove Me To This?* 1979.

Malki Museum Press for Wendy Rose's "To some few Hopi ancestors," "Walking on the Prayerstick," "The well-intentioned question," "Long Division: A Tribal History," "Protecting the burial grounds," "I expected my skin and blood to ripen," "Three Thousand Dollar Death Song," "Learning to understand darkness," "Detective Work," "For Mabel: Pomo basketmaker and doctor," "The man who dreamt he was turquoise," "The parts of a poet," "Mount St. Helens/Loowit: An Indian Woman's Song," "Poet Woman's mitosis," "Builder Kachina," "epilog," from *Lost Copper*, 1980.

Ms. Magazine for Wendy Rose's "Julia."

Red Earth Press and the University of New Mexico Press for Linda Hogan's "Blessings," "Oil," from *The Remembered Earth: An Anthology of Contemporary Native American Literature*, edited by Geary Hobson, 1979 and 1981.

Spawning the Medicine River, a publication of the Institute of American Indian Arts, for Charlotte de Clue's "The underside of trees," "61," "Healing."

Spinsters Ink for Paula Gunn Allen's chapter "The Bearer of the Sun Arises," from *The Woman Who Owned the Shadows*, 1983.

Strawberry Press for Paula Gunn Allen's "Suicid/ing(ed) Indian Women," "Poem for Pat," "Womanwork" from *A Cannon between My Knees*, 1981; for Diane Burns's "Our People," "Big Fun," "For Carole," "Houston and Bowery, 1981" from *Riding the One-Eyed Ford*, 1982; for Joy Harjo's postcard, "Moonlight," 1980; for Wendy Rose's "Long Division" from *Long Division: A Tribal History*, 1976 and 1982.

Thunder's Mouth Press for Joy Harjo's "Origins," "Remember," "Your Phone Call at Eight A.M.," "Talking to the Moon," "Moonlight," "Talking to the Moon #002," "Cuchillo," "Two Horses," "Ice Horses," "Noni Daylight Remembers the Future," "The Blood-Letting," "She Had Some Horses," "New Orleans," "What Music," "The Woman Hanging from the 13th Floor Window," "Anchorage," "For Alva Benson," from *She Had Some Horses*, 1982.

The editor acknowledges, with respect, the prior publication of the following works by these presses and journals, as well as the individual authors' permission to reprint copyrighted material.

Alaska Journal for Mary TallMountain's "Naahoolooyah."

Casa Editorial for Carol Lee Sanchez's "Conversations from the Nightmare," from *Through the Microscope.*

Denver Quarterly for Judith Mountain Leaf Volborth's "Vihio Images."

Holt, Rinehart and Winston for Louise Erdrich's "Jacklight," "Painting of a White Gate and Sky," "Turtle Mountain Reservation," "The Strange People," "Balinda's Dance," "The Lady in the Pink Mustang," "Snow Train," "Dear John Wayne," from *Jacklight*, 1984.

Holy Cow! Press for Roberta Hill Whiteman's "Beginning the Year at Rosebud, S.D.," "Midnight on Front Street," "Lines for Marking Time," "Star Quilt," "Dream of Rebirth," "The Long Parenthesis," from *Star Quilt*, 1983.

Loretto Heights College for Linda Hogan's "Daybreak," "Daughters, I Love You," "The Women Are Grieving," "Black Hills Survival Gathering," "The Women Speaking," from *Daughters I Love You*, 1981.

The Massachusetts Review for Rayna Green's "Mexico City Hand Game," "When I Cut My Hair."

Neek for Nora Dauenhauer's "Seal Pups," "Kelp," "Rookery," "Genocide."

New America for Paula Gunn Allen's "Donna," "Robin."

North American Review for Louise Erdrich's "Scales."

Northward Journal for Nora Dauenhauer's "Tlingit Concrete Poem."

Shantih for Judith Mountain Leaf Volborth's "Self-Portrait."

Shenandoah for Louise Erdrich's "Turtle Mountain Reservation."

Sinister Wisdom for Joy Harjo's "The Blood-Letting"; Linda Hogan's "New Shoes"; Wendy Rose's "The Indian Women Are Listening: to the Nuke Devils."

Taurean Horn Press for Carol Lee Sanchez's "Prologue," "Tribal Chant," "The Way I Was," "Open Dream Sequence," "Quotes from a Review," "Yesterday," from *Message-Bringer Woman*, 1977.

Tundra Times for Nora Dauenhauer's "Winter Developing," "Skiing on Russian Christmas."

University of California–Los Angeles–Native American Studies for Paula Gunn Allen's "Madonna of the Hills," "Rain for Ka-waik," "San Ysidro, Cabezon," from *Shadow Country*, 1982; Judith Mountain Leaf Volborth's "Three Songs to Mark the Night," "Dusk Chant," "Vihio Images," "Goat Woman

Dares," "Corn Woman Remembered," "How Came She," "Iron Door Woman," from *Thunder Root*, 1978.
WAY for Mary TallMountain's "Once the Striped Quagga."
Wingbow Press for Carol Lee Sanchez's "Grandfather's Coming Back," from *Coyote's Journal*, 1982.

The editor acknowledges, with respect, the first publication, or one of several prior publications, of authors' works previously noted, by the following journals and presses.
Contact II for poems by Joy Harjo and Wendy Rose; *Frontiers* for poems by Louise Erdrich; *Greenfield Review* for poems by Joy Harjo and Wendy Rose; Greenfield Review Press for poems by Wendy Rose; *Northern Light* for a poem by Mary TallMountain; *Shantih* for poems by Mary TallMountain, Wendy Rose and Judith Mountain Leaf Volborth; *Heresies* for a poem by Joy Harjo; *Shenandoah* for a poem by Louise Erdrich; *Conditions 7* for a poem by Joy Harjo; *River Styx* for poems by Joy Harjo and Wendy Rose; *Cedar Rock* for a poem by Joy Harjo; *Dodeca* for poems by Wendy Rose; *From the Center* for a poem by Wendy Rose; American Indian Visual Communications Bank for poems by Wendy Rose in *Poetry of the American Indian Series*; the University of Arizona Press for a poem by Wendy Rose in *The South Corner of Time*; Houghton Mifflin Company for poems by Wendy Rose, Joy Harjo, Judith Mountain Leaf Volborth, and Paula Allen in *The Third Woman*, edited by Dexter Fisher; *Journal of California Anthropology* for a poem by Wendy Rose; *Sybil-Child* for a poem by Wendy Rose; *A Journal* for a poem by Wendy Rose; *Native Perspective* for a poem by Wendy Rose; Puerta del Sol for poems by Joy Harjo in *The Last Song*; *Artists for Survival* for a poem by Joy Harjo; *Thunderbird* for a poem by Joy Harjo; *National Women's Studies Newsletter* for a poem by Joy Harjo.

Photographic Credits

Photograph of Paula Gunn Allen by Joseph Bruchac
Photograph of Joy Harjo © 1983 by Eve Domingsil
Photograph of Carol Lee Sanchez by Thomas E. Allen
Photograph of Mary TallMountain © 1980 by B. Ullrich Zuckerman
Photograph of Judith Mountain Leaf Volborth by Robin Enwright
Photograph of Annette Arkeketa West by Sherry Henson